Multon Hanson
4333 Corvallis Ave N
Crystal MN 55428

Marketing and Leasing of Office Space

Nancye J. Kirk, Publishing Coordinator
Peggy Jo Schleker, Project Editor
G. Patrick Charuhas, Jacket Designer
Sarah V. Mustoe, Production Assistant

Marketing and Leasing of Office Space

Duane F. Roberts, CPM®

IREM Institute of Real Estate Management
of the NATIONAL ASSOCIATION OF REALTORS®
430 N. Michigan Avenue, Chicago, Illinois 60611

Acknowledgments

Cole, Dustin A., ed., *1978 Downtown and Suburban Office Building Experience Exchange Report*. Copyright © 1978 by BOMA International. Reprinted by permission of Building Owners and Managers Association International, 1221 Massachusetts Avenue, NW, Washington, D.C. 20005, 202-638-2929.

Cutlip, Scott M. and Allen H. Center, *Effective Public Relations*. Copyright © 1964, 1971 by Prentice-Hall, Inc., Englewood Cliffs, New Jersey. Reprinted by permission of the publisher.

The Real Estate Board of New York, Inc., 1968. *Standard Method of Floor Measurement for Office Buildings*. Reprinted by permission of the publisher.

Forms or other documents included in this book are samples only; IREM does not endorse their use. Because of varying state and local laws, competent advice should be sought in the use of any document, form, exhibit, or the like.

Throughout this publication, masculine pronouns have been used to refer to individual leasing agents, property managers, executive officers, prospects, tenants, and the like regardless of whether they are men or women. This was done for the sake of convenience and does not imply that any or all these persons are or should be men.

Copyright © 1979
The Institute of Real Estate Management
of the NATIONAL ASSOCIATION OF REALTORS®
All rights reserved.
This book or any part thereof may not be reproduced without permission of the publisher.
International Standard Book Number: 0–912104–42–2
Library of Congress Catalog Number: 79–89774
Printed in the United States of America

To
Duane and Hazel,
Dian,
Miles, Marny, and Travis
with affection and gratitude

Foreword

The Institute of Real Estate Management of the NATIONAL ASSOCIATION OF REALTORS® is an organization of professional property managers who have distinguished themselves in the areas of education, experience, and ethical conduct. IREM offers property managers and the public an expansive program of educational courses and seminars, textbooks, and audiovisual programs. *Marketing and Leasing of Office Space* has been prepared as part of this professional program.

About the Author

Duane F. Roberts, CERTIFIED PROPERTY MANAGER® (CPM®), is Vice President of Marketing for Joseph C. Canizaro Interests in New Orleans, Louisiana. In this capacity, he is responsible for all phases of the marketing effort, including tenant improvements, construction, industrial construction, advertising and public relations, leasing, space planning, and interior design. Roberts joined the firm in February 1978, as Leasing Manager of Canal Place, a mixed-use $300-million project in New Orleans.

A native of Nevada, Roberts has 15 years of experience in construction, property management, leasing, and marketing management. Previously, Roberts served as Vice President in charge of leasing for Del E. Webb Realty and Management Company in Phoenix, Arizona. He also was property manager of Rosenzweig Center, a mixed-use project in Phoenix, and responsible for leases with national firms in Cincinnati, Ohio; Kansas City, Kansas; Denver, Colorado; Houston, Texas; Phoenix and Tucson, Arizona; and Shreveport and New Orleans, Louisiana. His experience also includes project management in the renovation of a 20-story, 50-year-old office building in Houston, Texas.

Roberts is the author of the cassette program, "How To Lease Office Space Profitably," published by the Institute of Real Estate Management.

Roberts attended the University of Nevada and the University of Utah in Salt Lake City and earned his CPM® designation in 1975. He is on the Editorial Advisory Board of Southwest Real Estate News and is a past member of the Board of Directors of Arizona Chapter of Building Owners and Managers Association, the Sales and Marketing Executives Association, and International Council of Shopping Centers.

In Recognition

The publisher is grateful to David C. Nilges, CPM®, Vice President of The T. W. Grogan Company, Cleveland, Ohio, and James E. Patrick II, CPM®, President of Patrick Properties, Inc., Phoenix, Arizona, for their interest and dedication to the production of this book.

The publisher also is grateful to Anthony R. Diana, CPM®, Anthony R. Diana Management, Inc., Edgewood, Maryland; Albert C. Harmon, CPM®, Dwelling Managers, Inc., New York City, New York; and Ronald M. Puntil, CPM®, Oliver Realty, Inc., Pittsburgh, Pennsylvania, who reviewed the manuscript prior to publication.

Permission was granted by Joseph C. Canizaro Interests to use numerous charts, graphs, forms, plans, and other illustrations throughout this book to support the concepts and ideas presented by the author. The publisher is grateful for the use of these materials.

Contents

Preface   xv

1 **The Leasing and Marketing Function**   1

   The Evolution of Office Leasing   4
   Property Management and Leasing   7
   The Marketing Process   9
   Summary   12

2 **The Product**   15

   The Building   16
      *Rentable Space. Tenant Improvements.
      Office Interiors. Lobby. Elevators.
      Stairways. Corridors. Janitorial Services.
      Life-Support System. HVAC System.
      Electrical System. Management.*
   The Building Environment   25
      *Prestige. Tenant Mix. Labor Pool.
      Transportation and Parking. Appearance
      of Surroundings. Neighborhood
      Amenities. Curb Appeal.*
   Summary   28

3 Rental Schedules — 29

Market Analysis   29
Regional Analysis. Neighborhood Analysis. Supply and Demand. Market Survey. Comparable Analysis.
The Pricing Process   43
Ownership Goals. High-Rise Office Building. Garden Office Building. Leasing Plan. Quoting Rental Rates. Pitfalls and Adjustments.
Summary   57

4 Market Segmentation — 59

Identifying Submarkets   59
Segmentation by Location. Segmentation by Size of User. Segmentation by Type of User.
Effect of Market Segmentation on Marketing Strategy   63
Market Research   64
Summary   66

5 Advertising — 67

Classification of Advertising Campaigns   68
Selection of Advertising Media   68
Print Media. Outdoor Advertising. Building Signage. Direct Mail. Broadcast Media. Portable Presentations.
The Advertising Campaign   76
Analysis of Advertising Effectiveness   77
Summary   77

6 Public Relations — 79

The Public Relations Program   80
Public Relations Vehicles   81
Press Releases. Promotional Aids. Community Involvement. Ceremonies. Business Entertainment.
Summary   86

Contents

7 Prospecting — 89

Locating Prospects   89
  Referrals. Canvassing. Cooperation with Other Agents. Other Prospect Sources.
Maintaining Leasing Activity Records   99
Summary   100

8 Agent Preparation — 103

Pre-Call Preparation   103
The Sales Presentation   105
The Art of Asking Questions   108
Accepting and Responding to Objections   109
The Trial Close   110
Summary   111

9 Qualification of Prospective Tenants — 113

Business Reputation and Stability   114
Operational Requirements   116
  Reception Area. Executive Areas. Departmental Areas. Special-Purpose Areas. Work Flow Allocations. Expansion Possibilities.
Aesthetic Requirements   126
Financial Limitations   127
Summary   129

10 Space Planning — 131

The Space-Planning Process   132
Developing the Preliminary Plans   134
Prospect's Review of Preliminary Plans   137
Estimating Improvement Costs   139
  Methods of Securing Estimate. Source of Cost Data.
Special Suite Design Considerations   143
  The Renewing Tenant. The Expanding Tenant. The Contracting Tenant. The Relocating Tenant. The New Tenant in Previously Occupied Space. The Tenant in a New Office Building.
Summary   148

11 The Formal Presentation — 151

Formal Suite Design Presentation 151
Building Tour 154
Finish Schedule 156
Payment Structure 156
Lease Proposal 157
Summary 160

12 The Lease Document — 161

Types of Leases 162
Lease Characteristics 163
Parties 164
Leased premises 165
Term 166
Rental 166
  Security Deposit. Rental Adjustments.
Use 169
Rights and Obligations 169
  Utilities and Services. Quiet Enjoyment. Maintenance and Repairs. Alterations. Hold Harmless. Insurance. Destruction. Eminent Domain. Substitution of Premises. Subordination. Sale or Assignment. Change of Building Name. Access to Premises. Default. Strict Performance. Surrender of Possession of Premises. Compliance with Laws. Compliance with Rules and Regulations. Assignment and Subletting. Insurance Rates. Attorneys' Fees. Additional Rental. Air, Light, and View Rights. Notice. State Law. Heirs and Successors. Reasonable Consent. Mortgage Protection. Addenda.
Summary 179

13 Exhibits and Other Lease Documents — 181

Supportive Exhibits 181
  Office Floor Plan. Workletter. Rules and Regulations.

Lease Alterations   187
Options   191
    Option To Expand. Option To Renew.
    Option To Cancel.
Special Provisions   195
    Parking. Directory Board. Painting,
    Floor Coverings, and Other
    Refurbishment Items. Services and
    Utilities. Rental. Miscellaneous.
Other Lease Documents   197
    Guaranty. Amendments to Lease.
    The Sublease. Assignment of
    Lease. Termination of Lease.
Summary   204

14   Negotiation   207

The Conceptual Basis for Negotiation   208
    Human Behavior. Perception.
    Leadership.
Benefits of Negotiation   209
Techniques for Negotiation   210
    The "When" Strategy. The "How and
    Where'" Strategy.
Summary   216

15   Concluding the Leasing Effort   217

The Close   217
    The Direct Close. The Indirect Close.
Landlord Acceptance of the Lease Documents   221
Follow Through   227
Summary   229

16   Salesmanship and the Leasing Process   233

Creating the Proper Impression   235
Assembling the Tools of the Trade   236
Managing Time   237
The Leasing Effort   240
    Defining the Role of the Leasing Agency.
    Gaining Knowledge of the Product.
    Establishing Rental Schedules.

Segmenting the Market. Promoting the Office Space. Locating and Qualifying Prospects. Planning the Space and Presenting the Design and Lease Proposal. Negotiating the Lease. Closing and Following Through.
Summary   244

Appendix   247

Glossary   271

Index   283

Preface

Property management is a specialized and rapidly expanding sector of the real estate profession. The leasing agent—the individual responsible for the marketing and leasing of office space—has become an important part of the effective, efficient management of real estate.

The leasing agent is not only educated and experienced in managerial and administrative skills but also commands an understanding of the market, the economy, advertising and public relations, maintenance, record-keeping procedures, salesmanship and negotiating techniques, and space planning and design. The leasing agent must be diplomatic, congenial, and professional at all times in order to interact positively with owners, tenants, prospects, peers, supervisors, contractors, architects, and the numerous other individuals who play integral roles in leasing efforts.

This book is written for the leasing agent who wants practical, comprehensive direction in the marketing and leasing of office space and who wants to continually develop, improve, and refine the methods and tactics used in the leasing effort.

If the reader is new to this challenging profession, a hearty welcome is extended to this business which is as exciting as it is demanding. If the reader has been engaged in this noteworthy calling for some time and has succeeded, the author thanks those individuals who have helped develop this business and therein enriched his life.

Many friends and associates have provided encouragement and reinforced the need for this book. The author is particularly indebted to Joseph C. Canizaro who contributed time, support, and inspiration. Joe is a master in his profession and deserves emulation. James

E. Patrick II, CPM®, kept the process moving with pats on the back and an occasional kick. A special thanks is extended to Helen Gilbert, Wanda Puzzio, and Doris Davis for typing the manuscript. Elaine Despenzero, the author's administrative assistant, is appreciated for managing his time and providing support. The author's colleagues at the Del E. Webb Realty and Management Company—George Reeve, CPM®, Rex Maughan, CPM®, Tom Reed, Marv Todd, CPM®, James Ganarelli, and Hal Belsher, CPM®—furnished an environment to learn the leasing, property management, and tenant improvement specialties, and the author extends his appreciation to them.

Joseph C. Canizaro Interests is a development organization, and the author's interaction with the various disciplines in the development process has been gratifying and a contributing factor to the writing of this book. Such individuals in the Canizaro group as Moon Landrieu (Administration), Tom Winingder (Development), Bill Erdelyi (Tenant Improvement Construction), Bill Hebeisen (Space Planning and Interior Design), Dave Richardson (Architecture), Bob Little (Retail Leasing), John Warren, CPM® (Property Management), and Lynn Jones (Advertising and Public Relations) provided the author continuous opportunities for learning.

Other interaction was with individuals involved in marketing, leasing, and property management, such as Bill Zei, GRI, Al Early, Dick Horn, Richard Cornwell, CPM®, Bill Whiteside, CPM®, Dick Lacour, Dave Alcorn, Tom Arnold, Skip Hiett, Mike Farley, Bob Kawa, Mike Brown, Ed Michalenko, Dick Kemp, and Marie Martel. A special thank you is extended to William L. Smith, who many years ago provided an opportunity in the construction industry for the author.

A very special acknowledgment is given to Peggy Jo Schleker, a writer and editor with the Institute of Real Estate Management, who worked with the author for many months writing, rewriting, editing, and organizing the information provided by the author. Her diligence, energy, good nature, and professionalism are commended and most appreciated.

Duane F. Roberts, CPM®

1 The Leasing and Marketing Function

In 1885, a new era in American architecture began in Chicago. Two years earlier, architect William Le Baron Jenney had prepared plans for what was to become recognized as the forerunner of the modern skyscraper. By late 1885, Jenney's plans had been transformed into the 10-story Home Insurance Building on the corner of Chicago's LaSalle and Monroe Streets. It was the first building constructed with a skeletal framework of iron and steel beams. With the Home Building's completion, the skyline began to appear on the urban horizon.

Jenney's creativity was influenced by the social and economic conditions of the time as well as an important historical event—the Great Chicago Fire.

Throughout the summer and early autumn of 1871, a drought had beseiged most of the Midwest, and Chicago was hardly immune to the dangers of sudden fire which accompany such a drought. Early on October 8, several blazes had broken out throughout the city, although none had done significant damage. Unfortunately, one small fire went undetected. The Great Chicago Fire was traced to a barn at 137 DeKoven Street, a muddy tract near Halsted and Twelfth Streets belonging to Patrick and Catherine O'Leary. Persistent lore attributes the beginning of the raging fire to Mrs. O'Leary's cow, which kicked over a lamp into the hay. The blaze was fanned by a dry, 30-mile-an-hour wind, which carried the flames north and east across the city. Confusion and insufficient fire-fighting equipment contributed to the disaster, as the fire reached uncontrollable proportions and ravaged through the city.

On the morning of October 11, 1871, a Chicago newspaper recorded the destruction in this way:

> During Sunday night, Monday and Tuesday, this city has been swept by a conflagration which has no parallel in the annals of history, for the quantity of property destroyed, and almost irremediable ruin which is wrought. A fire in a barn on the West Side was the insignificant cause of a conflagration which has swept out of existence hundreds of millions of property, has reduced to poverty thousands who, the day before were in a state of opulence. . . . It is at this moment impossible to give a full account of the losses by fire, or to state the number of fatal accidents which have occurred. So much confusion prevails, and people so widely scattered, that we are unable for a day to give absolutely accurate information concerning them. . . . We also hope that all will leave with, or at No. 15 South Canal Street, a memorandum of their losses and their insurance giving the names of the companies. (*The Chicago Tribune*, October 11, 1871, Volume 2, Number 6, p. 1.)

The fire eventually began to burn itself out and, doused by an hour-long rain on October 10, left only smoldering ruins of a once prosperous and growing metropolis. The toll of the blaze, which burned over an area of approximately 2,000 acres, included 18,000 buildings and property valued at $196,000,000; 90,000 were left homeless; and an estimated 300 people died. The only architectural survivor was the Water Tower, a mile north of the Chicago River.

Leading politicians and ambitious, aggressive businessmen were not defeated by the Great Fire. Immediately, they planned to rebuild the city. John Stephen Wright, who had helped build Chicago before the disaster, was asked as he walked through ruins what he saw for Chicago's future. He replied, "Chicago will have more men, more money, more business within five years than she would have had without the fire."

Wright's prediction came true. Within a year, businessmen such as Marshall Field, Potter Palmer, Cyrus H. McCormick, Philip D. Armour, Gustavas F. Swift, William Ogden, and others began to develop the midwestern city with their generosity, know-how, and civic consciousness. And for architects and engineers, the Great Fire triggered new ideas: Do away with the vulnerable, wooden city and replace it with steel and concrete. The businessmen and the builders thus collaborated to build a new city that was to etch the skies.

The Chicago Fire was a key reason for the development of the skyscraper. By the later 1800s, the agrarian society, once the backbone of American life, was giving way to the effects of the Industrial Revolution and the accompanying trends toward urbanization. As commercial and industrial real estate in major business centers dwindled, its value soared. The need for more concentrated building and more efficient use of urban land became apparent. No longer were one- and two-story frame buildings suitable. The quest for commercial space drove buildings higher, enabling a single parcel of land to accommodate many businesses rather than just a few.

The enterprising Jenney and his contemporaries were able to meet the challenges that confronted them because of three developments in building construction: the elevator, iron and steel frames, and advances in laying foundations.

The mechanized passenger elevator provided access to upper stories of tall buildings. In the 1850s, elevators were steam powered and could travel only a few stories; in 1870, the first hydraulic elevator was installed in a Chicago building; in 1877, the hydraulic passenger elevator came into general use; and by 1887, the first electric elevator appeared. The seemingly distant journey from the first floor to the fifth—or tenth—floor became quick, safe, and accepted by tenants.

With the use of iron and steel frames for building, load-bearing masonry or brick walls could be replaced and greater heights could be achieved. With masonry construction, as a building grew taller, the thickness of the walls at the base of the structure necessarily grew greater. Consequently, tall masonry buildings required thick supportive walls and permitted few windows on the lower floors. If, on the other hand, the skeleton of the building could be built with iron and steel and masonry merely used to cover the frame, greater heights could be reached without adding excessive weight and windows could be used more extensively. Cast-iron beams had been tested in the early 1800s to determine the design that could support high-rise buildings. Jenney capitalized on this research and went one step further, substituting Bessemer steel rolled beams for wrought iron in part of the Home Insurance Building. An architect of the late 1800s commented on these structures and what it would take to make them accepted places of work: "Occupants seek convenience, secureness and light, all this, of course, combined with a shine of elegance."

The third technological advance was in the laying of foundations so that construction on even the swampiest field was possible. This was especially important in Chicago, a city situated on mud flats. Frederick Baumann, a mid–1800s' architect, prescribed some fundamental rules in laying foundations:

Concrete work, at best, is random work that may and may not do good service. Upon hard and practically incompressible ground it will, under all circumstances, accommodate itself to the deflection of the ground caused by superincumbent loads, and thus may, if circumstances occur, be of positive and very serious damage to the structure under the law of convex deflections as before demonstrated. The Chicago material for bases is: Dimension stone, hard lime rock, of most [sic] any dimensions, from eight to twenty inches thick, and with even beds. There can be no better material in the whole world than this dimension stone. (Frank A. Randall, *History of the Development of Building Construction in Chicago,* [The University of Illinois Press, Urbana, 1949] p. 18.)

These strides in building construction combined with the imagination of architects gave stimulus to a trend that soon was to be followed across the nation. Dankmer Adler and Louis Sullivan, Daniel Burnham and John Wellburn Root, William Holabird and Martin Roche, and a young Frank Lloyd Wright—all recognized participants in the renowned Chicago School of Architecture—introduced and refined the city skyline, making the skyscraper a part of a rapidly developing urban nation. In doing so, they unknowingly laid the foundation for a new profession within the real estate industry.

The Evolution of Office Leasing

By modern standards, 10- to 15-story buildings would not be considered skyscrapers, but people living at the turn of the century were very much in awe of the new commercial buildings and the heights they reached. Although some businessmen were receptive to these lofty, skeletal structures, many others were apprehensive and considered occupancy in them to be unsafe. Tenant complaints focused on elevator rides that were too long, the comparative isolation of the top floors, the threat of being trapped by fire, and the fear of height. Structural blunders, such as poor heating systems and office arrangements and inefficient lighting, brought about by inexperienced architects further contributed to the doubts about locating in high-rise office buildings.

Interestingly, the same type of ingenuity needed to solve the technical problems of building skyscrapers would be needed to combat the psychological problems of their occupants. Prospective tenants had to be found and then convinced that the skyscraper was here to stay and destined to become a way of life for American business. The marketing of office space took on an added dimension, and the specialization within the broad field of property management—the leasing of office space—was born. The towering office building became an element of urban Americana that would continue to grow, change, and improve, and the leasing agent would be a contributor to its success.

By the 1920s, economic prosperity ruled, the high rise was accepted, and the office building became a popular form of investment. Although property managers were still little more than rent collectors, the need for management was becoming more recognized, especially among absentee property owners. At the same time, the office leasing function was becoming somewhat sophisticated. No longer was the emphasis on convincing businessmen that skyscrapers were safe. They also were being persuaded that the new, tall buildings offered numerous benefits that could improve their companies' profits.

Furthermore, office leasing agents were being confronted with still another problem: a severely overbuilt condition. Skyscrapers soon became symbols of business success, and more and more institutional developers were constructing them, as witnessed by the Singer Building and the Woolworth Building in New York City. Speculators created too much space for too few tenants, causing the competition for those tenants to become fierce.

When American living seemed to be at its zenith and everyone was enjoying the Roaring Twenties, the Stock Market Crash occurred in October 1929, plunging the nation into a severe economic depression. Businesses failed and tenants moved out. Real estate investors could no longer make mortgage payments, and the buildings they once owned fell into the hands of lenders, including banks, insurance companies, and other financial institutions. Virtually unskilled in managing and leasing office buildings, the lenders-turned-owners desperately needed the assistance of experienced property managers. It was during this period that professional real estate management had its genesis with the founding of the Institute of Real Estate Management in 1933.

Especially hard hit by the Depression was the office building sector of the real estate market. Too much office space had been developed during the highly speculative 1920s. With many companies going into bankruptcy during the Great Depression, the condition of too much office space and too few occupants was heightened. Luring those few firms that did remain required innovative marketing techniques and unique skills. The specialization of office building leasing continued to evolve as it sought to stabilize the office building industry. All too often, however, the only way to secure tenants was to reduce rental rates to unheard-of lows.

Even some of the period's most notable buildings had trouble finding tenants. It took 10 years, for example, to fill the Empire State Building which, when completed in 1931, added 40 acres of office space to the New York office market.

History tells the rest of the story of how America lifted itself from the depths of the Great Depression. By 1935, the real estate market had begun to improve with the rest of the national economy. Although recovery came more slowly to the office building sector than to the industrial, retail, and residential sectors, it did arrive.

Three technological advances that were made during this period were largely responsible for improvement of the office building industry. The first was improved lighting systems, specifically fluorescent lighting, which increased the value of interior office space that did not receive light from windows. The second advancement was in the refinement of air conditioning, and the third was the development of acoustical treatments that eliminated sound problems between offices. These developments were to have a major impact on the future of office building construction and on building desirability and, consequently, marketability.

With the outbreak of World War II, urban real estate entered a period during which the demand for professional property management of any kind began to decline considerably. The nation's resources were invested in the war effort, not in development of real estate. Space was scarce, and it was easy to get a tenant for any kind of building. Given these market conditions, there simply was no apparent need for management skills. It was not until the late 1950s that supply caught up with demand, vacancies began to appear, and the importance of experienced property management again was recognized.

The 1960s particularly experienced a surge in office building construction. This boom resulted from the overall growth of business, the fact that the office setting had become the work place for nearly three quarters of the population, and the desire on the part of companies to have prestigious addresses and previously unknown comforts and amenities.

The office building boom even extended to suburbia. With so many individuals owning a car, America had become mobile, opening the way for development of homes away from city centers. Once residential suburban areas were established, retail shopping centers and industrial areas soon followed. The decision to move offices from city hubs was based upon the preference for having the office close to the home and the lower cost of suburban land. Further construction of suburban office buildings was spurred on by development of the interstate highway system. Leasing agents realized that these buildings created new challenges, and their marketing efforts focused on the buildings' accessibility to major thoroughfares.

The 1970s was a decade that began with severe oversupply and ended with an equally severe shortage of office space. The seventies opened with office building managers and leasing agents struggling to fill huge volumes of vacant space. Most of America's large cities, including its suburbs, were overbuilt. The office construction of the late 1960s created a tenant's market for space, with record absorption rates prompted in part by the vast amount of space available for the asking. Compounding the problem of soft markets were increasing operating expenses, which raised the minimum rentals investors needed to keep their buildings in the black. By 1976, the market had begun to strengthen and soon the tables had turned until, two years later, vacancies throughout the U.S. were dropping and rental rates rising. Although good news for rental agents, the outlook was grim for companies that needed additional office space. By 1979, the developers who had been burned during the recession just a few short years ago were getting back into action, making an effort to meet pent-up demand.

Property Management and Leasing

As the history of the office building industry shows, the office leasing function developed as a specialization out of the broader property management function. Today, two basic approaches to operating an office building are common. On the one hand, an owner may contract with a real estate management agency both to handle leasing arrangements and oversee the physical operation of the property. On the other hand, the management and leasing functions may be treated as separate entities, the owner hiring a leasing or rental agent to handle rentals of the property and a building manager or managing agent to supervise the building's physical operation.

From this it can be concluded that an individual agent may perform either (1) both management and leasing functions or (2) strictly the leasing function. For simplification, this text discusses the role of the leasing agent as a separate entity and focuses on the responsibilities associated with the leasing function as distinct from the overall management function. Likewise, although an agent may be responsible for leasing space in one or more office buildings in scattered locations, for simplification this text assumes that an agent is involved with only one building. In any event, the policies outlined, the procedures suggested, and the professionalism with which they should be carried out remain the same in all situations.

The leasing agent's function requires skill in personal selling. When properly combined with a knowledge of marketing theory and technique, this skill enables the agent to interpret the features of a given office building in terms of benefits to potential tenants.

The agent's performance also depends on familarity with other disciplines: law and its impact on lease documents and building construction; economics and its relationship to price and market factors; psychology and human behavior and their effect on understanding, persuading, and negotiating with prospects and tenants; technology and its applications to mechanical and electrical systems and construction; and architectural and interior design and their connection with planning office space. The ability to interrelate all of these skills and disciplines determines the success or failure of the leasing effort.

More often than not, an owner seeks the services of a professional property management firm because an office building has lost occupancy, resulting in a serious loss of revenue. In such an instance, when an office leasing agent's expertise is called upon to boost a sagging rent roll, leasing as a specialty is propelled into a leadership position.

Similarly, current economic considerations have forced many office building developers to partially prelease their new projects. Not only is this considered prudent, but major lending institutions rarely will fund a project that is wholly speculative. In some instances, that portion of the product that must be preleased before the commencement of construction is substantial. The manufacturing of the product, therefore, follows the marketing function. To sell office space before it exists, a task force of specialists is created. This task force is composed of a leasing agent, architect, space planner, property manager, and developer. To create a cohesive group that will focus on the task at hand, a leader is needed. Because the goal is to obtain one or more major tenants, the leasing agent often will be placed in that leadership role.

Because leasing plays such a vital part in the overall management process, some larger agencies establish leasing hierarchies or teams.

For example, several buildings may be managed by one management company, with all leasing activities coordinated by a director of leasing, who oversees the leasing manager or agent at each building. Leasing agent trainees also may be assigned to each of the properties. The hierarchy and job descriptions may vary from company to company. A smaller management company may have only a few leasing agents who report directly to management. Regardless of how the leasing staff is organized, the responsibilities assigned to and performed by staff are key to the success of the management company as well as the office buildings under its stewardship.

Leasing is an on-going process that requires meticulous organizational skill on the part of the leasing agent. Support of leasing agents can be indicated at regularly scheduled staff meetings. Not only do these meetings permit leasing agents to report on the progress being made in their leasing ventures, but they also can be used to inform, educate, and motivate the participants.

The Marketing Process

In order to achieve a position of leadership within the profession of real estate management, the leasing agent must have a working knowledge of marketing theory and practice. Marketing is an essential business function. The College of Commerce and Administration at Ohio State University in its "Statement of the Philosophy of Marketing of the Marketing Faculty" defines marketing as "the process in a society by which the demand structure for economic goods and services is anticipated or enlarged and satisfied through the conception, promotion, exchange, and physical distribution of such goods and services" (Columbus, 1964). Pursuant to office leasing, marketing embraces all the activities necessary to bring office space together with the tenant.

Like any other business function, to be effective, marketing requires a plan. While the input for the plan should come from various sources, the leasing agent is responsible for its coordination and preparation. This marketing plan is the result of seeking practical solutions to merchandising problems, performing research, and deciding how much time and money should be spent in the marketing effort.

Planning may be done in a simple, informal fashion or in a scientific, formal manner. In either event, it must be done. The degree of success the leasing agent has in marketing office space depends in large part upon the nature of market planning. The more scientific the planning process, the more it forces the leasing agent to establish marketing goals and reduce aimless efforts.

While the nature of a marketing plan will vary according to need and preference, a comprehensive plan includes six components:

Situation Analysis. The purpose of the situation analysis is to determine an office building's place in the office market, especially as perceived by potential tenants. Doing this requires that all information be gathered relative to a building, such as market potential and funds to be spent on product development and promotion. This analysis traditionally includes many facts and details about the market in which the building seeks to secure a place.

Statement of Marketing Problems and Opportunities. The statement of marketing problems and opportunities reveals what the product will face in the marketplace. If the situation analysis is properly prepared, it should be simple to anticipate problems and opportunities. For example, a problem would come to light if it were revealed that there is a substantial amount of vacant space in competitive buildings. Conversely, an opportunity would apppear if it were discovered that there is a great demand for the particular class of office space offered by the subject building. In either event, the recognition of apparent problems and opportunities forms the foundation for the rest of the marketing plan. A plan should be devised so that it capitalizes on the opportunities and avoids or overcomes the problems.

Statement of Marketing Objectives and Payout Calculations. Having identified and evaluated marketing opportunities, the leasing agent can focus on those to which resources should be allocated. Initially, marketing objectives should be established. Marketing objectives should be quantitative in nature. They should include the share of the market to be obtained, rentals to be achieved, and the amount of square feet to be leased within a specified time period. Subsequent to establishing these objectives, the leasing agent should determine the cost of meeting them. With quantitative marketing objectives and accurate cost calculations, this portion of the marketing plan will become the means of evaluating the overall plan's effectiveness.

Statement of Marketing Strategy. The method by which marketing objectives are to be met is referred to as marketing strategy. In developing strategy for leasing office space, the agent has four controllable variables with which to meet the demands of the marketplace: the product, pricing structure, promotional activities, and distribution system. These four elements, collectively known as the

The Leasing and Marketing Function   11

marketing mix, are used to reach the consumer regarding a new product or service. Each of the elements in the marketing mix must be closely examined and evaluated. The element or elements to receive greater emphasis than the others must be determined by the leasing agent and management. The decision made about the marketing mix will provide guidelines for the agent as to how to reach prospective tenants and convince them of the value of the subject property.

The use of the marketing mix is applied readily to the leasing of office space. On the surface, the product is the actual building that a leasing agent takes to the marketplace. However, a more thorough study of the product reveals that it also includes the services that are provided for tenants of the building, the amenities found in and around the building, the flexibility of making tenant improvements, the labor pool available to office users, and many more factors.

The price of office space is determined by the demand for it. The pricing structure of office space refers primarily to the rental schedule that is established in order that the building will properly represent itself in the marketplace. However, pricing structure also includes any concessions, discounts, or special allowances that may be offered to lure tenants.

Promotional activities include advertising, public relations, personal selling, and other similar tools that may be used to communicate with office users and induce them to lease space within a given building.

Distribution is concerned with delivering the product to the marketplace. In the context of office leasing, the leasing agent is the channel of distribution, inasmuch as the agent is the catalyst in the transfer of office space from developer to tenant. Personal selling is the key to the distribution segment of the leasing effort.

Again, the leasing agent must examine the components of the marketing mix in order to determine which elements within each should receive greater emphasis. Within the promotional mix, for example, both advertising and personal selling are important. Creating an effective promotional mix requires properly allocating time and resources between advertising and personal selling efforts according to their relative importance. Similarly, there is room for variation within the pricing component of the marketing mix. For example, rental schedules usually are structured so that higher rates are charged for prestigious top-floor areas than for space on lower floors.

In addition to utilizing the marketing mix concept, the leasing agent also will find it worthwhile to apply the concept of market segmentation. Market segmentation refers to the dividing of the overall market of office users into submarkets who share common characteristics, such as location, size, and nature of business. The reason for defining the appropriate submarkets, or target markets, is to enable the leasing agent to adopt a strategy specifically tailored to attract and hopefully secure the office users within a given segment of the market.

Action Program. The action program defines the means, or tactics, of implementing the strategy. For example, if the strategy is to use advertising extensively, the action program states whether to use in-house staff or employ an advertising agency to design a campaign with the marketing objectives in mind. Similarly, since emphasis is placed upon personal selling in the promotion of office space, the approach to be taken and time to be spent on personal selling efforts are defined in the action program.

Calendar and Budget Summary. By imposing a time frame and budget allocations on a marketing plan, management has a device for controlling it. A calendar and budget summary permits the market expert to evaluate the implementation of the marketing plan and its effectiveness.

Knowing the basic principles of marketing enhances the agent's ability to achieve the agency's goals through skills in planning, analyzing, and executing. Indeed, marketing skills complement the specialized leasing effort, being an effective means to a necessary end: the leasing of office space. By understanding what marketing is, what is involved, and what efforts need to be invested in the marketing function, the leasing agent is better prepared to meet the obligations to ownership, management, prospects, and tenants.

Summary

The function of office leasing resulted from a demand created by the introduction of the skyscraper in the late 1800s and early 1900s. Tenants, apprehensive about locating in this new type of structure, needed special attention which demanded creative marketing skills. Later, as the skyscraper grew in acceptance and became wildly popular among speculators, innovative marketing approaches were needed to find tenants for a severely overbuilt market.

Today, not only are the leasing agent's skills significant to the merchandising of office space, but the design and execution of a marketing plan are equally important. The marketing plan is a short-term business tool to organize and direct the agent's marketing efforts. The understanding and application of basic marketing principles provide the agent with the equipment to transform prospects into long-term, satisfied tenants.

The leadership role that a leasing agent can play both in the development and management processes of an office building is great. Through preparation, knowledge, and staff support, the leasing agent can contribute significantly to the success of an office building as an investment vehicle.

2 The Product

An office building is a structure that is partitioned into smaller work spaces and designed to house persons performing professional, managerial, and clerical—as distinct from industrial—activities. Office buildings can be found in all shapes and sizes and locations, ranging from one-story cinderblock buildings in small towns to multistory superstructures in major metropolitan areas. Regardless of the size or design of the building, as soon as a leasing agent obtains a rental listing, full responsibility must be assumed for marketing and leasing its space.

The first step in the assumption of a new leasing account should be a personal tour of the building. Preferably, the building's owner or a representative of ownership will be on hand. In the case of a building to be constructed, a thorough inspection of all architectural plans and construction details should be made. In any event, the purpose of this inspection is to familiarize the agent with the total product to be marketed and leased.

On the surface, the leasing agent's product is the building in which office space will be leased. Indeed, it is the office space itself with which the agent will seek to secure a share of the market. Yet when taking into account the full impact of tenant needs and wants, it becomes clear that the actual physical structure is only part of the total product.

The product is composed not only of rentable space. It is also made up of public areas, elevator and mechanical systems, the management team that provides services and maintenance, neighborhood restaurants and shopping facilities, parking and public transportation, and the available labor pool. Consequently, the product is a bundle of tangible and intangible characteristics designed to satisfy tenant needs and wants.

To make informed marketing judgments and provide sufficient information to prospective tenants, the leasing agent must make a thorough analysis of not only the building itself but also the total environment within and around the building. The agent will use the data gathered in this evaluation to create a marketing plan appropriate to the building.

The Building

The analysis of the product begins with an examination of the physical structure and condition of the building, its maintenance, its safety and security, and any plans for future improvements. Based on this analysis, the leasing agent will be able to recognize the factors that make the product desirable and intelligently and knowledgeably relay these assets to prospective occupants.

Rentable Space

The most important concern of a leasing agent is the building's rentable space. The appropriate strategy for marketing this space will depend on: (1) How much is available; (2) the largest block of contiguous space; (3) the smallest tenant reasonably possible considering the layout of the building; (4) the building's bay depth, or distance from the corridor wall to the rear window or wall. Once this information is secured, the agent can begin to determine to whom the product will appeal and how the appeal should be made.

Critical to analyzing rentable space from a marketing standpoint is knowing how it is measured. The area on which a tenant will pay rent generally is referred to in terms of rentable square feet. This rentable area may differ from usable area, in that the tenant may be charged for all or a portion of space occupied by public corridors, air conditioning facilities, and the like. Occupants of multiple-tenancy floors may feel deceived if an agent fails to inform them that the square footage used to calculate rent includes a share of the floor's public areas and thus exceeds the actual usable office space. Some standard method of measurement must be adopted so that all parties involved in the renting of space will know exactly what is being leased and misunderstandings can be avoided. The Building

The Product

Owners and Managers Association (BOMA) has developed a method of measuring office space that is used extensively by owners, managers, and leasing agents. (Figure A.1 in the appendix describes the BOMA space measurement standards.)

The BOMA method first explicitly defines rentable area for single-tenancy floors and multiple-tenancy floors, as well as retail areas within an office building. The rentable area on a single-tenancy floor is calculated by measuring from the inside finish of the permanent outer walls. From this gross rentable area, deductions are made for stairs, elevator shafts, pipes, ducts, heating and ventilating rooms, janitorial and electrical closets, and other areas not available to the tenant. Toilet facilities are included in the rentable area, if they are available to the tenant exclusively.

The rentable area of a multiple-tenancy floor first requires measurement of all individual rentable areas on that floor. Each single rentable area is determined by measuring from the inside finish of the permanent outer walls to the inside finish of partitions that separate office areas. In measuring space on both single- and multiple-tenancy floors using the BOMA method, no deduction is made for areas attributable to columns and projections necessary to the support of the building.

Although the BOMA method is the most commonly accepted means of measuring office space, others are used. One alternate method of measuring space is the New York method, which received its name from its place of origin and most commonly is used by East Coast leasing and management firms. (See figure A.2 in the appendix for a complete explanation of the New York method.) If neither of these methods is adhered to, the one used in the locality of the building should be applied. In this way, space in the building will be offered in the same way that space in other buildings is offered.

The primary reason for differentiating between rentable area and usable area, regardless of the method of measurement, is to determine the loss factor. The loss factor, the difference between rentable and usable area, has an impact on the marketability of office space. Leases are based on rentable area, which generally is greater than usable area. If a building has a high loss factor, it will be more difficult to merchandise than one with a low loss factor. The lower the loss factor, the more efficient the building.

For instance, using the BOMA formula, assume a floor in a building has a rentable area of 12,000 square feet and a usable area of 11,000 square feet. The loss factor would be 8.3 percent (12,000 −

11,000 = 1,000; 1,000 ÷ 12,000 = 8.3). If another building measured according to the BOMA method has a rentable area of 12,000 square feet and a usable area of only 9,500 square feet, the loss factor would be 20.8 percent (12,000 − 9,500 = 2,500; 2,500 ÷ 12,000 = 20.8). All other things being equal, if the rate per rentable square foot were the same for the space in the two buildings, a tenant probably would choose the building with the lower loss factor.

Tenant Improvements

A prospective tenant's ability to make improvements to office space is an important factor in choosing an office site. For this reason, the leasing agent should know what leasehold improvements are permitted by ownership.

If a building is new, an agent should have a quantity allowance sheet for building standard improvements (such as the one illustrated in figure 2.1). This sheet lists in units various square foot rela-

---

Figure 2.1

Quantity Allowance for Tenant Improvement Items

Standard Interior Partitions—one (1) lineal foot for every 12 square feet leased.
Standard Demising Partitions—one (1) lineal foot for every 60 square feet leased.
Standard Interior Doors with Frame and Hardware—one (1) for every 300 square feet leased.
Standard Corridor Doors with Frame and Hardware—one (1) for every 1,200 square feet leased.
Standard Acoustical Ceiling throughout the Demised Premises.
Standard Recessed Lighting Fixtures—one (1) for every 80 square feet leased.
Duplex Electrical Outlets—one (1) for every 125 square feet leased.
Light Switches—one (1) for every 350 square feet leased.
Telephone Outlets—one (1) for every 300 square feet leased.
Wall Finishes—one (1) prime coat and two (2) coats standard paint finish.
Venetian Blinds—one (1) standard 1-inch narrow slat venetian blind furnished and installed at all windows.
Flooring—Building Standard Carpet throughout.

---

tionships for installing such items as partitions, doors, and electrical outlets. Some developers of new office buildings use a dollar per square foot allowance rather than a spatial allowance.

The Product

If the space being leased was previously occupied, the agent must know how much remodeling or decorating the landlord will do for a new tenant. A landlord's contribution for decorating previously occupied space usually is expressed in dollars per square foot or as a percentage of total lease rental value. This allowance, however, like many other terms and conditions of a lease, is negotiable.

Office Interiors

When a potential tenant appraises the desirability of an office site, the design possibilities of the interior space are important. A prospect will visualize what can or cannot be done with the number of windows, the view, lighting, the ceiling height, the depth of the office from corridor to wall, and the width of the office between support columns. Since layout possibilities are a primary tenant concern, the flexibility offered by the design of a building can contribute to its marketability.

The quality of the decor and its general conformity (or lack thereof) to the image of an ideal office interior should be evaluated. In touring a building, a prospect will be comparing it mentally to the best building in town. The selection of an office location is made on the basis of comparability to such an ideal building. The agent's responsibility is to see that this comparison places the product in a favorable light.

Lobby

The initial impact made by the lobby often sets the tone of a building. A lobby's lighting, cleanliness, style, maintenance, and general appearance contribute to product desirability. Neat and well-designed graphics and directories are also indicative of a well-planned and well-maintained building. Each of these items, though easily ignored, is significant in creating a positive initial impression on prospective tenants. Some buildings are designed with extensive ground-floor space for retailers. The quality and appearance of these shops are also critical, as is the operation of news and tobacco stands that may be located on the lobby level.

Elevators

Elevator service has become almost mandatory in any building more than two stories tall. While most people take good elevator service for granted, poor service can drive existing tenants out of a building and discourage prospective ones from renting.

Three factors are important in the evaluation of an office building's elevator system: (1) the appearance of elevator entrances, cabs, and, when applicable, operators; (2) the operating facility and newness of the equipment; and (3) the location of the elevator banks.

First, the general appearance of elevators should be flawless. The cab should be clean, with floor and wall coverings and paneling well maintained. Ventilation and lighting should be adequate, and, when applicable, operators should be well groomed and tastefully uniformed.

Second, the efficiency at which elevators operate is a primary consideration in evaluating an office building. Businessmen justifiably are concerned about the expediency with which employees and goods can be moved. If elevator service is inadequate, the amount of time wasted while waiting for elevators can be considerable. While employers certainly will be concerned about their employees wasting time in this manner, there will be equal concern about clients or business associates who must spend an undue amount of time waiting for elevators when on their way to conduct business.

Signal control elevators and automatic hatchway doors are indicative of fast-moving equipment and looked upon as assets to those interested in expediency. To fully evaluate the speed at which elevators operate, four factors must be considered:

1. The height of the building.
2. The number of tenants and employees per floor.
3. The anticipated number of visitors as well as employees in the building.
4. The type of tenancy. (For instance, multifloor tenants may need elevator service between floors for daily business functions. Also, tenants whose staffs work in shifts will need elevator service throughout the day and night.)

These four elements affect the speed with which elevators can move and thus play an important part in determining if a building's elevator system is an asset in marketing the product.

In addition to moving people, an efficient elevator system is designed to move furniture, equipment, and supplies as well. For this reason, a freight elevator can make a building a more marketable product. The greater its availability and accessibility, the more valuable a freight elevator is. Even if a tenant never needs to use the freight elevator once move-in is complete, it is still an ongoing asset. If a freight elevator is available for transporting goods, passenger

The Product

elevators can be devoted to doing what they were designed to do—move people—and their efficiency will improve.

Finally, the location of elevator banks is important. Tenants should not have to walk great distances to find elevators. Elevator banks in older office buildings often are on outside walls, creating poor accessibility. On the other hand, elevator systems in newer office buildings usually are centrally located, as are stairwells, restrooms, and other public areas. Such placement is quite convenient and favored by tenants who require easy accessibility of elevators.

Stairways

While stairways are especially important in garden office buildings for enabling tenants to travel between floors, their value in elevator buildings should not be overlooked. In fact, they take on added importance in a high-rise office as an alternate exit route in the event of fire or other emergency. For this reason, stairways should be as accessible and well maintained in high-rise buildings as are those in garden offices that are used on a routine basis. Only if this kind of care is given to stairways will the agent be able to use them as a selling point.

Stairways should be well marked and well lighted. At all times the flooring should be clean, unobstructed, and free of debris. Stairwell walls should be clean and in good repair. All too often, as a building ages, the stairtower is the last area to be maintained. However, the public use of stairways demands periodic painting and reflooring.

It is advised that each floor be clearly marked on stairwell doors. In a garden office building, a directory of the tenants on that floor should be posted. This enables clients and visitors to do business with tenants without encountering travel difficulties.

Corridors

Just as the lobby creates an impression on those who enter a building, public corridors are further indication of building quality. Wall coverings, corridor graphics, floors and floor coverings, doors, entrance ways, and lighting should all be evaluated for neatness, coordination, tastefulness, and maintenance attention.

Janitorial Services

A well-kept, spotless building sells itself to potential tenants; therefore, good janitorial service is an important factor in marketing a building. Most buildings are cleaned five nights a week. Whether the cleaning is a contracted service or performed by a building's employees, it most likely will be administered according to cleaning specifications that list each cleaning function and how frequently it is performed. The leasing agent must be familiar with a building's standard janitorial services, as well as be able to answer questions about tenant charges for janitorial services not otherwise provided.

Life-Support System

Security and protection services—often referred to collectively as a life-support system—are provided as a benefit in most office buildings. Depending on the size of the structure and the kind of tenants, the system may range from simple to complex.

Several steps should be taken in appraising the quality of a life-support system. To begin, a perimeter survey should be performed to locate potential danger points. Such danger points might include fire doors, unlocked windows, and adjoining roofs that permit easy access to the building; poorly lit areas that encourage crime; and landscaping that provides a potential hiding place for criminals. The absence of troublesome situations like these is a selling point for the building. In the eyes of a prospect, guard forces and a closed circuit television system will be considered the further measure of an effective life-support system.

The security inside a building also must be judged. Especially in high-crime areas, the visibility of security is as important to many tenants as the security system itself. Still, the system must be properly administered: Is a guard in the lobby a threat or an obvious sign of security? Are security officers armed? Are security officers from guard services or are they uniformed employees?

Assessment of a building's communications system likewise is important in determining a product's advantages in the marketplace. Is it possible to contact all tenants within the building if a problem arises? Does the system extend to access areas, such as the freight entrance and lobby?

Fire control is an essential part of a life-support system. City codes, which may dictate the installation of sprinklers, smoke detectors, fire alarms, and fire extinguishers, must be adhered to. Any additional fire control devices or plans will make the building more desirable. Stairwells, which may be needed for escape purposes, should be well marked and well lighted. A plan to evacuate the building should fire break out needs to exist, the plan should be posted in

The Product 23

conspicuous locations, and fire drills should be performed periodically.

Similarly, if procedures have been designed for possible power shortages, waterline breaks, bomb threats, and civil disorders, and prospects are made aware of them, they will take a positive outlook on the building's management. In all matters, the value of a building's life-support system as a selling tool is based on what is easily seen and what can be conveyed during a discussion or tour of the subject building.

HVAC System

The HVAC—heating, ventilating, and air conditioning—system contributes to the product make-up. Oftentimes, prospects consider moving from older buildings to newer ones in order to take advantage of improved comfort for themselves and their employees. However, if an up-to-date climate control system has been installed in an older building, this can be an important selling point, especially among those occasional tenants who prefer older buildings to newer ones.

It is important for the agent to know the facts and benefits of a building's HVAC system. The energy crisis, which apparently has become a part of daily life in the United States, has made office building owners whose tenants have full-service leases painfully aware of the resultant spiraling costs of utilities. If a building has implemented energy conservation techniques, which benefit everyone, a prospect should be told about it and the effect on utility costs fully explained. Many building operations have been forced to reduce energy-consuming services as a means of offsetting rising utility costs. Office users who previously expected and received extensive hours of operation may discover air conditioning or heating being shut off at 5:00 P.M. and on weekends. Prospects will want information regarding a building's scheduled hours of operation and may require that these services be provided beyond normal business hours. The agent must be familiar with the tenant cost per hour for providing additional utility services.

The leasing agent also should be alert to the type of heating and air conditioning systems, how they are controlled, and the number and location of zones per floor if mixing boxes are used. (A zone is an area whose temperature can be controlled by a thermostat separately from other areas on a floor in order to satisfy the demand of tenants in that area.) Other systems are available as well. If a building is equipped with a sophisticated climate-control mechanism, the agent should evaluate it from a marketing standpoint. For example, if a building has a variable air volume system, which uses individual ceiling units to allow thermostatic controls in virtually every office, this is a selling feature. The building operating engineer should be consulted on the mechanical facilities and asked to give the agent a tour to explain and clarify the system.

Electrical System

Like the HVAC system, the building's electrical system also can be important as a selling point of a building. Lighting systems are designed to produce an approximate number of foot-candles of illumination at desk-top level. Some buildings, however, have reduced design light levels to conserve energy usage. The light level to be provided should be known by the agent. Some larger prospective users even may inquire as to the KVA (kilo volt amps) per floor; the agent should be able to answer these technical questions as well.

Some office space plans require the installation of numerous duplex and telephone outlets through the floor. Such installations may require drilling through a concrete floor, which is usually costly. Photocopying machines and other special-use electrical equipment, such as large coffee makers, may require separate electrical circuits or heavy duty lines. Furthermore, in consideration of the technical advancements in today's businesses, computers are becoming commonplace. With their required additional electrical and air conditioning demands and extended hours of operation, computers can produce a serious electrical expense burden. These extraordinary expenses often are charged to a tenant's account. The leasing agent should know these costs, as well as any other policies affecting special electrical equipment.

Management

The reputation of a building's management is usually a key factor in the selection of office space. Unresponsive management is a prime reason that tenants seek space elsewhere. Consequently, the quality and quantity of services provided by management are crucial to the evaluation of a building as a marketable product.

While management's primary responsibility is to the owner of the building, it must balance this obligation with responsibility to tenants. The effective manager knows how to be sympathetic to tenant requests and understanding of their problems while dealing with them firmly but politely.

The Product

There are, essentially, two types of professional office building management. One way of managing a building is through a full-time building manager who is an employee of the building. The building manager is fully responsible for the operation of the building, possibly through employees if the building is of sufficient size.

On the other hand, the owner may contract with a managing agency to oversee the building's operation. The managing agency is a firm that manages properties for various clients. To clarify the agreement between a managing agent and building ownership, a management agreement is negotiated. The purpose of this contract is to spell out the responsibilities of the two parties and give the agent the necessary authority to act in the name of the owner. For smaller properties, it is advantageous and sometimes essential to employ a managing agent, since they could not economically support the services of a full-time qualified building manager.

Regardless of the method of managing an office building, the selling point lies in the professionalism of the individual and/or agency responsible for its operation. An indication of such professionalism is designation of the management company as an ACCREDITED MANAGEMENT ORGANIZATION (AMO®) or the individual property manager as a CERTIFIED PROPERTY MANAGER (CPM®) or both. The AMO® and CPM® designations, awarded by the Institute of Real Estate Management to those who exhibit high standards of experience, ethics, and education, are a reflection of the high degree of service that tenants can expect.

The Building Environment

Once the agent becomes knowledgeable about a building's physical structure and its rentable space, attention should be turned toward those intangible attributes that increase the desirability of a building and make it a more marketable product.

Prestige

Class consciousness is very much a part of any business. On a personal scale, class awareness is brought about by the existence of classes or groups of people who are ranked by the members of the community in socially superior and inferior positions. Like individuals, businesses are aware of their common status with respect to other businesses on certain social and economic levels. Each business sees itself as belonging to a specific class, and it will want to locate its office in a building that is compatible with this image. For example, a small, ambitious brokerage firm would do well to locate in a city's financial district near larger, prestigious brokerage institutions. Likewise, a promising, new advertising agency may wish to locate its offices in a building where reputable, established agencies are situated. Because a prestige building or address often is important to businesses in search of new office space, a leasing agent should develop a sensitivity to the prestige association and its effect on the leasing of office space.

Tenant Mix

Whom a tenant shares a building with is very much a factor in the selection of office space. For this reason, the leasing agent should evaluate a building's tenant mix and determine how that mix affects its marketability.

Office building tenant mix refers to the type or types of business operations being carried on within a building. Certain tenants will, on the one hand, attract one type of tenants and, on the other hand, drive others away.

Professional tenants, for example, often do not want to be associated with business operations that have anything less than the same kind of prestige they enjoy. For this reason, attorneys, architects, and other professionals may be hesitant to work in a building that houses what they consider to be nonprofessional activities. Often the ground-floor tenant of a building determines the tenant mix. If a bank is located on the lower floor, for instance, it may attract tenants in need of the financial services it provides. If, on the other hand, the ground floor is occupied by a wholesale clothing establishment, it is likely that less favorable tenants would be lured.

In any event, a consciousness is aroused as a prospect perceives a certain company image to be maintained if not upgraded through association with other tenants.

Labor Pool

Most office users will want to locate in an area that assures them of an available labor source that is appropriately trained to meet their employment needs. If a building is located so that the labor pool would benefit a prospect, an agent should be certain to have the appropriate facts and figures ready to present.

Transportation and Parking

An office building may house numerous tenants with hundreds of employees. Further, there will be many other individuals who come

The Product

and go to transact business with firms located there. How these people get to the office and leave, either to return home or to carry on business matters elsewhere, is a concern of tenants. Accessibility to trains, buses, subways, and taxis is vital, with availability to major thoroughfares and expressways, airports, and bus and train depots being equally important. It is the agent's responsibility to know the modes and operations of transportation in the vicinity of the building.

Parking is an amenity in which prospects are interested as well. Oftentimes, neighborhood parking facilities are sufficient. Even better, many buildings have their own facilities. This is especially true of suburban office buildings and is one of their biggest selling points. Some cities have codes which dictate that a minimum number of parking stalls, based upon the rentable square footage of a building, must be provided. In other cases, the parking space allowance is left to the developer's conscience and business acumen.

The leasing agent should be aware of management policies regarding parking facilities with respect to: (1) tenant charges, if any, for parking; (2) the ratio of parking spaces to the building's area; and (3) supplementary parking and its cost.

Appearance of Surroundings

The value of an office building is directly related to its surrounding areas. Unsightly vacant lots, deteriorating structures, unkempt lawns, and untidy streets and sidewalks are all deterrents in convincing prospects to lease space in a building.

Conversely, attractive plaza and seating areas and bike and walking paths can contribute to the list of the surrounding area's attributes. The landscaping outdoors as well as indoors plays a crucial role in the formation of overall first impressions projected by a building. The general appeal of the environment is a plus in marketing the product, and the agent should be prepared to call a prospect's attention to it.

Neighborhood Amenities

Influencing a potential tenant's building choice may be the availability of certain amenities in the immediate area, such as restaurants, banking facilities, and shopping areas. In some cases, not just the amenities but rather variety of the amenities is a key factor in choosing an office site. For example, having several restaurants with diverse price ranges within a building's neighborhood is far preferable to having one or two expensive restaurants. The needs of all the persons who will work in the office building, from corporate presidents to mail room clerks, must be taken into account in evaluating a building's marketability.

Likewise, the physical relationship of the office to needed facilities, such as a post office, government offices, courthouses, and banks, is judged important by some office users. It is important that an agent develop a keen awareness of accessible neighborhood amenities and their benefits to potential tenants.

Curb Appeal

The curb appeal—overall asethetic image and building appearance—projected by a building creates a first impression even before a prospect walks in the front door. Hopefully, this impression is a positive one. Curb appeal is produced by a building's design, its aesthetic appeal as an entity, and its unique relationship with its surroundings. An attractive, well-maintained building always will appeal to prospects and will be one of the leasing agent's most valuable marketing tools.

Summary

The product is much more than office space available for lease. It is a total working environment created by the building's physical structure and condition, the management team, and the ancillary facilities and amenities available to tenants. In order to effectively market the product, a leasing agent must know everything possible about the product. An inspection and evaluation of all the tangible and intangible characteristics that make up the product are basic to creating a sound marketing plan for an office building. The product knowledge that is gained will be invaluable in convincing prospects that the building is a wise choice for tenancy.

3 Rental Schedules

No single factor dictates rental rates that may be charged for office space. Rather, to establish a realistic rental schedule, many variables must be considered. Data about the marketplace, the economy, the competition, the objectives of the marketing plan, the goals of ownership, and the product itself must be weighed. By scientifically analyzing all of the factors, the leasing agent can set rental rates that will maximize occupancy levels and rental income.

Consequently, the first step in setting a rental schedule is to perform an in-depth analysis of the office market, including a study of the neighborhood and region in which the building is located and the nature of the competition. One of the rules in determining rental rates is that they always must be a true reflection of the market. This is true whether a rental schedule is being set for space in a new building or an addition to an older building or vacated space in an existing building.

Market Analysis

Market analysis is the collection and study of economic, demographic, and other data in order to ascertain the supply of and demand for office space, market trends, and other factors useful in the leasing effort. Prior to performing an analysis of the office market, it is necessary to understand precisely what a market is. Although various definitions have been given to the term "market," it is essentially a group of consumers with certain needs to satisfy, money to spend, and a willingness to spend it. Thus, there are three factors for the leasing agent to consider in analyzing the office market: tenants with needs, their purchasing power, and their buying behavior.

From this it can be concluded that performing a market analysis demands an integration of many disciplines. A leasing agent must understand economics, finance, and management. Furthermore, because human behavior is a factor in leasing activities, an awareness of sociology and psychology is important, too.

To begin a market analysis, a study of both the national and regional economies must be undertaken. The leasing agent should determine if the economy is receding, vacillating, or experiencing a general growth period and the factors contributing to the prevailing economic condition. These factors influence not only rental rates but also marketing techniques to be used. Also involved in a market analysis are studies of the subject property and comparable properties. By doing this, the strengths and weaknesses of a given building as it relates to similar properties can be judged. The leasing agent can use this information not only in marketing the building by capitalizing on its strong features but also in assigning appropriate, competitive rental rates.

Regional Analysis

The chiefly statistical part of the market analysis is the regional analysis. The term "region" has no specific definition. Generally, however, a region is the city or metropolitan area in which a building is located and which has an economic impact on it. From a study of existing conditions and apparent changes occurring in the region, the leasing agent can sight or predict trends that will affect both immediate and long-range merchandising efforts.

Several factors must be considered when performing a regional analysis, including economic, demographic, psychographic, and geographic trends and conditions. Data pertaining to these factors will help the leasing agent establish realistic rental rates that will achieve marketing objectives.

Economics. Statistics should be gathered about the region's money market and labor market. This information can be analyzed to determine the stability or instability of the economy and provide some guidelines in determining the purchasing power of office tenants within the region. An available labor pool encourages businesses to take root or remain in an area, as they will be ensured of the needed personnel to perform office work.

Rental Schedules

Data also should be collected regarding production, distribution, and consumption of goods and services in the area. From this an agent can determine the type of business enterprises that are located within the region and can be considered prospects for the subject building. The financing methods available in the region and the nature of the mortgage market likewise are worthy of study. This information should suggest if funds are available for financing new construction, remodeling, and renovation.

Any governmental controls on real estate can have a major impact on rental rates. Thus, zoning restrictions, local property tax laws, and development restraints and their application to the building should be studied. For example, zoning laws may forbid the existence of laboratories in office buildings located in certain regions and thus restrict tenancy of certain businesses.

Overall, economic conditions of a region enable the leasing agent to determine the buying power of users of office space and assist in setting rental rates within this purchasing capacity.

Demographics. Demographics refers to social statistics, including age, race, density, distribution, wealth, education, occupation, nationality, and religion of the region's population. Since the type of people who live in an area and the type of businesses located in an area influence its economy, demographic statistics can lead to conclusions about the behavioral patterns of the region's population. For instance, if the demographic study reveals that the area has a stable residency, the leasing agent can use this information to lure a major corporate headquarter tenant that is looking for a stable, high caliber labor pool to avoid employee turnover. Certain socio-economic groups tend to be more stable, make long-term investments, such as buying homes, and have more disposable income. Therefore, more money circulates and is invested in a region occupied by these groups, providing a high level of economic stability. An office building in an urban or suburban area with an established, secure community will be able to attract a reputable tenancy at higher rates than can be charged for space in a building in a region with a less desirable demographic structure.

Psychographics. Psychographics deals with a lifestyle measurement of the consumers in the area in which a building is located. Tenant interests and tenants' opinions of themselves provide clues as to what may motivate prospects to seek space. From this psychographic information, the leasing agent can select the type of promotion that most likely will attract interest. For example, the agent may have space available in a renovated building in a city's financial district (e.g., Wall Street in New York or LaSalle Street in Chicago). Knowing that well-established successful law firms and financial institutions already exist in the area, a psychological appeal can be made to new, aspiring law firms interested in developing an image of prestige and prosperity.

Geographics. Geographic variables are those which pertain to the size of a city or region, the climate, and whether a prospect is interested in an urban, rural, or suburban setting. Geographic information may suggest the types of businesses that locate within a region and how a given office building may fulfill those business needs. For example, an agricultural studies center may require a region that permits its regional office to be located in a large city yet has laboratories and planting fields nearby in a rural area. This might be necessary if office personnel find it necessary to travel to the experimental station regularly. A geographic study of the region would reveal that an office building's location facilitates this type of travel.

Neighborhood Analysis

Another part of the market analysis is the neighborhood analysis. Its concern is with the area immediately surrounding the subject property and which has a direct impact on its operation and productivity.

The actual sizes of neighborhoods vary. A neighborhood may cover several square miles or, in a large urban area, a few square blocks. Often natural elements, such as lakes, rivers, and hills, well-known buildings, or monuments mark the boundaries of neighborhoods. Once the neighborhood's borders are determined, the agent must pursue the pertinent details about it in order to answer these questions: What is its occupancy level? What is the neighborhood absorption rate? Does this rate represent continuous growth, or is the neighborhood characterized by a cyclical pattern of progression, regression, and stability? What is the growth of business in the area? What is the transportation situation? Is government or major industry coming into the neighborhood? What makes the neighborhood desirable or undesirable?

The aesthetics of a neighborhood—landscaping, greenery, maintenance of surrounding territories, views, etc.—have a major impact on the community's desirability and consequently on rental rates. If the environs are appealing and tasteful, this indicates a keen interest by local residents and owners to maintain, if not up-

Rental Schedules

grade, the neighborhood's image. Therefore, a well-kept business neighborhood with a stable tenancy is a benefit in marketing a building. Furthermore, a building in such a neighborhood can command higher rates.

An aesthetically pleasing neighborhood usually indicates economic strength, which in turn suggests loan availability, investment potential, and other available resources.

Supply and Demand

A comprehensive market analysis moves from a general statistical profile of the region and the neighborhood to detailed studies of the office building market itself. Data that indicate the supply of and demand for office space within a building's immediate neighborhood must be gathered and the relationship of the supply and demand factor to rental rates analyzed.

To explain the nature of demand and supply and its effect on marketing strategy, three market conditions, simplified for explanatory purposes, are presented in figure 3.1. In example A, supply

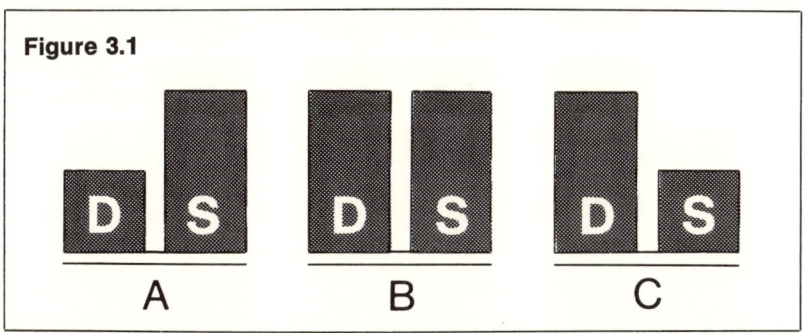

Figure 3.1

outdistances demand; hence, marketing has a definite role. A leasing agent must actively compete against others for the few tenants that do exist. Example B indicates a condition of equilibrium between demand and supply. Although marketing efforts must continue, no hard-sell is required, as business will flow in naturally. In example C, demand far exceeds supply. This does not call for an abandonment of marketing efforts but rather a creative de-marketing program. (A recent example of such a situation was seen in the energy industry, which had to curtail its goods and services due to severe shortages. This, however, did not mean dismissal of marketing programs. Rather, a service-oriented marketing approach was adopted. For instance, some utility companies launched programs aimed at saving energy by suggesting conservation tactics.)

In reality, the situation illustrated in example C most likely will not exist within the office market, at least on a national scale. James C. Downs Jr., CPM®, in *Principles of Real Estate Management* (Chicago: Institute of Real Estate Management, 1975, p. 251), refers to this market condition:

> Although in some buildings, 100 percent occupancy has been recorded for brief periods, the level of general business activity over the long term has failed to support a demand sufficient to utilize all of the country's office space. Moreover, the dynamics of office building construction have been such that, when a point of high average occupancy is reached, new structures are built, thus introducing new units.

While the supply and demand factor has an impact on the kind of marketing program required, it also influences the assignment of a rental schedule. Demand for office space creates a condition in which space can be priced at whatever the market will bear. The more secure the product and more intense the demand, the greater the value of the space, all other things being equal. This was the case in the late 1970s, when the demand for office space far exceeded supply, driving rental rates upward to unheard-of levels. Conversely, when supply outdistances demand, value falls. As a result, in setting a rental schedule, the leasing agent must gather information on the level and strength of the demand for office space within the area and relate it to the supply of that space.

Market Survey

In conjunction with the market analysis, up-to-date information on competitive office buildings near the subject property must be sought. A market survey provides this kind of data. Government agencies, real estate consultants, and bank research departments often perform comprehensive market surveys which are made available to leasing agents. If a market survey has not been made by one of these agencies, the leasing agent should undertake the task.

In performing a market survey, data is gathered about all the office space that is in the vicinity of and competitive with the space in the subject building. Generally, buildings of similar size and type should be taken into account.

If the business center itself is small, the leasing agent may find few similar office buildings. In such a case, the survey should focus on

Figure 3.2

Office Market Survey

Subject Building _____ Address _____

Age _____ Number of Stories _____ Owner _____ Address _____ Area _____ Class _____

Owner Phone _____ Management and Leasing Entity _____ Address _____

Management/Leasing Phone _____ Comments _____

Building Name								
Survey Date								
Net Rentable Area								
Square Feet Occupied								
Square Feet Vacant								
Largest Block of Vacant Space								
Square Feet Competitive								
Square Feet Noncompetitive								
Services								
Rates								
Concessions (if any)								
Parking — Rates								
Parking — Availability								
Tenant Improvement Allowance								

those buildings that contain similar rentable areas. For example, the market survey for a building in a small business center might be limited to buildings containing between 2,500 and 5,000 rentable square feet.

In performing a market survey, government-occupied buildings usually are not included. Likewise, buildings under construction and older structures undergoing renovation and not being used are excluded. These buildings are omitted from the survey because they are not competing with the subject for tenants. However, these buildings should not be altogether ignored. They may be used in subsequent surveys as a function of additional supply, inasmuch as they will have an impact on future market conditions.

Once the scope of the survey is established, the agent conducts a fact-finding interview with the owner, management, or leasing entity controlling each building. The purpose of these interviews is to determine occupancy and rental levels within the market area. To aid in this procedure, an office market survey form, such as the one shown in figure 3.2, is useful. A market survey form generally asks for each competitive building's name, address, geographical area, rental rates, and other pertinent data. In addition, regardless of the format of the market survey form that is used, it should ask for the building's classification and the amount of competitive and noncompetitive space.

Office buildings are classified in order to evaluate their competitiveness. Buildings in the market survey are designated as Class A, B, or C. Class A buildings are the most prestigious and usually command the highest rent; class C buildings have obvious defects and usually the lowest rent; and class B buildings fall in between the two in quality and price. The classifications primarily parallel quality and price levels; however, other factors may be reflected, such as character of tenancy, landlord or management reputation, and location.

Office space studied in the market survey must be further categorized as either noncompetitive or competitive. Noncompetitive office space is that which is occupied by a building owner or long-term tenants (those whose leases have 10 or more years remaining), since this space is not available to satisfy immediate demand. Competitive space is the space in which there is possible turnover within the next 10 years.

When a comprehensive market survey is completed and the data verified, the buildings should be grouped first into defined neigh-

Rental Schedules

Figure 3.3

Central Business District/North

	A	B	C	ALL CLASSES
Number of Buildings	6	9	6	21
Rate Range	$7.00-$12.00	$6.50-$8.00	$4.00-$6.70	$4.00-$12.00
Net Rentable Sq. Ft.	1,742,890	1,443,093	378,217	3,564,200
Competitive Sq. Ft.	1,528,210	1,195,998	306,217	3,030,425
Non-Competitive Sq. Ft.	214,680	247,095	72,000	533,775
Sq. Ft. Vacant	200,341	5,398	37,500	243,239
Sq. Ft. Occupied	1,542,549	1,437,695	340,717	3,320,961
% Vacant	11.5%	0.3%	9.9%	6.8%
% Competitive	87.7%	82.8%	80.9%	85%
% Competitive Vacant	13.1%	0.4%	12.2%	8%
Largest Block of Space Vacant	30,000	2,000	7,000	30,000

Figure 3.4

Statistical Summary of Class A Buildings

Area	Number of Buildings	Net Rentable Square Feet	% of Total Space in Survey	Rate Range	Competitive Sq. Ft.	Sq. Ft. Vacant	% of Competitive Sq. Ft. Vacant	% of Net Rentable Sq. Ft. Vacant	% of Total Space Vacant in Survey
CBD—South	5	2,021,962	18.2%	8.00-12.00	1,408,849	64,237	4.5%	3.2%	7.0%
CBD—North	6	1,742,890	15.7%	7.00-12.00	1,528,210	200,341	13.1%	11.5%	21.8%
Westbank	2	227,000	2.0%	8.50- 9.00	227,000	17,987	8.0%	8.0%	2.0%
Metairie	8	619,741	5.5%	8.00-10.25	580,361	71,956	12.3%	11.6%	7.8%
Orleans Parish (Outside CBD)	2	102,000	0.9%	8.00- 9.00	102,000	35,000	34.3%	34.3%	3.8%
New Orleans East	0	0	0%	—	0	0	0%	0%	0%
Totals	23	4,713,593	42.3%	7.00-12.00	3,846,420	389,521	10.1%	8.3%	42.4%

Rental Schedules 39

borhoods and then into classes. An example of such organization is found in figure 3.3. This chart represents the findings of a survey of office space performed on the northern portion of the central business district in New Orleans, Louisiana, in June, 1978. If such a comparison is performed annually, local trends and cycles will become evident and a comparison may be made to the previous year's data to determine the supply and demand factor.

Additional analyses can be made from the tabulated results. For instance, figure 3.4 is a statistical summary of class A buildings developed from a series of surveys like the one in figure 3.3. These analyses provide details about the office market that will aid the leasing agent in further evaluating the competition and proceeding with establishment of a rental schedule.

A common reason for unprofitable marketing programs is failure to correctly and completely evaluate the competition. The market survey is the first step in undertaking this crucial evaluation. The survey is performed to determine the amount of competitive space, and the data are further analyzed to uncover the means by which the competition will retaliate. The potential of new competition entering the market also is taken into account. It must be realized that new buildings seemingly always are being constructed, and thus the nature of the competition is constantly changing. A property's future depends on the planning done in the present. The information gathered in the market survey should be evaluated to answer the following questions: (1) How much competitive space is there? (2) What are the competition's histories in the market? (3) What is the total market share of the competition? (4) What are the pluses and minuses of competitors' marketing programs? (5) What are the financial resources of the competition?

Comparable Analysis

The information gathered for the market survey sets the stage for an in-depth analysis of three or four buildings. The buildings chosen for analysis must have characteristics in common with the subject building, including environment, general location, services, and other amenities. When performing the market survey, buildings were grouped into classes based on quality and price levels, character of tenancy, location, and landlord and management reputation. Subsequently, the comparables should be selected from the same market classification and neighborhood as the subject.

To complete a proper analysis of selected comparables, detailed

Figure 3.5

Field Research—Office Building Rentals

	No. _____
Project Name _____	Page _____ of _____
Address _____	Area _____
Directions _____	Census Tract _____
_____	Phone _____

Owner/Agent Contact _____

Type of Building   __Downtown   __Medium-rise   Year Completed _____
                    __High-rise   __With Other   Under Con-
                    __Walk-up   Retail Uses   struction _____
                    __Suburban   __Other_____   Completion Date _____

Building Size: Gross Building Area _____   Net Rentable (office) _____
Prime Tenant/Owner Net Rentable Area _____   Commercial Area _____
Off-street Parking Space _____   Garage Space _____
Location Data: (trend, convenience, appearance, quality, features)
    Rated: __Above Average   __Average   __Below Average
Comments: _____
Occupancy: (Rental History) _____

Services Provided:
__All utilities included in rent
__All except lighting
__All except air conditioning
__Cold water
__Hot water
__Heating fuel
__Air conditioning power
__Elevator service
__Elevator starter
__Full cleaning service   __Days
  __Contract   __Employees
__Covered garage   __Spaces
__Open parking space
__Security guards

---

studies must be undertaken. Two checklists developed by the Institute of Real Estate Management are invaluable guides in completing a physical analysis of selected comparable buildings. One of these checklists is designed for inspecting the exterior of an office building (see figure A.3 in the appendix) and the other is designed for inspecting the building's interior (see figure A.4 in the appendix). If properly completed during a tour of the comparable buildings, these

Rental Schedules

Figure 3.5 (continued)

Facilities Provided:
Heating   ___Central for building
                 ___Central for each unit
Air   ___Central for building
Conditioning   ___Central for each unit
                 ___Through-the-wall unit
                 ___Window
Paneling   _____
Vinyl Walls   _____
Drapes   _____
Carpeting   _____
Parking   ___Off-street; ratio
                 ___:___
                 ___Inside garage; ratio
                 ___:___
                 ___No off-street parking
                 ___Nearby public parking _____

Lease Required   ___How long? _____
Rental Analysis: (as of _____)
Percentage of Occupancy _____   Number of Square Feet Vacant _____
Average Rate Occupied Space per Net Rentable Area $_____
   Range $_____ to $_____
Asking Rate for Vacant Space _____
Terms _____
Computation of Net Rentable Area _____
Percentage of Public Areas Included _____
Escalation: ___Taxes Only ___All Operating Expenses
Other comments: _____
_____

forms will provide needed information about their condition and character. A field research form, as shown in figure 3.5, will augment this information as to rental rates, vacancy factors, facilities and services provided, and lease conditions.

Figure 3.6 is an example of a comparable analysis worksheet. This form facilitates the comparison of the subject building to its competitors. In addition to noting certain objective information,

Figure 3.6

Comparable Analysis Worksheet

	Subject Building	Building 1	Building 2	Building 3
1. Name of Building				
2. Building Address				
3. Owner				
4. Management				
5. Leasing				
6. Rental Rates				
7. Parking Availability				
8. Parking Rates				
9. Age of Building				
10. Net Rentable Area				
11. Percent Vacant (Current)				
12. Character of Tenancy (Major Tenants, Number of Business Categories Prevalent)				
13. Exterior Appearance and Design				
14. In-Building Amenities (Restaurants, Banks, etc.)				
15. Main Lobby Appearance				
16. Elevator Appearance and Efficiency				
17. Upper Elevator Lobbies and Public Areas				
18. Restroom Facilities				
19. Floor Load Capacity				
20. Lighting (Type of Fixture and Foot Candles)				
21. Electrical Service (KVA/Floor)				
22. HVAC System				
23. Tenant Area Appearance				
24. Acoustical Qualities (Office Areas)				
25. Security				
26. Life-Support Systems				
27. Tenant Improvement Allowance				
28. Area Amenities (Restaurants, Parking, Banks, etc.)				
29. Access (Automobile)				
30. Public Transportation				
31. Other				
32. Building Class				

Rental Schedules

the leasing agent also is asked to subjectively judge such items as exterior appearance, space design, and total atmospheric value. Once a worksheet is completed with data on each of the comparables, the findings can be measured against the subject. By doing this, the weaknesses and strengths of the subject as they relate to the competition will become evident.

Should a comparison reveal the need for physical improvement of the building, an appropriate recommendation should be made to management or ownership. Any upgrading that can be done will lead to another "plus" in marketing the product. Conversely, the analysis may reveal the competition's weak areas; this knowledge too can help in the marketing efforts. Marketing emphasis, however, should be placed on the subject's superior points rather than on the negative aspects of competitive buildings. Belittling the competition may be more injurious than beneficial to the leasing agent and the product.

The Pricing Process

The comparable study leads to one of the most common methods of assigning rental value—the comparative approach. Based on (1) the study of comparables and (2) the degree to which the subject is more or less desirable than the comparables, a competitive rental value may be assigned to the product's space. This rental value is referred to as the base rate. This is the rate that is deduced from the comparable analysis as the competitive rental rate for the typical space within the building. As such, the assignment of the base rate hinges on considering the average rental for the building as a whole.

Even though the subject building may be far more desirable than the competitors, it does not always follow that the base rental rate may be established at a proportionately higher level. Office space rents, like prices of other products, have economic limits; in other words, there is a point beyond which renting the space would not be economic to tenants. As a consequence, the office space would not bring the higher price, and vacancies would result.

As indicated, pricing based on comparisons with similar properties provides the agent with a per-square-foot base rental rate. However, the process of assigning rental rates within a building is influenced by additional factors. The location of a particular office suite within a building may be a factor in the pricing process if it has an impact on prestige, view, convenience, or other desirable amenities. For example, a view of the Golden Gate Bridge from a San Francisco office building or the snow-covered Rocky Mountains from a Denver high rise could command a 10- to 20-percent higher rent than otherwise identical space without such a view.

In light of this, most leasing specialists approach the task of assigning value to each space within a product by adjusting the base rate upward or downward on a mathematical rating scale according to its desirability.

The recognition that certain areas within an office building are better or worse than other areas first was brought to light during the Depression by two Chicago building managers, Leo J. Sheridan and Waldemar Karkow. Realizing that the quality of an individual office space was important to the rentals that could be asked, these two managers devised what has become known as the Sheridan-Karkow formula for pricing space within a building.

Under this formula, the typical office space was defined to be an 18- by 25-foot area facing the most important street on a building's eighth floor. This was the space to which the base rate was assigned. This typical office then was used as the standard to compare all factors increasing or reducing the rental value of the remaining space within the building. According to Sheridan and Karkow, the conditions that affect rental rates and for which price adjustments should be made are exposure, elevation, width and depth of the office area, and the corner influence. By applying these factors and relating the value of all space within a given building to the typical office at the base rate, the Sheridan-Karkow formula provided a method of establishing an equitable rental schedule that assured tenants of getting what they paid for.

While the Sheridan-Karkow formula is by no means recognized today as a universally accurate method of assigning rental rates within an individual office building, it did lay the groundwork for the scientific pricing process that has come to the fore.

Leasing agents now recognize that each type of office building has unique characteristics and consequently demands unique pricing techniques. Experience with one type of office building does not necessarily guarantee success in establishing accurate rental rates for another type of building structure. Space in high-rise office buildings must be evaluated differently than space in garden offices.

Prior to embarking on a scientific pricing process based on the type of office building, however, the leasing agent first must give some consideration to the objectives of the building's ownership.

Rental Schedules

Ownership Goals

Regardless of what the market analysis and study of comparables divulge, the leasing agent cannot establish a rental schedule without first turning attention to the financial objectives of ownership. Specifically, the agent must be mindful of the minimum acceptable rent that will meet the owner's expected yield on the real estate investment.

In order to understand the impact of ownership's goals on the rental schedule, the leasing agent must understand the financial framework out of which the ownership's return is realized. Essentially, the owner's return on equity invested is the cash flow realized by the property. Cash flow is calculated in this way:

	Gross Scheduled Income
Less	Vacancy Factor and Rental Loss
Equals	Effective Gross Income
Less	Operating Expenses
Equals	Net Operating Income
Less	Debt Service
Equals	Cash Flow

In order for the building and the investor to survive economically, a rental schedule must be established that covers operating expenses and debt service. On top of this bare minimum, the cash flow expected by the owner must be computed. This minimum return requirement will form a foundation on which to create an acceptable minimum rental schedule. Given this minimum, the leasing agent can pursue the pricing of office space according to the type of building.

High-Rise Office Building

There is no universally accepted definition for low-, mid-, and high-rise office buildings. However, a suggested guideline to distinguish buildings of varying heights is: low rise, up to five stories; mid rise, six to 10 stories; and high rise, 11 stories or more. With the advance of structural engineering techniques, there seems to be no limit as to how high a high-rise office can be, although the more typical high rise is usually in the 20- to 40-story range.

Pursuant to these guidelines, it is worth noting that the locale of an office building determines in large part its classification as either a low, mid, or high rise. For instance, a 15-story building in New York would be overshadowed by nearby skyscrapers and consequently might be considered a mid-rise building. In a small urban area, on the other hand, a 15-story building could be the town's tallest office and consequently would warrant the considerations due a high rise.

In any event, when pricing space in a high-rise office building, two factors deserve study: vertical considerations and horizontal considerations.

Vertical considerations relate to the social and psychological motivations of having an office in the uppermost portion of a high-rise building. Height is directly related to achievement. The top one or two floors of an office building represent coveted space by many firms; therefore, great demand exists for it. The high demand for the prestigious high-rise location can command higher rates and the rental schedule must reflect this.

This by no means implies that the ground-floor location is the least valuable space in a high rise. Quite the contrary, ground-floor space is in demand and commands a high rental rate. The ground floor of many buildings offers certain definite advantages to retail tenants. For example, if pedestrian traffic is high, good visibility and identity is provided automatically and can be further enhanced by street-side signage. Building graphics also play an important role in attracting public attention to retail tenants. Too, if the building is large enough (e.g., 500,000 square feet or more), the retail tenant can reasonably assume that the persons who work in the building create a captive market. Banking facilities, restaurants, office supply stores, and boutiques generally are regarded as especially successful retailers on the ground floor of an office building.

If a high demand exists for ground-floor space, a premium can be added to the rate. It may be advantageous to consider the benefits of a percentage lease, under which retail tenants pay a minimum rental against a percentage of gross sales.

Thus, the ground floor as well as the top one or two floors can command premium rates. The space in between should be priced accordingly, based on predicted demand, with the base rate given to the typical space. Consider, for example, a 20-story building. By adjusting the base rate upward in proportion to the increased desirability, the rate for the top-floor space can be determined. Moving downward through the building, the price is discounted when it is warranted.

To price office space accurately, it is necessary to be physically in the building. Rental rates cannot be assigned from an agent's desk, as all of the senses must be engaged. For example, a view must be con-

Rental Schedules

sidered from a similarly located window on all floors. Is the view from the twelfth-floor window less appealing than from the fifteenth floor? If so, the price should be discounted; if not, it should be the same. The outcome of weighing vertical considerations should be a rental schedule that realistically charges for space on desirable floors and discounts for space on undesirable ones.

Naturally, in pricing space, the leasing agent cannot physically tour a building that is under construction. In this case, a careful analysis of the building site and its surrounding area, coupled with the agent's experience, must be relied on to accurately place a rental value on space throughout the structure.

Once the price is assigned to all space in the building, the rental schedule is tested against the competition. First, the agent studies a suite in the subject building and all of its advantages are considered. A tour through a similarly located suite in a similar, nearby building then is conducted to determine if the subject compares favorably and its rates are competitive.

Just as vertical location within a building may affect rental value, demand also can be predicted for certain locations on a given floor. These are horizontal considerations. As mentioned previously, suites with such desired views as mountains, lakes, rivers, oceans or skylines can be priced higher than those without such vistas. For example, in Chicago, unobstructed views of the downtown area and Lake Michigan can be seen from many high-rise office buildings and, as a result, suites with these views command more rent.

Elevator exposure is another important horizontal consideration that can have an impact on pricing. Some types of tenants, law firms, specifically, almost always demand office suites that have impressive entrances immediately visible to clients as they step out of elevators. In consequence, on multi-tenant floors, areas near elevators can be assigned higher rates than those without this exposure.

Even weather influences pricing, as it may persist in creating negative tenant attitudes and lowering demand for certain exposures on a floor. In the southwestern United States, for example, some tenants are hesitant to locate on the west side of a building where the afternoon sun, even with today's sophisticated air-conditioning systems, can be intense and create employee discomfort.

Garden Office Building

The garden office building, which is usually one to three stories, often is referred to as a suburban office building because of its typical location. Garden office buildings occasionally are located in clusters and collectively referred to as a complex or office park. In most cases, this type of office building is conveniently located in an environment that provides many needed and desired amenities. The suburban office building tends to offer an abundance of free parking and a closeness to airports and major highways and streets. Because of the services provided, tenants who locate in these buildings often require proximity to suburban areas. For example, an insurance office would need accessibility to its customers concentrated in a residential area. Likewise, a suburban building may be able to offer advertising possibilities to a service-oriented tenant, especially if signage is permitted and the building is located on a major thoroughfare. Suburban buildings often are closer to employees' homes, and the fact that restaurants, banks, and shopping facilities have expanded into the suburbs makes this type of office space even more appealing.

The advantages of the suburban office building, such as tenant convenience, parking, customer convenience, and tenant identity, directly affect the assignment of rent. However, because of the energy crisis, particularly rising gasoline prices, the suburban labor force—and, therefore, the leasing of suburban office buildings—may change significantly.

The nature of the change is yet to be determined. On the one hand, the suburban labor force has easy access to downtown offices in those cities in which efficient rapid transit is available. Similarly, improved inner-city residential alternatives, which may detract residents who otherwise might choose suburban lives, are making downtown offices more popular. On the other hand, since many office workers continue to live in suburban areas, an argument can be made for the growing importance of suburban office buildings as employees choose to work closer to their homes. This could be especially true in cities where no sophisticated mass transit exists. In either event, the leasing agent whose listings include garden office buildings must keep close watch of the market trend.

Mindful of the changing nature of the suburban office market and based on a study of comparable buildings, the leasing agent can establish a competitive base rental rate. As with the high rise, the criteria for pricing space within a specific suburban office building can be grouped into two main categories: vertical considerations and horizontal considerations. Again, the space must be priced while the agent is physically inspecting it, if possible.

While the general principles of applying vertical and horizontal considerations to suburban office buildings are the same as with high-

Rental Schedules 49

Figure 3.7

Square Feet

12,000	20	$9.00
12,000	19	9.00
12,000	18	9.00
12,000	17	9.00
12,000	16	9.00
12,000	15	9.00
12,000	14	9.00
12,000	12	9.00
12,000	11	9.00
12,000	10	9.00
12,000	9	9.00
12,000	8	9.00
12,000	7	9.00
12,000	6	9.00
12,000	5	9.00
12,000	4	9.00
12,000	3	9.00
12,000	2	9.00
14,000	GROUND FLOOR	9.00
230,000		

Market rate range for class A space is $8.50-9.50. Ground-floor market rate ranges $9.00-10.00. Owner-requested rate is $9.00 per square foot.

By pricing all space at $9.00 per square foot, gross possible fixed rental is $2,070,000.00.

PARKING

rise buildings, the effect of these factors differs. For example, the top floor in a garden office building may not carry with it the prestige assigned to the top floor of a high-rise building. In fact, the upper floor in a three-story walk-up office may require discounting, inasmuch as getting to it is an inconvenience. However, hydraulic elevators whose maximum efficient height is about four floors often are installed in multiple-floor garden office buildings. If the inconvenience is eliminated and enhanced views are created, the rent may not need to be discounted. In fact, this may warrrant an increase over the base rent.

Likewise, horizontal considerations with respect to view, elevator or stairway exposure, and the weather can have an impact on rental rates.

To judge accuracy in pricing suburban office space, the leasing agent should test the subject's prices with those of comparable buildings, adjust accordingly, and compare the results. The final solution with the agent's recommendations then may be submitted for ownership approval.

Leasing Plan

A leasing plan is the formal expression of the leasing agent's judgment as to realistic rental rates and the types of tenants that would be suited to certain spaces within an office building. Such a plan delegates blocks of space vertically to full-floor and partial-floor tenants, giving consideration to the depth of the anticipated market of large users and allowing for their expansion on contiguous floors.

To describe a leasing plan and further explain the scope and method of pricing office space, it is best to study the situation of a hypothetical building. While a leasing plan should be developed for all types of office buildings, the concept is more vividly illustrated with respect to the high-rise office. Consequently, consider a building that has 19 stories, an attached parking structure, and an expanded ground floor. It contains 230,000 rentable square feet (using the BOMA standards for multi-tenant floors). A comparable analysis reveals that the competitive base rate is $9 per square foot per year. Figure 3.7 depicts this building priced within the limits of market conditions and applying the projected $9-per-square-foot rate to all the space in the building. With this rental schedule, the gross scheduled rental income would be $2,070,000. This rental schedule would allow an agent to lease quickly the coveted space worth more than $9 per square foot; the space worth less than $9 likely would remain vacant.

Rental Schedules 51

Figure 3.8

Vertical Leasing Plan

Square Feet

Sq Ft	Floor	Tenant Type
12,000	20	Major Tenant
12,000	19	
12,000	18	
12,000	17	
12,000	16	Multi-Tenant Floors
12,000	15	
12,000	14	
12,000	12	National Firm
12,000	11	
12,000	10	Multi-Tenant Floors
12,000	9	
12,000	8	Full Floor User
12,000	7	
12,000	6	Multi-Tenant Floors
12,000	5	
12,000	4	
12,000	3	Full Floor Users
12,000	2	
14,000	GROUND FLOOR	

PARKING

230,000

Figure 3.9

Vertical Leasing Plan—Rental Schedule

Square Feet

Sq Ft	Floor	Rate	Total	
12,000	20	$10.00	$120,000	Market rate range for class A space is $8.50-9.50. Ground floor ranges $9.00-10.00. Owner's requested rate is $9.00 per square foot. By pricing floors more closely to demand, a gross scheduled rental of $2,096,000, or $9.77 per square foot, can be achieved.
12,000	19	10.00	120,000	
12,000	18	9.75	117,000	
12,000	17	9.75	117,000	
12,000	16	9.50	114,000	
12,000	15	9.50	114,000	
12,000	14	9.25	111,000	
12,000	12	9.25	111,000	
12,000	11	9.00	108,000	
12,000	10	9.00	108,000	
12,000	9	8.75	105,000	
12,000	8	8.75	105,000	
12,000	7	8.75	105,000	
12,000	6	8.50	102,000	
12,000	5	8.50	102,000	
12,000	4	8.25	99,000	
12,000	3	8.25	99,000	PARKING
12,000	2	8.25	99,000	
14,000	GROUND FLOOR	10.00	104,000	
230,000				

Rental Schedules

Figure 3.8 illustrates a possible leasing arrangement that accounts for vertical considerations, or a vertical leasing plan. Depending on the depth of the market for large users and any preleasing that may have occurred, other plans would be possible. Note that ample space delegated for multi-tenant use is placed between the major tenants in anticipation of their future expansion.

Upon physically inspecting the building and pricing the space intelligently using only vertical considerations, rates range from $8.25 to $10.00 per square foot, for an average of $9.11 per square foot. The gross scheduled income increases from $2,070,000 to $2,096,000. (See figure 3.9.) This rental schedule not only increases scheduled income, but also enables the agent to lease the less desirable space on the lower floors.

Similarly, horizontal considerations may be incorporated into a leasing plan. Figure 3.10 depicts the results of applying a premium to the rate for space with a desired view. The rates range from $8 to $10 per square foot, or an average of $9.20 per square foot. This again increases gross scheduled income—to $2,115,500. Priced at a lower rate, the garage side of the structure should lease as quickly as the side with the view. The rates for space on the eighth, eleventh, twelfth, fourteenth, nineteenth, and twentieth floors contain no premium for the view, inasmuch as they are designated for single-tenant usage.

By increasing or decreasing rates to coincide with projected demand based on desirability, all of the building should be leased. Concurrently, the gross scheduled income is greater than would otherwise be projected.

Even if the leasing plan concept is adopted and scientifically applied, an agent should be flexible in assigning rent schedules because of the numerous variables that affect rates. Strong markets, for example, achieve maximum rental rates, whereas in weaker markets, rents must be discounted in order to attract tenants. If the agent anticipates an upward trend in the market, these lowered rents should be tied to short-term leases.

Quoting Rental Rates

The leasing agent generally is put in the position of determining how rental rates are to be quoted. The price of office space usually is expressed in terms of a unit price per square foot. However, while in some regions rents are quoted on an annual basis, in others it is done on a monthly basis. For instance, one leasing agent might quote the

Figure 3.10

Desired View Leasing Plan—Rental Schedule

Square Feet

Sq Ft	Floor			Rental	
12,000	20	$10.00	$10.00	$120,000	Market rate range for class A space is $8.50-9.50. Ground floor ranges $9.00-10.00. Owner-requested rate is $9.00 per square foot.
12,000	19	10.00	10.00	120,000	
12,000	18	10.00	9.75	118,500	
12,000	17	10.00	9.75	118,500	
12,000	16	9.75	9.50	115,500	
12,000	15	9.75	9.50	115,500	Results achieved by considering demand created by desirable view. Possible gross scheduled rental of $2,115,500, or $9.20 per square foot.
12,000	14	9.25	9.25	111,000	
12,000	12	9.25	9.25	111,000	
12,000	11	9.25	9.25	111,000	
12,000	10	9.25	9.00	109,500	
12,000	9	9.25	9.00	109,500	
12,000	8	9.00	9.00	108,000	
12,000	7	9.00	8.75	106,500	
12,000	6	8.75	8.25	102,000	
12,000	5	8.75	8.00	99,000	
12,000	4	8.50	8.00	99,000	
12,000	3	8.50	8.00	99,000	PARKING
12,000	2	8.50	8.00	99,000	
14,000	GRND. FLR.	10.00	10.00	140,000	
230,000					

Rental Schedules

rent as $9.00, meaning $9.00 per rentable square foot per year, while an agent in another city might quote the rent as $.75, meaning $.75 per rentable square foot per month. The method that traditionally is used in the agent's locale should be followed.

In some instances, the rate is quoted as a monthly rent. For example, the price of a 1,500-square-foot suite, based on a rate of $7.50 per rentable square foot per year, might be quoted as $937.50 per month. This frequently is true of space in a building in which previously occupied suites that already are constructed are being offered.

When a lease is drafted, it typically will show the total annual rental as well as the unit rate. The total rental is based on the unit rate multiplied by the rentable square footage occupied. It is worth emphasizing that the rentable square footage may differ from the usable square footage. This again points out the need for the leasing agent to be able to determine the rentable square footage according to the method customarily used in the region.

Pitfalls and Adjustments

Once an agent has established a rental schedule, there is always the question of its accuracy. The answer will be reflected in the market's response. Ideally, the unit rate is set as discussed in this chapter, and tenants lease space throughout the building. Realistically, space may not have the anticipated demand or be leasing well. In such a case, the agent may ask, "Should the space be offered at a lower rate?" The answer is usually no. One thing that can be done is to increase the price of those areas that are leasing beyond expectations. This action will cause the pricing imbalance to level off and increase the building's income. It also may be necessary to take other steps to entice positive market reaction.

To attract interest, many owners, brokers, and agents structure financial concessions or bonuses into their leases. For example, they may try to induce prospects to sign leases by offering one month's free rent or over-building-standard tenant improvements or the landlord may agree to absorb the tenant's moving expenses. If the tenant is leasing space in another building, the landlord may assume the tenant's obligation thereunder.

A rent concession generally is in the form of a waiver of rent for a specific period of time. To understand the impact of concessions on a building's net operating income, the leasing agent must understand the concept of effective rate.

For example, three months' free rent in a 36-month lease is an

8.3 percent discount (3 ÷ 36). If the quoted and accepted rate is $9.00 per square foot but three months' rent is conceded, the effective rate becomes $8.25 ($9 × 8.3% = $.75; $9.00 − .75 = $8.25). However, if the end-term rental is at or near market at lease inception, the building then has a meaningful rental to adjust upon renewal.

If a free-rent period of three months is granted on a lease calling for a monthly rental rate of $5,600, the concession is worth $16,800 ($5,600 × 3) to the tenant. However, this does not necessarily represent a loss of $16,800 to the property's income stream. Only if the leasing agent were able to rent the office to another tenant for $5,600 a month without offering the concession would the waiver be seen as a cost. If the space were to remain vacant during the three-month concession period, then granting the concession actually costs nothing. The leasing agent should see concessions as a possible means of obtaining tenants without incurring a cost to do so.

Likewise, in order to close a deal, it may be necessary to structure other financial inducements into a lease which also will have an impact on effective rates. Changing market conditions cause demand to increase or decrease. If market conditions make such financial incentives necessary, the leasing agent must consider them. Similarly, the investment goals of ownership regarding cash flow requirements and the desire to sell or hold the property will greatly affect pricing and the degree and amount of concessions.

Unfortunately, many leasing agencies spend more time convincing owners to give concessions than they do selling buildings' benefits to prospective tenants. Office space should not be given away; it should be sold.

While concessions can help solve a leasing problem if it appears that rental rates are too high or the market has changed, the leasing agent also may be faced with the problem of pricing space too low. Tenants may sense that prices for inexpensive office space may have been set incorrectly and sign leases quickly. Consequently, if rents are immediately accepted, this should be a sign that upward adjustments may be necessary. If, however, a scientific pricing process has been followed, drastic pricing changes should not be required on a regular basis.

It is worth noting that 100-percent occupancy of an office building is not necessarily a sign of a proper rental schedule. In fact, many leasing agents probably would agree that every building should have some level (maybe three to five percent) of vacancy. A 100-percent occupancy level must be achieved at fair rental rates. Otherwise, the in-

Rental Schedules 57

come to the property will not be maximized, and the leasing agent will not be fulfilling a basic obligation to the owner.

Summary

A rental schedule for an office building cannot be assigned haphazardly. The process requires an understanding of economic factors, market conditions, competition, ownership goals, and horizontal and vertical considerations. By weighing each of these variables, the agent can lend experience and intuition to the establishment of realistic rental rates.

No rental rate is exact. A rental schedule represents nothing more than an estimate of value. However, the precise estimate is the one based on in-depth research and analysis. The accuracy of a rental schedule can be ascertained only by the public's reaction to it and be reflected in occupancy records.

4 Market Segmentation

In order to establish effective marketing strategy, in-depth knowledge of the market is necessary. The office market consists of all those companies and individuals who use office space. However, office requirements for these users vary significantly, and, thus, no single building will be able to attract every user. Rather than attempting to appeal to the mass market of office users, it is more effective to focus on those specific types of users whose requirements are compatible with what the given office building has to offer. To do this, the overall office market must be divided into submarkets. Each submarket is composed of office users who share certain characteristics. For example, companies that have similar operations and business functions might be in one submarket; those that are of similar size, such as full-floor users, or multi-floor users, or those requiring approximately 2,000 square feet, might be in another submarket. This division of the marketplace into submarkets, or market segments, is referred to as market segmentation.

The purpose of market segmentation is to identify those groups of office users to whom marketing efforts should be directed, consequently identifying what are commonly termed the target markets. Once target markets are defined, marketing strategy can be tailored to appeal to these office users.

Identifying Submarkets

The very character of an office building usually establishes arbitrary limitations on the types of office users whose needs it can fulfill. Consequently, the kinds of submarkets appropriate to a given building may be identified by performing an analysis of the building's suitability for specialized use.

One of the most notable office characteristics that can aid in identifying submarkets is location. Another is size. Still another is architectural design. Depending on the nature of these characteristics, a building might appeal to one type of user and not another. From this it can be concluded that one way of identifying submarkets is by location, another is by company size, and another is by the kind of company.

Segmentation by Location

One of the first market segments that should be identified is that one made up of all office users already located within the same business area as the subject building. Quite often a company is satisfied with its location within a city but nevertheless must relocate. It may need additional space, newer facilities, special amenities, or other items not available in its current building. Or there may be dissatisfaction with the existing building. Whatever the reason, when relocation becomes necessary, it is likely the company will begin its search for new space in the immediate area. Leasing strategy should be designed to capitalize on this type of situation. Thus, segmentation by location is important to the leasing effort.

In order to identify office users in this way, the business area in which the building is located must be identified. Prior to performing the neighborhood analysis as part of the process of setting rental rates, it was necessary to define the boundaries of the neighborhood in which the building is located. This same neighborhood can be used in segmenting the market according to location. A list of all buildings within these boundaries whose rental rates are comparable to the subject is prepared. The firms occupying the buildings on this list make up a key submarket that requires the leasing agent's attention.

It is possible that prospects in the immediate business center are paying a lower rental rate than is being asked for space in the subject property. This factor is not necessarily defeating to the leasing efforts. If office users are compensated by an increase in satisfaction—improved working environment, better services, more favorable amenities—higher rent is quite acceptable.

Pursuant to this, major firms often locate their offices in newer buildings with higher rates, not merely for status but for personnel reasons. They recognize that a pleasant, satisfactory working environment may reduce expensive employee turnover, attract better employees for the same payroll dollar, and increase employee production. Hence, the prevailing attitude is that the additional rental dollar will be well spent.

As with any rule, there are exceptions to the one of directing initial marketing efforts toward companies located in the vicinity of the subject. For example, suburban office buildings often draw from central business districts, and new buildings can attract large users that are relocating their facilities from other cities. Notwithstanding these situations, the submarket of nearby companies is usually considered to be a target worthy of special attention.

Another method of segmenting the market according to location has to do with the nature of the neighborhood in which the building is located. For example, an office building located near local or federal courts probably would be attractive to the legal profession. In this case, lawyers would constitute a submarket worthy of marketing emphasis. In the same vein, a building near a hospital complex would be attractive to medical practitioners, who would compose an identifiable submarket for this leasing effort.

Segmentation by Size of User

Another method of segmenting the market is according to the size of the user, specifically as it relates to the design of the office building. Developers occasionally construct buildings that satisfy only large users, excluding the small tenant. If there are few large users within the proximity of the subject building, the search would have to extend beyond the immediate neighborhood, possibly even to other metropolitan areas.

On the other hand, some office buildings are designed specifically for smaller users. A garden office complex may be designed for several smaller tenants, such as quick-copy printers, insurance claim offices, income tax services, and dentists and doctors. This is not to imply that small buildings necessarily are designed for small users, nor large buildings for large users. It is the design of and the availability of space on each floor that determines the nature of the tenancy. An office building in a central business district, for example, may be more accommodating to many tenants engaged in the same business (e.g., lawyers, stock brokers) than to a few multi-floor users.

Segmenting the market according to tenant size comes into play particularly in re-leasing situations. If a small tenant moves out of a building, obviously it becomes necessary to find another small tenant to replace it. As long as the agent has identified submarkets according to size, finding prospects for replacement should not be a difficult task.

Segmentation by Type of User
Some office buildings are more compatible with one type of user than another. When this is the case, segmenting the market according to the type of user may be worthwhile. Office users can be classified into four major groups: (1) government, (2) corporate, (3) institutional, and (4) service.

Office space for the federal government is controlled by the General Services Administration (GSA). If the federal government is to become a potential tenant, the leasing agent must be aware of the requirements set for its users by the GSA. There are also some unique considerations in dealing with local and state governments. For instance, since these agencies usually are funded on an annual basis, one-year leases are the rule. Although longer terms can be arranged, this requires the structuring of special lease clauses.

In any event, the government is the largest single user of office space and should not be ignored. Even though securing government tenants requires familiarity with limitations and restrictions imposed on and by them, contact should be maintained with individuals or agencies responsible for the acquisition of government office space.

The corporate submarket includes the administrative headquarters and, occasionally, branch offices of publicly held corporations. Generally included in the corporate submarket are the giants of industry and other major business concerns in manufacturing, trade, and transportation.

A corporation's industrial or manufacturing division tends to be located in a suburban or rural area, where land is relatively inexpensive and labor and other needs can be filled. On the other hand, the administrative division usually will prefer to locate in a major metropolitan area. This is attributable to two key factors. First of all, the sale of the product that is manufactured requires proximity to the marketplace, which is in urban areas. Similarly, the supportive services that administrative offices need are more readily found in downtown areas. Consequently, if an office building is located in a metropolitan area and its design is compatible with corporate offices, the corporate submarket should be identified. For example, a large office building with an extensive block of vacant space might be considered as a relocation site for corporate offices.

Oftentimes large corporate relocations are controlled by consultants. Contacts with these consultants should be established and maintained as one way of being aware of corporate offices as potential tenants.

While corporate office users tend to be found primarily in major metropolitan areas, institutional office users are more evenly dispersed throughout the country. Included in the institutional submarket are insurance companies, banks, utility companies, brokerage firms, and the like.

Service industries are those that have no product to sell, just their services. Among the more common service industries are real estate offices, accounting firms, advertising and public relations firms, and such professionals as lawyers, medical practitioners, and architects. Since service industries do not necessarily require the concentration of population that is found in large cities, they may locate virtually anywhere.

Understanding the needs of these submarkets allows the agent to approach companies within them with utmost confidence. For example, if space is available in the financial district of a metropolitan area, the building's attraction to stock brokerage firms and banking facilities is maximum and should be capitalized on by the leasing agent. Awareness of the type of tenancy that already exists in a building's neighborhood, either urban or suburban, is the first step in being able to attract those tenants to the building being leased.

Effect of Market Segmentation on Marketing Strategy

Market segmentation is not an end in itself. Its purpose, rather, is to identify specific types of firms toward which the marketing effort should be aimed. Having defined the target markets, attention may be turned to identifying the way to appeal to these users. The message relayed through advertising (discussed in chapter 5), public relations (discussed in chapter 6), and the continuous personal selling efforts of the agent must be made with these targets in mind.

In order to guarantee that an effective marketing strategy can be formulated from the identification of target markets, two rules should be followed when the office market is segmented: (1) The submarkets must be reachable, and (2) the submarkets must be substantial in size. Only if these qualifications are met will the efforts invested in segmenting the market yield maximum results.

If a submarket is identified that cannot be reached, then defining that submarket is pointless. It must be possible to get promotional materials in the hands of these users. With certain consumer goods (e.g., household cleaners, dental hygiene products), interest in the product can be aroused by sending samples to potential customers. But office space cannot be distributed. The only way to reach potential users is to successfully distribute information about the building to them.

Submarkets also must be large enough in size to warrant directing leasing efforts to them. Only if the submarket is of sufficient size will the amount of time and money spent cultivating the firms within it be profitable to the leasing agency. For example, if an identified submarket were made up of film distributors, it is likely that no more than two or three companies within that submarket would be found. Such an undersized submarket probably would not justify the endeavors of the leasing agent.

Market Research

Market segmentation is not a one-time-only process. The office market continually changes, and, consequently, the submarkets within the overall market change as well. What may have been an identifiable submarket at one point may become quite heterogeneous within a short period of time.

To keep aware of changes in the market and the effect these changes can have on the submarkets that have been targeted for attention, market research is necessary. Market research is the systematic and ongoing process of collecting information about changes in tenant occupancy, building construction and remodeling and demolition, outside influences causing fluctuation in supply and demand, and other variables that might precipitate a shift in the needs and wants of office users.

For example, consider a simplified, hypothetical case: An agent is leasing space in a professional medical building that has a low occupancy rate. Faced with the dilemma of determining what type of promotion should be used, market research can provide direction. For instance, it could reveal that a new hospital complex is soon to be constructed within a mile of the subject. Hence, the medical office building can become an attractive site for doctors who will practice at the new facility. As the agent considers the change that will occur in the market and the benefits of the building, the appropriate mar-

Market Segmentation

keting tactics will come to light. In this way, market research sharpens the understanding of the environment in which the product exists and gives direction to the leasing effort.

Changes in the rental market will have a definite impact on the degree of success of a leasing program. Repetitive market surveys can provide valuable information about absorption rates (the estimate of the rate at which office space will be leased or occupied each year) and pertinent supply factors. Other market data can be accumulated and from it projections made regarding population changes, local economic and financial trends, employment, construction and housing, retail sales, and consumer profiles. Professional market research firms may be hired to perform surveys, or a leasing firm may do its own research and analysis.

If a firm has access to a computer, it can be programmed to provide current, valuable information on the marketplace including office users within the target markets. The input for such a computer program generally is provided to the programmer by the firm's leasing agents. For example, each agent may be required to fill out a prospect card (as referenced in chapter 5, figure 5.2) for every interview. The information indicated on this card is then fed into the computer. As the accumulation of data becomes substantial and if the system is updated periodically, it can become a useful source of market information for the agent. Depending on the program, the system may allow retrieval of detailed information about office space users as to location, area occupied, and lease expiration date. The name of the agent who supplied the input also might be programmed for future reference. For example, such a system may make it possible to retrieve a list of:

1. All office users within a specified city zip code that occupy 2,000 to 5,000 square feet and whose present leases will expire in three to nine months.
2. All office users in a city whose input was provided by a specific agent and which currently occupy 2,000 to 4,000 square feet.
3. All companies currently leasing space in a specific building.

Obviously, the kind of information provided by an information retrieval system can be quite valuable when market segmentation is adopted as part of the marketing strategy. For instance, if the agent determines that one of the target markets is all those users who occupy fewer than 5,000 square feet, the system may be able to provide a list of firms that fall into this category. Likewise, if the subject property is located in zip code 60012, by retrieving a list of all office users who have this same zip code, the agent has segmented the market by location and can begin calling on these companies.

The information requested can be as broad or as narrow as the leasing agent needs, since a computer program can be designed to provide as much or as little information as necessary. If an agent does not have such a computerized system available, it would be profitable to visit an agency that does and see how that system works for its agents.

Summary

Office requirements for office users vary. As a result, no one building will be able to attract every user in the marketplace. It is imperative to focus on specific types of office users whose requirements are compatible with the subject property. To accomplish this, all office users must be divided into segments or submarkets. All of the users in each of these submarkets shares a common characteristic, such as office location or size. Likewise, office users can be segmented according to the nature of their business operation, specifically government, corporate, institutional, or service. The purpose of market segmentation is to enable the leasing agent, through study and understanding of the marketplace, to identify those target markets to whom marketing strategy should be directed.

Because the market is dynamic, it is necessary for the agent to study it on an ongoing basis. Constant changes reflected in tenant occupancy, building construction, and remodeling and demolition must be evaluated in order for marketing efforts to be carried out effectively. Market surveys that analyze data relating to population changes, local economic and financial trends, construction and housing starts, retail sales, and consumer profiles give guidance in tailoring the leasing efforts to the proper submarket. Whether the agent performs the research, contracts for the services of a research firm, adopts a computerized system of information retrieval, or uses a combination of these, the data gathered will provide a clearer picture of the office market and how that market should be segmented and approached.

5 Advertising

One of the key considerations in creating a marketing plan for office space is the marketing mix, which takes into account the product, the pricing system, the distribution structure, and promotional activities. Since each of these components must be weighed in preparing an effective marketing plan, it follows that at some point the leasing agent must turn attention to determining what combination of promotional activities will achieve the goals of the marketing plan and, more specifically, the goals of the marketing strategy. Various tools are available to the agent, including public relations, personal selling, and, the focus of this chapter, advertising.

Advertising is a hybrid business function, a tactical representation of marketing strategy in art, words, and thought within the framework of commercial requirements. It is used to influence attitudes in such a way as to generate sales and, hopefully, profits, for both the leasing agency and the building's ownership. For the leasing agent who is promoting and leasing office space, advertising becomes the means of supplying product information to potential tenants. Without advertising, they might never learn of an office building's availability.

Advertising is the purchase of time (radio and television) or space (periodicals, outdoor) and therefore is not to be confused with public relations, in which no direct purchase is involved. Business advertising is mass, nonpersonal, paid communication. Its purpose is to provide information, shape attitudes, and promote a building's image. Advertising—from the Latin *advertere* which means "to turn to"— turns the attention of a target audience to a particular product. Because the leasing agent wants to attract the attention of a specific group of office space users, advertising is very much a part of the leasing function. Advertising can be especially helpful in stimulating interest in a building suffering from a declining occupancy, introducing a new building to the market, or reintroducing a renovated building.

Classification of Advertising Campaigns

An advertising campaign is a coordinated series of promotional activities that revolve around a common theme. Advertising campaigns may be classified into one of two general categories: primary demand and selective demand.

Primary demand advertising is designed to introduce a generic type or class of product rather than for a specific brand. For example, smoke alarms are a general product type. When they were introduced to consumers, primary demand ads were used to establish the product in the marketplace.

On the other hand, advertising with selective demand assumes that the consumer is aware of and comprehends a type of product and seeks to differentiate a specific brand of that product from competitors. For instance, selective demand advertising urges consumers to buy the XYZ brand smoke alarm. Through selective demand advertising, a product is shown to be different and better than its competition.

In the leasing of office space, primary demand is assumed. It is known that the demand for office space exists. It is the principles of selective demand that are relevant to the leasing efforts. A relocating firm or a newly established company will be looking for a specific amount of space in a building that offers certain amenities and services, a prestigious address, transportation conveniences, and the like. These office users know what they want but not where to find it; selective demand advertising can give them direction.

Selection of Advertising Media

The selection of the appropriate media for waging a selective demand advertising campaign is important to the campaign's success. The selection is not based on trial and error but rather on the results of a systematic process requiring research and understanding of the total

Advertising

marketing picture. Some of the important factors that influence the selection of media include these:

1. The product.
2. The target market.
3. The monies allocated for advertising.
4. The objectives of the advertising campaign.
5. Competitors' advertising campaigns.

The establishment of advertising policy and the selection of media are often the responsibility of the leasing agent. However, that policy and decision should be discussed with experts and the actual preparation of the advertising should be handled by them as well. The expertise, whether provided by in-house staff or an outside agency, is critical to success in the use of advertising. Nonetheless, the logistics of advertising and the basic principles behind it should be understood by the agent responsible for leasing office space, as mistakes and misdirected energies can be quite costly.

Goods and services can be promoted through numerous media. However, not all of them have proven to be successful in leasing efforts. Effective vehicles for promoting office space are newspapers and magazines, billboards and signs, direct mail, television and radio, and portable presentations. Again, expertise in advertising becomes invaluable in the use of these vehicles. The advertising specialist can determine which vehicle will reach the target audience and prove a wise investment.

Print Media

The print media—including newspapers, magazines, and journals—collectively represent one of the most important vehicles available for office space advertising. Of the various print media, newspapers are the most popular in capturing advertising dollars. Newspaper advertising is advantageous for several reasons. First, it offers more regional flexibility than other media. A newspaper's circulation area may include an entire city or even several cities; it may even offer circulation to specific neighborhoods and suburban areas. Second, if the newspaper in which an ad is placed has prestige and recognition in the community, the building advertised will be seen as a reflection of this image. Third, newspaper advertising offers intense coverage, in that newspapers are so widely read, especially among the type of people who would be in positions to make decisions about leasing space. Fourth, newspaper advertising is timely. An ad can be placed or cancelled within one or a few days' notice. Therefore, it is easy to keep advertising information up to date.

There are disadvantages as well: Most newspapers are read hastily and discarded; the material in newspapers is timely and therefore, gets stale quickly. Consequently, newspaper ads do not have a lengthy impact and must make an immediate impression. Furthermore, ad reproduction is not of maximum quality and details are lost. If a picture has to sell the product, considerable thought should go into the selection of the photograph to be used for newspaper reproduction.

As mentioned previously, the actual preparation of all advertisements, including those placed in newspapers, should be in the hands of specialists. Nonetheless, the leasing agent should be aware of the most common formats for newspaper ads and how they are created.

Newspaper ads fall into two categories: classified ads and display ads. Classified ads (or want ads) are small notices, usually one column wide, placed in special classified sections of daily and weekly newspapers, Sunday newspapers and supplements, and specialized newspapers. Publishers dictate the type size and layout of classified ads yet satisfactorily accommodate the buyers of space. Classified advertising has not always been determined to be a cost-effective means of promoting office space. The leasing agent is advised to research its usefulness and measure results to determine if the benefits of the expense are worth the investment.

A display ad is usually more than one column wide and has a border framing a headline, informative copy, possibly an illustration, and a company or building logo. Obviously, such an ad is more noticeable than a classified ad. Consequently, it is usually more expensive.

While display ads commonly are associated with newspapers, they also appear frequently in other print media that take advertising, such as magazines, trade journals, and professional directories. To determine which publications would be effective vehicles for promoting office space, the leasing agent must research the reading habits of prospective tenants, specifically those in the building's target market. Based on the results of this study of reading habits, the agent can decide which publications would be likely to reach the proper individuals. For example, if a building is located within the financial district of a city, the agent leasing its space might consider advertising in local business and financial magazines which

Advertising

may be read by financial businessmen. By advertising to specific markets, waste of advertising dollars can be avoided.

Publishers of periodicals may establish guidelines as to the size and style of type, arrangement of headlines and body text, and other visual devices. Such restrictions are imposed to ensure that the graphic character of the ads is compatible with the character of the publication. They should not discourage the agent from advertising in magazines, journals, and professional directories since it does offer advantages, including these:

- Advertising in certain publications can be a relatively inexpensive way of reaching target markets.
- Ads tend to reproduce well in black and white as well as color.
- Periodicals have a long life. People tend to keep them and read them longer than newspapers.
- Prestige publications lend prestige to an office building advertised in them.

Naturally, the advantages are partially offset by disadvantages. The lack of flexibility is the key drawback. Although some nationally distributed magazines run regional advertising, not all of them do. This inability to fit copy to local situations can be a detriment. Too, last-minute changes in copy are virtually impossible. Nonetheless, when an advertising budget is being drafted, display advertising in periodicals should be evaluated as a possible way to advertise office space.

Outdoor Advertising

Outdoor advertising is another medium used to promote the availability of office space. The increased number of automobiles coupled with the growing population has resulted in a high degree of mobility and consequently a high exposure of outdoor advertising to consumers. There are several types of outdoor advertising—billboards, electric spectaculars, painted displays, and transit ads. The key to effectual outdoor advertising is in selecting the appropriate type for the situation.

Leasing firms generally find billboards useful in these types of situations:

1. When there is a need to produce activity for the leasing firm rather than a particular building.

2. When a new, large office building is being introduced to the market.
3. When the market's knowledge about a building, such as one that has been extensively remodeled, must be altered.

In order to reserve billboard space, it is necessary to go through an outdoor advertising firm. Most firms offer programs that rotate advertisements among billboards throughout a selected market area. In this way, billboards achieve increased exposure of a property to the market.

Electric spectaculars are large illuminated signs with special lighting and action effects. Usually custom-made and located in important traffic centers, electric spectaculars draw attention to a new office building or complex.

Painted displays are illuminated or nonilluminated bulletins or wall panels painted on roofs or sides of buildings in cities and along highways. Likewise, a painted display may be found on the fencing often placed around an office building construction site. Even though painted displays may be somewhat costly, they may be potentially profitable if they are located where enough interested businessmen will see them. If such displays are used, they should be repainted regularly. Otherwise, they will reflect a poor image of the building or agency being promoted.

Transit advertising is the term used for signs on or in trains, subways, buses, taxicabs, and other public transportation vehicles and the stations from which they operate. The cost usually is reasonable, and studies have shown that readership of and retention of information given in transit ads is high.

Building Signage

Signs placed on or near a building being leased are commonplace and considered to be valuable promotional tools for the leasing agency. However, a building's curb appeal can be tarnished by a large, distasteful "For Lease" sign. An attractive, functional environment is more effective than the largest of signs. A prospect is not interested in leasing the sign; the building should promote itself. The effective sign merely informs the prospect that office space is available and indicates to whom inquiries should be directed.

The sign should be tastefully designed and compatible with the architecture of the building and should be erected in an inconspicuous location so that it fully but subtly does the job it is sup-

Advertising

posed to do. If the sign must attract the attention of automobile traffic, it should be perpendicular to the traffic flow and easily readable by persons in moving vehicles. The lettering on the sign must be large enough to be readable to passers-by, and the aesthetics must be pleasing.

Sign maintenance is mandatory. A sign should always be in an upright, vertical position. If it is vandalized in any way, it should be repaired or replaced immediately, before the building's image is tainted.

Direct Mail

Direct mail and direct advertising are still other means by which the leasing firm can effectively promote office space. The difference between the two is subtle: Direct mail is a printed promotional piece sent through the mail; whereas if the same promotional piece is given to prospects personally by salespeople, it is direct advertising. For the purpose of this discussion, the term direct mail will be used to refer to both types of promotional activity.

Direct mail is one of the most effective means of educating a market about an office building and its amenities and services and creating a desired image. There are both limitations and advantages to direct mail advertising, yet the latter far outweigh the former in leasing of office space. Generally speaking, the gains of direct advertising are these:

1. If the right lists of potential tenants are secured, the target markets can be reached with limited waste of circulating materials.
2. Since the release time of direct mail is controlled by the leasing agency, advantage can be taken of business conditions and other opportunities in the marketplace.
3. The graphic possibilities of direct advertising are only as limited as the creator's imagination.
4. There is a personal touch in direct ads in that they can be addressed to specific parties.
5. A direct mail campaign can be implemented without competitors being aware of it.
6. The target market can be reached in a short period of time.
7. Direct mail encourages response from the audience; a promotional piece received in the mail is a reason to call for information about the building advertised.

8. Direct mail is selective; a specific audience can be reached by such a campaign.

Limitations of direct advertising are these:

1. Finding or developing appropriate mailing lists can be difficult.
2. Direct ads often connote to the public "junk mail." Therefore, direct ads should be well designed, well written, and colorful to create a positive impact on the reader. Individuals with specialized skills can create attractive and attention-getting pieces. This not only would help to combat the "junk mail" image but would stimulate readership of the message.
3. Direct mail can be extremely expensive, both from the standpoint of skyrocketing mailing costs and producing and printing quality, eye-catching pieces.

A direct mail advertisement may take various forms, with the final decision based on the market to be reached, the image to be conveyed, and the information to be relayed. It may well be worth the investment of an expertly designed piece in order to captivate a specific audience. "Expert" does not necessarily mean expensive. It does mean, however, that the direct mail piece must fulfill its purpose. The six most popular formats of direct mail are these:

1. Broadsides. A broadside is a folder that opens up into one large ad. Each page may be an ad in itself. Because of its size, a variety of graphic styles can be used.
2. Form letters. A form letter with a personalized address and salutation can be quite effective and often is used to begin a direct mail campaign.
3. Circulars. Circular ads, often called leaflets, are not mailable by themselves but rather are additions or inserts in other pieces.
4. Postcards. Inexpensiveness and high attention value make postcards a useful and effective direct mail piece. The intention of a postcard is to get immediate attention and stimulate direct action.
5. Portfolio. A portfolio is a collection of advertisements and other promotional pieces. The multi-ad approach promotes a building by giving testimony of its value.
6. Brochures. The brochure, the most commonly used direct advertising piece, is a pamphlet that describes the building being leased or the agency handling the account or both.

Advertising

Of these six types of advertising pieces, broadsides, form letters, postcards, and brochures are the most useful in a rental advertising campaign. Still, any of the other direct mail pieces can help create or enhance a prospect's image of the product and serve as an effective frontrunner for the personal selling efforts of the agent. In all instances, if follow-up is feasible and can be done in a timely manner, it should be pursued.

One of the most valuable direct mail pieces is the brochure. It can explain and answer the questions a prospect may raise about the product and generate interest in it. There is no rule of thumb on how lavish or plain a brochure must be. The purpose and objective of the brochure dictates its design and content. Items often included in a brochure are the features and benefits of the product; the building and neighborhood amenities; maps and photographs of the product and its neighborhood; and other pertinent facts that might arouse prospect interest. For instance, the brochure might offer information about the building's management or architect, the background of the leasing agent, and the credentials of ownership. This data is especially applicable if the building is owned or managed or was designed by a prestigious company or individual, as is the case with Rockefeller Center in New York, the First International Bank Building in Dallas, or Pennzoil Place in Houston.

Broadcast Media

In the leasing of office space, broadcast media—including radio and television—have had an enormous impact on advertising programs and, consequently, advertising budgets. If broadcast media are used to advertise office space, the objectives of the campaign, the target markets, and a distinct message must be specified. Experts in the field should be consulted to design the ad depending on the medium that is used.

Radio advertising requires special care in selecting proper stations and programs, times of day, and the type of listenership. Despite the in-depth attention that must be given to a radio ad campaign, it should be considered because radio is a flexible and timely medium that can reach a large segment of the market.

The use of television as a means of promoting office space is a more delicate decision to make because of the expense involved and the potential waste if a target audience cannot be reached. It is usually unprofitable in a large metropolitan area where, because the mass audience is so large, it is quite costly. However, a leasing agency in a smaller area may find the use of local television a successful means of promotion. Again, experts in the field of broadcast media should be consulted prior to implementing a television advertising campaign.

Portable Presentations
In order to point out all the advantages of an office building to a potential tenant, the leasing agent may find it worthwhile to use portable presentations, such as drawings, models, slide programs, movies, and easel presentations. These have been proven to be convincing ways of promoting office space. Although some presentations can be costly to produce and require expertise, their ability to gain the confidence of the viewer and encourage a prospect to lease office space merits consideration. Once available, the agent may be able to set up—in either the agent's or prospect's office—a portable presentation that could convert a prospect to a tenant.

If the prospect cannot tour the building, a model or accurate artist's drawing can serve as an effective alternative, thereby increasing the prospect's interest level. And, the prospect should be able to visualize the firm as a tenant. Furthermore, many office buildings are marketed before they are constructed. In these preleasing situations, color renderings and models are essential, in that they provide the only view of the completed property.

The Advertising Campaign

The leasing agent should not regard each type of advertising medium as a separate and distinct entity that is used independently of the others. Rather, they should be seen collectively as a means of coordinating an effective advertising program based on a single promotional theme. To whatever degree each promotional device will be used to promote an office building, the overall promotional scheme should be harmonious with the entire marketing plan and with the building's image.

There are two keys to a successful advertising campaign. The first is to establish a theme compatible with the building, then maintain and reinforce the theme throughout the campaign. If the building being leased is a modern but conservative high rise, all of the advertising material should reflect this contemporary but unostentatious image. The second key is the agency's ability to coordinate

Advertising

the efforts of the entire promotional team, including both in-house artists, designers, and salesmen and outside advertising agencies. Based on knowledge of the selling points of the product, market conditions, and the use of the various advertising media, the leasing agent should be equipped to successfully build and organize an effective campaign around a single promotional concept.

Analysis of Advertising Effectiveness

Knowing what types of advertising media are available for use in leasing efforts is only the first step in creating an effective advertising campaign. The agent also must know how much to spend for advertising. To do this, an evaluation of the effectiveness of advertising is necessary.

The cost of promoting office space can be computed on a cost-per-prospect basis. This is simply a matter of maintaining an accurate record of the number of prospects produced by each advertisement, verifying the cost of that advertisement, then calculating the cost of producing each prospect. The most effective medium is the one that produces the greatest number of prospects at the lowest cost.

For example, assume that a display ad placed in a local business magazine costs $1,200. If the ad produces six prospects, the cost per prospect is $200. On the other hand, assume a billboard advertising campaign costs $10,000, but only 10 businessmen contact the leasing agent because of it. The cost-per-prospect factor is $1,000. Obviously, the magazine ad is much more cost effective than the billboard.

As a rule, a leasing agent will have some idea as to how many prospects will be needed to obtain a single signed lease. This data, together with the cost-per-prospect factor, can be used in establishing an advertising budget. This relationship relies heavily on market conditions, the nature of the building being leased, and the experience of the leasing agent. In any event, once this factor is determined and based on the cost of producing prospects via the various advertising media, the leasing agent should be in a position to establish a realistic advertising budget in which every dollar is a sound investment.

Summary

The basic principles of advertising must be understood by the leasing agent if an effective campaign for promoting office space is to be waged. Mistakes and misguided efforts are costly and wasteful. Necessary precautions should always be taken and advertising specialists' guidance obtained to make advertising cost-effective.

Many different advertising media may be adopted. The avenue a firm ultimately takes is determined by marketing objectives and the funds made available to this portion of the promotional mix.

Whether print media, direct advertising, broadcast media, or portable presentations are used to promote office space, it is imperative that a coordinated campaign be planned, records of prospect traffic be kept, and cost-effectiveness be measured. Only by performing this analysis can the leasing agent be sure that the purchase of time and space is worthwhile and profitable.

6 Public Relations

Public relations is a business function used to secure publicity and market exposure by means other than advertising. As explained in chapter 5, advertising is a purchased form of mass communication. Public relations, on the other hand, involves no direct purchase and is a more subtle approach. Its purpose is to develop good rapport and a reciprocal understanding between the leasing agency and the general public and between the agency and present tenants.

Public relations encompasses a variety of activities ranging from making a speech to issuing a press release. Two authorities in the field, Scott M. Cutlip and Allen H. Center, summarize in *Effective Public Relations* (Englewood Cliffs, New Jersey: Prentice-Hall, Inc., 1971, p. 10) the functions which come under the umbrella of public relations:

> The daily practices of public relations consist of a multitude of little tasks and a few big tasks. It is the application of common sense, common courtesy, and common decency. It can be doing favors for others. It can be pleading a cause in the area of public opinions. It can be entertaining a visitor. It can be preparing a speech of giving one. It can be a news conference or the dedication of a new building. It can be as important as providing counsel on real estate practices. It can be helping a newswriter get a story from a press-shy executive. To show the immense variety of public relations situations, you need only look at your own daily routine. Public relations techniques are everywhere, but you do not become aware of them until you realize that the actions you take to improve your relationship with the public you serve are—public relations.

The Public Relations Program

Cutlip and Center also cite in their text four basic steps that should be integrated into a public relations program to ensure its success:

1. *Research-Listing.* This means probing the opinions, attitudes, and reactions of persons concerned with the acts and policies of an organization, then evaluating the inflow. This task also requires determination of the facts regarding your organization. *"What's our problem?"*
2. *Planning-Decision Making.* This means bringing these attitudes, opinions, ideas, and reactions to bear on the policies and programs of an organization. This will enable it to chart a course in the mutual interests of all concerned. *"Here's what we can do."*
3. *Communication.* This means explaining and dramatizing the chosen course to all those who may be affected and whose support is essential. *"Here's what we did and why."*
4. *Evaluation.* This means evaluating the results of the program and the effectiveness of techniques used. *"How did we do?"* (Englewood Cliffs, New Jersey: Prentice-Hall, Inc., 1964, p. 108.)

By continuously being mindful of these steps, a leasing agency can ensure that public relations is recognized as an ongoing business activity. Each of the steps should be assigned equal value and given equal attention; in this way, the marketing objectives, inasmuch as they are achievable through public relations efforts, should be met. The application of these four steps to a leasing agency's public relations program is not difficult. For instance, an agency in the southwestern United States sets out to develop one of the first underground office buildings in a large metropolitan city in the same geographical area. The energy savings, reduced maintenance, and improved security are just some of the benefits to be gained from the underground concept. However, with such innovative construction taking place in the city, the public relations firm employed by the leasing agency feels the need to educate the public on this concept and its benefits and raise interest so that by the time the building is completed in approximately two years, the concepts and advantages of such a building will be understood. Ultimate acceptance of the building will come when the building is complete and potential tenants and the general public can tour and evaluate it.

The public relations program for this project includes the four steps suggested by Cutlip and Center, specifically: (1) research of the public relations problem; (2) adoption of plans to emphasize the building's aesthetics, safety, security, and quietness; (3) ongoing communication with the public through photographs and showings of the model, announcements of the kickoff of construction and all leasing activity, and, later, a press tour; and (4) evaluation, upon completion of the building, of the effectiveness of the strategy used.

To create or maintain a positive public image, a leasing agency first must audit its present position with the public. This calls for intense and objective self-evaluation. The purpose of this introspective study is to create a framework upon which a program can be built and a sound public position be maintained or cultivated. As James D. Downs Jr., CPM®, emphasized in *Principles of Real Estate Management* (Chicago: Institute of Real Estate Management, 1975, p. 360):

> The only purpose of critical self-examination is to establish a course of action. It is useless for the businessman to acquaint himself with the deficiencies of his organization unless he is willing to act to remedy the conditions responsible for such deficiencies. Too often, a business operates in a well-defined "rut." Executives and employees fall easily into crystallized routines from which it is extremely difficult to extricate themselves.

Having determined how the agency is perceived by the public, it then is prepared to undertake the second step outlined above and set definite objectives, specific strategies, and detailed tactics for a public relations program. Generalities are wasteful and may send a public relations program off into aimless directions. Alternate plans for meeting objectives should exist for back-up purposes. Public opinion and response is so varied that a once-successful strategy may fail when it is implemented a second time. Every public relations plan must be evaluated regularly to determine its ongoing effectiveness.

Public Relations Vehicles

Because of the importance of public relations, relevant promotional activities should be planned and implemented with care. Like advertising, public relations can be directed by in-house personnel who have training and experience in the field. However, it is not uncommon for a leasing agency to contract with a public relations firm to oversee its public relations program. If the decision is made to use an outside firm, the firm must be experienced and in-tune with office leasing methods, aware of the image to be conveyed, and suited to the specific needs of the project. Inadequate and improper public relations can destroy the image of the office building and the leasing agency.

Several tools are commonly used to enhance an agency's public image and, in turn, the image of a building being leased. The most popular are press releases, ceremonies, and community involvement. The image to be projected and the promotional budget dictate the appropriate methods to be used in order to achieve marketing objectives.

Press Releases

The press release, sometimes known as a news release, is one of the most widely known and extensively used public relations tools. It is a newsworthy announcement or publicity item issued to the press. A press release should be clear, straightforward, and timely and give only the facts, never opinion. The length is dictated by the importance of the facts being announced. When applicable, illustrations should be included.

The mechanics of preparing a press release are not complicated and should be understood by the leasing agent. A review of the sample press release in figure 6.1 calls attention to a few simple guidelines:

1. The agency or company name and address are found at the top of the page. The upper right-hand corner includes the date and the name and phone number of the individual who submits the release.
2. On the left-hand side of the page, near the top, instructions for date of release are indicated. This will read "For Immediate Release" if that is the case or "For Release on or after (date)" should that be required.
3. The actual copy—the story itself—should be typed double spaced using one side only with ample margins on all sides. To indicate the end of a news release, one of the following sets of marks is used: "30," "###," or "***."

A news release issued by a leasing agency can be used to provide information about space being leased or improve the image of the agency itself.

For example, the development of a new office building listed with the agency offers an excellent reason for a series of news releases about ground acquisition, development plans, major tenants, ownership, selection of architect, contract award for construction, and the management entity. Preleasing progress, status of the various states of construction, and innovations in construction materials or pro-

Figure 6.1

DURNHAM DEVELOPERS	NEWS
500 Main Street (208) 344-1212	RELEASE
Boise, Idaho 83702	

FOR IMMEDIATE RELEASE   CONTACT: Martha McGregor
                                                                                       Public Information
                                                                                       (208) 344-1215

REYNOLDS SQUARE TO BE RENOVATED BY NEW OWNERS

The Reynolds Square office building, located on the corner of Hawkins Street and Howard Boulevard in downtown Boise, Idaho, has been purchased by Durnham Developers, according to James H. Wilson, Acquisitions Vice-President.

Wilson reports that the 63-year-old, 8-story building will be completely renovated in order to attract many of the new businesses currently flourishing in the downtown area.

The building consists of 110,780 square feet of rentable space and a full basement. According to Wilson, the basement will be installed with screened-off, insulated areas to provide storage space at no extra charge to tenants.

Every effort will be made to preserve the expansive ground floor lobby, which contains several fine examples of art deco, including a variety of brass bas-relief.

A central air-conditioning system will be installed, as well as a small gymnasium and whirlpool bath on the fifth floor for the lunch-hour use of health-conscious executives.

"We expect to repaint the entire interior," Wilson stated, "as well as lay durable but attractive carpeting on the exposed cement corridors." Wilson also expects to place energy-saving light fixtures at a variety of points.

The Reynolds Square office building is currently 70 percent occupied, but Durnham Developers intends to launch a major promotional campaign once renovation is complete. According to Wilson, target date for completion of total renovation is January 3, 1983.

According to Wilson, once renovation is complete, rents will be raised. Space in the Reynolds Square Building currently rents for an average of $5.00 a square foot. Wilson said he could not quote an exact figure for 1983 rents but stressed occupants will definitely find the building a more attractive, comfortable headquarters for their operations.

---

cedure are other news release ideas. Older office buildings also can be the subject of press releases. A remodeling or renovation program, a lease signed with an important tenant, or the naming of a new management or leasing agency merits a news release. In all instances, each time a building is named in the newspaper or on radio or television, its image will be improved. If each press release notes the name of the specific agency handling the leasing of the building, the agency's image will be heightened as well.

Press releases can be sent to the broadcast media, newspapers, and trade and business periodicals. As news releases are so much a part of a public relation's program, the development of good rapport with members of the press is an asset. It would be advantageous to know the real estate and business editors of local newspapers and trade publications and keep them informed of leasing activity.

Promotional Aids

Promotional aids, often referred to as "hand-outs" or "give-aways," include a diversity of creative items ranging from paperweights to rulers to ashtrays to pens and pencils. Most importantly, each of the aids carries the name of the leasing agency or the building being promoted.

Give-aways, while often used as part of ongoing promotional campaigns, are especially valuable during warm-up periods while canvassing. Their purpose is to remind the prospect of the agent's firm and product. If the item is to have a positive impact and not be discarded or its importance taken lightly, it should be well made and tastefully designed.

One give-away item, popular during preleasing of space in an office building under construction, is a hard hat that bears the agency or building logo. Inexpensive yet effective, the hard hat can be given to each serious prospect prior to the tour of the building. The tour itself enables the prospective tenant to get a sense of the building as a potential place of business and provides a one-on-one, on-site opportunity to ask questions about the product. If the hard hat is personalized with the prospect's name, it indicates the seriousness of the agent in obtaining the prospect as a tenant.

Community Involvement

A viable means of establishing a relationship between the leasing agency and the public is through involvement in the community. One way to be visibly active is through speaking engagements. Opportunities to talk to the public are many. Real estate boards, mortgage bankers, appraiser societies, home builders organizations, and apartment associations are just a few of the many trade associations which the leasing agent could address. Special local seminars could be held to inform the public about a new office building project or the renovation of an older building.

It might also be worthwhile to speak to community associations. For instance, the leasing agent might address the local Rotary Club about a new building that is to be constructed, placing emphasis on what it would mean to the local economy. This could be especially valuable if the proposed building is being met with somewhat of a negative public reaction. By addressing local organizations, a strong public image can be created not only with the real estate industry but with the broader business world as well.

Speaking to the public increases visibility and establishes good lines of communication with representatives of potential tenants as well as the general public. However, to successfully use this public relations tool, the agent must be able to speak before a group. An agent inexperienced in public speaking would best forego this type of endeavor until some experience is gained or classroom teaching received. If not properly prepared or equipped, the image of the agency, as well as that of the agent, could be damaged.

A leasing agent who is genuinely interested in community affairs indicates this interest by getting involved. While there is personal satisfaction in such participation, the agent also gleans positive results from a business standpoint: The individuals met through this participation can result in referral sources or prospective tenants for a building, while the agency obtains public recognition.

Leasing agents will find their public images further enhanced if they become members of professional real estate organizations, such as the Institute of Real Estate Management (IREM), Building Owners and Managers Association (BOMA), Sales and Marketing Executives Association (SMEA), and local and national real estate boards. Not only is the agent's professionalism upgraded through such membership, but, by being an active participant, valuable information can be learned through these organizations' publications and by attending seminars and meetings. Trade associations also encourage colleagues who share similar professional interests to develop rapport and exchange practical experience.

Ceremonies

Office buildings often present numerous opportunities for conducting ceremonies that attract the interest of the local news media. New office buildings, ground-breaking ceremonies, topping-out ceremonies, and grand openings are but a few media events that can be planned. The objective of these events is to attract the interest of the press, thereby obtaining coverage and creating interest in the office building being leased.

If such an event is of major local significance, the leasing agent should capitalize on it in order to enhance both the agency's and the building's public image. For instance, when breaking ground for a new office building, the city's mayor, the area's U.S. congressman, or the governor might be invited as a guest speaker. This would make the event even more newsworthy and encourage the press to cover it. In this way, positive editorial comment on local television and radio and in the newspaper may be generated.

In order for important events to make the desired impact on the public, detailed planning is necessary. Serious consideration must be given to invitations and the invitation list, press kits, transportation of dignitaries, entertainment, food and beverages, and the site of the ceremony. The extent to which this is done depends on the size of the event. A major media event is public relations at its zenith and to be interesting and entertaining should be handled by professionals. Obviously, these events can be costly, and their cost effectiveness must be analyzed. If public relations activities are carelessly planned and executed, the pitfalls are rampant. However, well-organized public relations programs have tremendous promotional possibilities and can go far toward generating goodwill with the general and business public.

Business Entertainment

Leasing agents often will entertain prospects, referral sources, centers of influence, and other individuals who are keys to successful leasing efforts. Many business decisions are made in the relaxed atmosphere of a restaurant over breakfast, lunch, or dinner. The person or persons with whom the agent is dining has an opportunity—away from the interruptions and activity of the office—to evaluate the agent's abilities. This opportunity to display professionalism and relay knowledge while creating a positive public image should be exploited.

Summary

In creating a comprehensive public relations program, the leasing agent is met with not one but two goals: To create a positive image of the building in which space is being leased, and to heighten the public's esteem for the leasing agency itself. Establishing and maintaining a positive image and gaining the support and confidence of the public requires that four steps be taken: (1) listening to the public in order to evaluate the existing image; (2) planning image-building programs; (3) communicating with persons whose cooperation is needed; and (4) evaluating the effectiveness of the public

Public Relations

relations techniques used. These steps can be applied both to the building's and the agency's public relations program.

There are several vehicles that can be used in a public relations program, among them being press releases, promotional aids, community involvement, ceremonies, and business entertainment. Each of these has its own design, mechanics, and objectives and can be used to enhance a building's or agency's public image.

A well-planned, well-executed program is needed to gain the recognition and respect of the public. Once this image is achieved, a leasing agency would do well to continually judge and, if necessary, upgrade its performance level as seen in the public eye.

7 Prospecting

Successful marketing of office space demands the leasing agent's continuous effort to attract prospective tenants. While well-designed advertising and public relations programs are profitable ways to promote an office building and its services and amenities, other methods are equally or more effective and should not be overlooked.

Locating Prospects

One of the best ways of obtaining names of prospective tenants is to establish personal contact with both representatives of firms that might be interested in leasing space and other persons who might have knowledge of such firms. The systematic search for potential tenants based on this concept of personal interaction is called prospecting and can be carried on in various ways. The most common techniques include developing a referral network, canvassing, and cooperating with other leasing agents. The leasing agent who adopts a methodical program of locating tenants using these prospecting methods should experience little difficulty either filling a new office building or finding replacement tenants for an older one.

Referrals

Satisfied tenants, business associates (e.g., furniture vendors, interior designers, mortgage bankers), persons in influential positions, and friends are often aware of firms in search of office space. If a strong line of communication is established with these individuals, referrals for possible tenancy may be generated.

A referral system is worthwhile for numerous reasons. Most importantly, time can be saved: First, appointments with prospective tenants usually can be made easily, especially if the contact agrees to act as an intermediary in arranging a meeting. Second, the referral acts as a kind of screening process, since it is doubtful the referral would have been made unless it was known that space was being sought. Indeed, the percentage of prospects who ultimately become tenants is often greater among those who have been referred by knowledgeable contacts than those obtained from other sources.

Few persons have as much potential value to a leasing agent as those who occupy positions of authority within a neighborhood or region. These are the people who make up what are known as centers of influence and have information about various businesses and the office space they occupy. They may even be in positions to apply pressure on these companies in their selection of office space. For example, consider an office building that has a bank on the ground level and some of the bank's departments on the second and third floors. The president of the bank will have a keen interest in the image or tenancy of the building and, therefore, may use his position to convince certain firms to lease space in it. The prospect is complimented by the interest shown by the bank president, enabling the building to secure a tenant compatible with the product and its image.

Persons who exercise this kind of authority may be found in a wide range of positions. Some may be active in city or state government and consequently responsible for local economic development and the rental of offices for these agencies. Others may be key figures in financial institutions and, based on their knowledge of financing instruments being negotiated, be aware of business expansion that is to occur. Members of chambers of commerce will know of new businesses that are about to enter an area and the plans of existing companies. Representatives of utility companies also may have access to information that could be valuable to the leasing agent in obtaining prospects.

Individuals who hold such positions of power should be cultivated and constant communication with them maintained. By keeping these people informed about plans for developing new offices, available office space, progress in leasing existing space, and relevant policy changes, these centers of influence can be enlisted in obtaining prospects.

Figure 7.1

Referral Source Card

Firm_____
Contact_____Title_____
Address_____City_____State_____Zip_____
Phone (____)_____Source Comment_____
Spouse Name_____Children_____
Interests_____

Contact Date	Remarks	Achievement

The astute leasing agent stays in regular communication with all referral sources via telephone, business breakfasts and luncheons, or personal visits. Such actions encourage ongoing cooperation. One method of ensuring that no contacts are forgotten is to keep an accurate record of persons who provide names of possible prospects. Usually an agent will use contacts to secure referrals over a period of time. Thus, it is important to maintain a file on contacts when they are called upon. The referral source card (sampled in figure 7.1) can be used for recording this information. A well-designed referral source card provides space to note the contact's title or position, place of employment, and telephone number. Information about the contact's spouse, children, and personal interests can be valuable as an "ice breaker" when a contact is called. Any sincere expression of concern about family and interests encourages the contact's support and allegiance. Preferably, these referral source cards will be organized in a tickler file, arranged in such a way that they will remind the leasing agent to get in touch with the contacts on a periodic basis. (Establishing a tickler file is discussed in the latter part of this chapter under Maintaining Leasing Activity Records.)

If a contact makes a referral, many leasing agents consider it good business practice to ask permission to use the source's name when approaching the prospect. The contact even may offer the leasing agent a business card to present to the prospect, write a note of introduction, or telephone the prospect recommending the agent's building. If a referred prospect ultimately becomes a tenant, this should be noted on the referral source card and the source should be given an appropriate acknowledgement of appreciation. A note of thanks or a suggestion that the new tenant use the services or goods supplied by the referral source is a thoughtful gesture that can lead to continued cooperation.

Canvassing

Canvassing is a difficult means of obtaining prospects; however, because it can be quite productive, canvassing must be included in every leasing campaign. Canvassing, sometimes known as cold prospecting or cold calling, involves visiting current office users within a defined area in the hopes of locating prospects. Usually, little or no information is known about firms that are contacted, their needs, or their financial status. The canvasser is hoping that by coincidence the call may uncover a company in need of office space.

The experienced leasing agent learns quickly to use various

Prospecting 93

resources in order to take as much of the unknown out of canvassing as possible. For instance, the agent can review the directory in a building to be canvassed to see if it lists the names of or at least offers some hint to the individuals who should be approached by the agent. The agent can pursue the status of prospective tenants through reference materials, such as *Standard and Poor's Register*. The agent also will want to find out who has the authority to make decisions regarding leasing of space and where this person can be reached. For example, the A-B Company may have a large, multi-floor, regional office in Omaha, but leasing decisions are made by executives in Chicago. Thus, the agent also must make a contact in Chicago. Newspapers and business journals print stories of business mergers, acquisitions, development of subsidiaries, and expansions, which can suggest needs for relocation or additional space.

The success of a canvassing program depends on the leasing agent's ability to gain access to executive-level personnel. Consequently, the agent should master the subtle art of being insistent without being abrasive. It is probable that the agent will be met with instant rejection. Only by being psychologically prepared will the leasing agent be able to carry on diplomatically despite a negative reaction. On the other hand, if a prospect shows even the slightest interest in the product, a promotional brochure should be left and a written reminder made to contact that prospect periodically.

When segmenting the office market, the leasing agent recognized that a key target market consists of firms currently located within the immediate area of the subject property. Canvassing can be one of the most effective methods of reaching this market segment. Canvassing efforts begin in areas closest to the subject building and progress outward in concentric circles. In this way, a thorough canvassing program results in a complete sweep of the territory. These face-to-face contacts usually provide a broad spectrum of relevant data about the marketplace. For example, through personal canvassing efforts, the leasing agent may learn which tenants are expanding, which buildings are full and thus are creating a pent-up demand, when certain leases are to expire, and what rental rates are being paid. The leasing agent creates from the information harvested a detailed profile of each of the subject building's comparables, and it further refines the agent's understanding of the market and is a guide in determining the most profitable marketing approaches.

Many leasing agents prefer to canvass by telephone rather than by personal solicitation, the attitude being that telephone calls can generate business from a latent market. Certainly, the telephone can save time, and some prospects may be more receptive to telephone calls than visits. However, a telephone call never should be regarded as a substitute for a personal visit but only as a way to determine if a company might be considering a move. If the response is positive, an appointment for a personal interview may be arranged.

If the telephone is used to locate prospects, some guidelines must be followed. A receptionist or secretary usually will answer the telephone. Confidently and politely, the agent should ask to speak with the person responsible for leasing office space but should not be surprised if the call does not initially go through to the appropriate individual. Once having reached the proper person, the call may be considered an interruption; therefore, after identifying himself, the agent should ask the prospect if the time is convenient for the call. This conveys recognition of the value of the other party's time and sets a positive tone for the conversation. If the time is inconvenient, arrangements should be made to call at another time.

The agent's voice must be pleasant and sure, and listening skills must be sharp. If the firm's representative reveals that the company may be interested in relocating or its lease expires in the near future, a personal appointment should be made. If the expiration date of the prospect's lease is remote (two years or more), the agent should note this and plan to pursue this prospect in the future.

Unfortunately, canvassing often is regarded erroneously by some as a waste of time. Only a few of the companies approached will have an immediate need for office space. In consequence, the ratio of the number of persons canvassed to successful rentals is generally small. Figure 7.2 graphically shows a hypothetical relationship. The market, the product, and the leasing agent's skills contribute significantly to the actual return on canvassing efforts. Furthermore, canvassing should be valued at least for its possible long-term results: Should a company have need for office space in the future, it is likely to contact the agent who stopped by and left a brochure describing an especially appealing building.

Cooperation with Other Agents

On occasion, leasing agents within an area cooperate with one another in obtaining prospects. If properly planned and administered, a program of agent cooperation can be mutually beneficial. Such a program operates in this way: If one agent has no space accommodating to a prospect's needs, the prospect is referred to another agent

Prospecting 95

Figure 7.2

Relationship between number of prospects canvassed and number of prospects still present at the various stages of obtaining a signed lease.

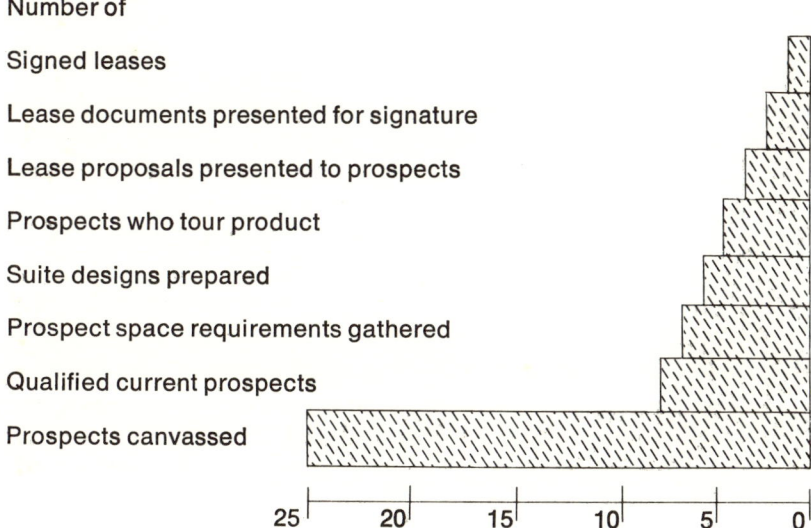

with a suitable product. Likewise, the first agent would be referred by the second agent if the reverse occurred. In either case, if the prospect leases space, the commission earned is shared by the two agencies.

To instigate a cooperative program, the leasing agent can send out a letter of introduction and a detailed product description to another agent or agents with established reputations. In a subsequent telephone call or personal meeting, the agents can make arrangements to help one another in responding to the needs of prospects. As a result of cooperative efforts several qualified leasing agents may be offering a single product to the marketplace.

Agent cooperation programs, however, are not without potential pitfalls. For instance, the question of which prospect originally belonged to which agency is sure to arise. If both companies' policies are defined at the outset and an agreement made in writing, many of the problems should be eliminated before they occur. For example, a policy to ensure problem-free cooperation might state that agents are to register their prospects on a first-come first-served basis, subject only to a letter from a prospect giving another agency the exclusive right to act on its behalf. Accurate record keeping is the key to mutually profitable cooperative leasing situations, with close attention to cooperating brokers' submittals being especially critical in preventing misunderstandings.

Other Prospect Sources

While promotional campaigns, referrals, canvassing, and broker cooperation programs may produce the greatest number of prospects, other sources should not be disregarded. For example, the Yellow Pages of the local telephone directory, which lists businesses by category, may be used as an inventory of potential tenants.

Likewise, the agent may obtain mailing lists that catalog companies by the type of business in which they are engaged. This could be invaluable to the agent who has identified a target market based on business operation. Certain mailing lists are arranged by zip code; hence, all of the businesses within a given area would be listed together. This would identify immediately those firms located near the subject building and would be useful in the organization and execution of canvassing efforts.

Walk-ins are another source not to be ignored. An individual seeking office space often will walk into an office building's rental office to talk to the leasing agent, usually in response to an advertisement that has been seen or an effective public relations program. Walk-ins occur more frequently in a tight market in which office space is hard to find than in a renter's market. The soft market demands adoption of a much more aggressive marketing strategy.

City directories are also a source of potential tenants. Listings in directories often are made according to building name (e.g., The Renaissance Center) or address (e.g., The Three-Thirty-Three Building). Listed below each building entry are subentries that list the building's tenants and their suites and phone numbers. This provides the agent with enough pertinent information to begin making contacts. One word of caution in using directories: They become outdated quickly. The agent should not proceed on information found in a directory until its timeliness has been verified through further research.

Figure 7.3

Interested Prospect Report

Agent _____

Building Proposed _____

Date _____ Approved _____

Prospect	Bldg./Address	Present Sq. Ft.	Exp. Date	Sq. Ft. Needed	Direct Mail	Telephone Contact	Personal Contact	Prospect Card Complete	Referral Request	Deliver Brochure	Tour of Site	Information Packet	Prospect Qualified	Gathering Prospect Space Requirements	Remarks

Figure 7.4

Prospect Card

Company _____ Address _____ Zip _____ Phone _____
Who Contacted _____ Title _____
Desirable Present Space: Condition: Good _____ Fair _____ Poor _____
Approximate No. Employees _____ Parking for _____ Cars/Comments _____

Company Does/Sells/Services _____
Now Occupies _____ Square Feet Pays: $ _____ Per Square Foot $ _____ mo. $ _____ yr.
Prefers What Area _____ Options _____
Lease Expires _____
Lead by: Cold Call _____ Phone to _____ Add _____ Phone from _____
Referral by: Broker _____ Other _____

Contacts	Showed	Call Back
Date:		
Date:		
Date:		

Maintaining Leasing Activity Records

As contact is established with potential tenants, appropriate records of this activity should be maintained. Not only is this beneficial to the leasing agent, but ownership or the agent's superiors may require ongoing reports on marketing endeavors. Because ownership is always interested in leased space as it translates into cash flow, accurate and timely reporting of the agent's progress in filling vacant space is critical to maintaining good rapport with ownership. Various kinds of records may be kept, each one designed to assist in leasing efforts.

An interested prospect report, sampled in figure 7.3, summarizes leasing progress and is appropriate for forwarding to ownership on a regular basis. The interested prospect report is designed to show a suggested progression of steps involved in office leasing efforts. (The latter half of figure 7.3 shows future activities.) To the left of the slash mark within each column, the date the task should be accomplished is recorded; to the right, the actual day of accomplishment is noted. When realistic deadlines are established, the chart sets goals for and measures progress made by the agent, as well as reveals to ownership what is being done to lease the building. Furthermore, the report serves as a means of keeping track of what attracted prospects to the building. This information can be useful when future leasing programs are planned. For example, if the records show that a certain $2,500 direct mailing produced no results, this promotional activity should not be repeated.

The fourth column of the interested prospect report makes reference to a prospect card. This card, sampled in figure 7.4, is a means of recording pertinent information about potential tenants. A card should be completed for every office space user to whom the agent speaks. The information noted helps the agent determine if the product matches the prospect's needs. If complete and accurate data is posted, the prospect card can become an organized, at-a-glance summation of vital information about the prospect and provide guidance in leasing efforts.

Prospect cards should be organized to create one of the agent's most important leasing tools, a prospect tickler file. As the agent talks to each office user, the company's lease expiration date or other information pertinent to relocation should be noted. From this, the leasing agent can determine when that prospect should be contacted again. Once call-back dates are posted on all prospect cards, the agent can establish the tickler file.

The tickler file is set up in this manner: The front of the file is marked with 31 sections, one for each day of the month; the next part of the file has a section for each month of the year. At the beginning of each month, the cards are pulled from that month and placed behind the date of the call-back. For example, during the month of June, all cards are pulled from the June section of the file. All call-backs for the first of June are placed behind the one, for the second of June behind the two, and so forth. Each day the number of call-backs the agent has may vary. Should an agent make a call-back and be told to call again at the end of July pending a decision to be made about relocation, the agent would note this on the prospect card and file it behind the section marked July. Thus, the agent would have a reminder to call that prospect the next month.

Oftentimes, the agent will have a card on a prospect who need not be contacted within the present year. These future prospect cards are filed alphabetically and separate from current prospects. At the end of each year, these cards would be reviewed for possible follow up. For example, at the end of 1980, a leasing agent would go through the future prospect cards and pull the cards of those office users to be contacted in 1981. These cards would then be placed behind the appropriate month—January call-backs would be placed behind January, February behind the appropriate month, and so on. If established and used correctly, the tickler file serves as a visible reminder of potential tenants and consequently encourages timely canvassing efforts.

Summary

Locating prospects is an integral part of marketing office space. The agent can obtain the names of prospects through a referral network, canvassing the office market, and cooperative efforts with other agents. Every possibility must be pursued. By adopting a methodical program of locating prospects, the task of acquiring tenants for a new office building or replacement tenants for an existing one become less difficult.

The perfect operational complement to this program of locating potential tenants is a system of rental progress record keeping. This system should encompass not only who is contacted but when con-

Prospecting

tact is made. The appropriate system of record keeping can be used to communicate with ownership on space being leased, as well as enable the leasing agent to keep track of progress in the overall leasing effort.

8 Agent Preparation

Once the leasing agent has obtained a list of prospective tenants, one of the most important facets of the merchandising of office space begins—that of personal selling. Although personal selling complements advertising and public relations campaigns which are aimed at the mass market, it is the means of establishing direct, face-to-face contact with a representative of a prospective tenant as well. Without this contact, it would be impossible to persuade the prospect to give serious consideration to a specific building as an office site.

The leasing agent should understand the fundamentals of effective salesmanship and establish a procedure for dealing with prospects in an affirmative and persuasive manner. This procedure should be implemented during the first meeting with the prospective tenant and maintained throughout the often lengthy series of meetings that will occur. If the procedure is sound yet flexible enough to permit a sales presentation to be tailored to a given prospect's needs and wants, the leasing agent should be met with ongoing success in the marketplace.

Pre-Call Preparation

A leasing agent becomes effective at personal selling only by being fully prepared before entering a prospect's door. At the outset, the agent should have ample knowledge of the office building being leased, including all of the tangible and intangible characteristics associated with it. If an in-depth analysis is conducted when the rental listing is obtained, the agent should be fully familiar with the product.

Second, the leasing agent should be acquainted with the office market, including the buying patterns of office space users and economic trends and conditions. The market analysis that was performed in conjunction with establishing a rental schedule should provide this information.

Third, the leasing agent should be as acquainted as possible with each prospect that is called upon. Only by understanding the motivations of the target market will it be possible to entice a prospect within that market to want to hear more. In conjunction with arousing prospect interest, the leasing agent also must begin to determine the viability of the potential tenant: Will the building satisfy the needs and wants of the prospect, and will the prospect satisfy the needs and wants of the building and its ownership?

The leasing agent must prepare a list of questions to ask the prospect. Specifically, information in three areas should be uncovered: the present lease situation, the company's future expectations, and the prospect's general attitude about the office space currently occupied. The potential tenant's responses reveal how accommodating the subject property is and suggest the directions the marketing efforts should take.

Not only will the leasing agent prepare questions for the prospect but also will get psychologically prepared for the meeting. The agent must be sensitive to responses, realizing that the prospect may be either receptive or apprehensive to the meeting and the questions asked.

Obtaining the detailed information necessary to determine prospect acceptability is not always easy. It can be safely assumed that a prospect will be unwilling to reveal likes and dislikes about the current space or the details of the present lease situation. Premeeting research and preparation by the agent can avoid much of the difficulty in uncovering this information that may be encountered over the course of one or more meetings with the prospect.

Pre-call preparation requires careful planning of the questions to ask the prospect, the appeal to make regarding the subject property, and the approach to take should the prospect be aloof or unresponsive. In short, every possibility should be anticipated. The reason for pre-call preparation is to individualize the presentation by recognizing the uniqueness of the prospect's needs and wants. In this way, a canned sales pitch should be avoided.

Agent Preparation

To assist in making a personal appeal, information about the prospect might be sought before a meeting is held. Although such data may be hard to find, the search is worth the effort. Even the slightest information about a prospect may suggest the extent to which marketing efforts should be carried out in order to create interest. For example, a prospect or tenant may be the regional sales office for a hospital equipment company. Several thoughts should come to mind: A sales force will enter and leave the premises regularly. The salesmen may transport the equipment to customers. Sales territories may extend from the immediate locale to a broad regional area. By confirming these thoughts when meeting with the prospect, a sales presentation can be tailored for this prospect: Building elevators are accessible and move with speed, which should be an advantage to the salesmen who enter and leave the building often. Adjacent parking facilities are close to the building and, to facilitate moving equipment, a freight elevator provides satisfactory service. The product's location is within a few minutes' driving time to several local highways, an interstate highway, and main arteries of the city.

Although this hypothetical case is simplified, this type of analysis and preparation is necessary. Not only does it strengthen the presentation, but it demonstrates the agent's genuine interest in the company and a willingness to maintain and even increase efficiency in day-to-day operations.

The time and energy required to obtain prospects, talk with them, and begin to qualify them is extensive; this time and energy must be invested wisely. Discussions that are tangent to the purpose and presumptuous thoughts regarding the prospect must be avoided. In order to achieve positive results in meeting with the prospect, the right questions must be asked, motivations and operational requirements be understood, and apprehensions and objections be accepted and discussed.

The Sales Presentation

The initial interview with the representative in charge of leasing space for the potential tenant may be arranged by appointment or may be the result of a cold call on the prospect. The effective presentation encompasses more than selling the product, its amenities, and its services. It is finesse, professionalism, product and market knowledge, and a mastery of the art of conversation that enables the leasing agent to achieve success.

Whether the agent is a novice or well seasoned at conducting meetings with prospects, nervousness and uncertainty may surface. One of the purposes of pre-call preparation is to override any momentary apprehensions.

Before meeting with the prospect, the leasing agent should introduce himself to the secretary or receptionist and state the nature of the business call. This should be done confidently so it is clear that a definite purpose is at hand and the agent is not put off by the secretary or receptionist. Oftentimes when the agent states the business at hand, the receiving party may well provide an important clue as to the prospect's interest in office space. For instance, a secretary who is quite aware of the supervisor's disgust with nonoperating air conditioning during a severe heat wave may convey these thoughts to the agent. The secretary's remarks certainly pave the way for the agent in tailoring the presentation to the prospect.

Upon entering the prospect's office and after the initial greeting, the leasing agent must be prepared to attract the prospect's interest immediately. There are several approaches that can be used. For instance, a perceptive glance around the office may reveal awards or photographs that the agent could inquire about as a warming-up conversation. The discovery of a prospect's "hot-button"—interests, hobbies, and the like—is an opportunity to begin earning immediate attention. These first few minutes also create a friendly, receptive atmosphere conducive to open communication. On the other hand, if the prospect was referred to the leasing agent, it might be more appropriate to start the conversation off with a reference to this mutual acquaintance. Less subtle methods of attracting attention are also possible. For instance, if the leasing agent is aware that the prospect is disturbed about the company's inability to expand, the prospect might be greeted with a direct question related to this matter, such as, "I understand your organization is expanding so quickly that you've outgrown your office and need to find more space elsewhere?" In any event, the first step is to attract the prospect's interest. Having accomplished this, attention can be turned to increasing desire for space in the office building being leased.

In order to appeal to the prospect, it is necessary to know why the company is seeking office space elsewhere. Some of the most common reasons why office tenants seek new locations are these:

Agent Preparation

- Expansion requirements that cannot be satisfied in the present location.
- Tenant's desire for a more prestigious location.
- Expansion of a contiguous tenant, causing a loss of lease.
- Inefficient layout created by expansions over a period of time.
- Inadequate curb appeal, building services, air conditioning, lighting, parking, and the like.
- Inconvenient location for customers, employees, or both.
- Desire to consolidate scattered offices or establish a new branch office.
- Unusual rental expenses, such as rate increases at renewal or remodeling costs for desired expansion.
- Need to attract better employees, improve employee morale, or reduce absenteeism and turnover.
- Desire to improve convenience to amenities such as public transportation, restaurants, banking and shopping facilities, and the like.

By knowing what is motivating the prospect to relocate, the agent can make a convincing appeal about how the features of the subject property can erase the existing deficiencies. This is not to suggest that the competition should be condemned. Criticizing is unnecessary and unethical behavior. It is demeaning to the agent and the agency represented. Such action especially should be avoided during a sales presentation, as it may be regarded as a subtle attack on the prospect who is a tenant in the building.

The most promising marketing approach is the one in which the agent is wise enough to take the time to listen, look at, and analyze the total picture. When the leasing agent can talk in actualities and specifics rather than in generalities, the more expertly the product can be shown to fit the prospect. If the prospect is a cardiologist seeking space in the agent's medical building, the agent can point out the accommodating electrical systems for the doctor's equipment, efficient lighting for examination purposes, meticulous janitorial services, and adjacent parking facilities for patients. These benefits may be the key attractions to the subject property and thus should be strongly emphasized by the agent.

For example, a prospect may seek new office space for a combination of reasons: Services are not up to par, expansion requirements cannot be met, and the president wants to be closer to home.

Rather than criticizing the present site's weakness, the agent can describe the fine services and space availability of the subject building. As for the latter reason, it is not unique and may cause personnel problems for the company. It may be easy to justify to employees a move based on the first two reasons, but the last one may not be well received. The leasing agent can help the president point out the benefits of relocating by acquiring employees' home addresses and charting public transportation and automobile routes from their homes to the new site. In this day of energy problems, such a service by the agent can impress the prospect who in turn can demonstrate the benefits of relocation to employees while satisfying business and personal requirements. Thus, the attentive, creative leasing agent solves the prospect's problems by highlighting the assets of the subject property—not condemning the competitor's building. By taking a creative, innovative approach toward solving the company president's problems, the leasing agent enters into the decision-making process by providing information and service and obtains the president's cooperation.

The Art of Asking Questions

Throughout the sales presentation, the leasing agent's emphasis is on getting as much information as possible about why the prospect wants to relocate, its expectations for future office space, and overall attitude about tenancy. A series of interviews undoubtedly will be required to gather the pertinent data. Furthermore, practice and experience in questioning helps ensure that the information sought during these interviews is obtained.

The right questions encourage participation, uncover hidden motivations, and lead to positive attitudes about the subject property. The leasing agent should be aware of the various kinds of questions that can be asked. Essentially, eight types of questions exist:

1. Direct question. "Mr. Prospect, to help you select the best space for your firm's requirements, may I ask several basic questions about your business operations?" Such questioning provides answers that will enable the agent to successfully proceed with the merchandising effort.
2. Indirect question. "If we knew what you were paying, we could be more realistic in our search for your new office location." This question is less abrasive than "What rate are you now paying?" and will elicit a more favorable response.

Agent Preparation 109

3. Question designed to make the prospect agree with the agent. "Am I right, Mr. Prospect, that you are interested in maintaining your quality of leasehold improvements, but you still need to expand?" A confirming response to this type of question lays a strong foundation for continued and open communication.
4. Feedback question. "As I understand it, Mr. Prospect, your main concern is the ability to expand in two years, isn't it?" This inquiry encourages the prospect's thoughts and demonstrates further the agent's genuine interest.
5. Leading question. "I wonder, Mr. Prospect, if you too feel the rental rate is the most important consideration in choosing office space location?" The leading questions uncovers the prospect's motivation for seeking space elsewhere.
6. Silent question. This type of question is asked with facial and body gestures to elicit more information. A raised brow or look of confusion on the prospect may be asking for clarification or convincing details.
7. Negatively disposed question. "Mr. Prospect, although ABC Company successfully used an elaborate office landscape design in its extensive office space, I wonder if it would work in your 3,000-square-foot office?" Caution and tact need to be exercised in asking this kind of question, as it could be offensive. A prospect very well could be insulted by the slightest suggestion that an idea may not be functional or feasible. Nonetheless, this type of question may be necessary when it is apparent that a prospect's request is physically or economically prohibitive.
8. Assumptive question. "Mr. Prospect, may I ask you if you have considered what effect new office space would have on the morale of your employees? Would their production increase?" Such a question encourages the prospect to discover benefits not yet realized.

As the leasing agent gains experience, the ability to ask the right question at the right time will increase. The art of asking questions is not mastered in a few meetings but is refined as the questions asked and responses given are evaluated over a period of time.

Accepting and Responding to Objections

It can be realistically assumed that prospects will raise objections. An objection, although not a signal to halt the leasing effort, must be dealt with and disposed of immediately. Objections may be raised for a number of reasons:

1. To put off decision making.
2. To imply that the presentation lacks clarity.
3. To try to conclude the meeting.
4. To express uncertainty about needs or a product's benefits.
5. To slow down the leasing process.

Whatever the reason, the leasing agent must be able to cope with them. Some general suggestions for confronting objections are offered:

1. An objection should not be disturbing or alarming.
2. The approach used in discussing objections will vary with the prospect: Every prospect is unique and must be approached on an individual basis. What works with one firm may not work with another.
3. The seriousness of the objection must be measured. Can a perceptive agent turn around a negative reaction to a more positive one?
4. A second recommendation should be offered when an initial one is rejected.
5. The art of listening must be perfected. When an objection is raised, what is the prospect really saying?
6. A positive direction must be established early on in the meeting. It is easier to return to a positive discussion once an objection is raised than if the discussion had been negative from the outset.

The most difficult objections to handle are those that are never raised. The leasing agent will never secure a tenant unless all the objections are out in the open and have been counteracted. The prospect who wants to "think it over" usually is harboring inner doubts about the agent or the office space being leased. The agent should encourage the prospect to discuss these doubts so that they can be opposed persuasively.

The Trial Close

Although intermittent objections and rejections are inevitable, they should not be regarded as hindrances to eliciting the desired reaction, which is acceptance of the presentation and thus a move

Agent Preparation 111

toward a signed lease. Asking what seems to be a minor question and getting an affirmative response is one step toward this level of acceptance. Imposing a question that tests the prospect's interest in the office space being leased is referred to as a trial close. It is important because it gives the agent an indication of how close the prospect is to making a decision.

For example, conversation may have revealed that the prospect's present conference room is too small. Pursuant to this remark, a trial close may be, "In planning your office layouts, if we increased the conference room seating from 12 to 20, would this be helpful to your business operation?" Aware of a specific prospect need, the agent can elicit a positive response. Two achievements are made with this question: The prospect gets into the habit of answering "yes" and begins to commit to the agent.

A trial close can produce a negative response as well. The agent need not be put off by the objection. Rather, the prospect should be reapproached with another question aimed at showing how the building can satisfy the business's needs and wants. The appeal should relate to dominant needs. When a prospect responds positively to an inquiry, a subtle compliment for a well-executed decision is in order.

Summary

The successful leasing agent, recognizing the importance of personal selling, adopts a program for persuasively appealing to prospective tenants on a one-on-one basis. Essential and basic to this program is the agent's preparation. The agent should be fully acquainted with the product itself, the office market, and the prospect being pursued. Armed with this knowledge, it will be possible to tailor the sales presentation to the prospective tenant by anticipating needs and wants and planning for the type of responses expected.

Part of this sales effort is determining if the building can satisfy the needs and wants of the prospect and if the prospect fits the tenancy of the building. To do this, detailed information about the prospect is needed. A willing prospect makes securing these details an easy task. However, more often than not, the prospect is unwilling, and numerous questions must be asked. The technique of asking questions is refined and the leasing agent becomes able to elicit the desired responses through practice and experience.

Throughout the series of interviews with the prospect, objections will be encountered. They should not be ignored but rather dealt with directly and spontaneously. This makes a prospect aware that the agent has the prospect's interests in mind and is capable of meeting them.

A leasing agent's self-preparation is necessary to deal effectively with both common occurrences and unique circumstances. Self-preparation gives the agent self-confidence, assures a successful presentation, and furthers the marketing efforts toward the signed lease.

9 Qualification of Prospective Tenants

The leasing agent is in a most unique marketing situation. The consumer is not buying a product, but rather the office user is leasing space for a specified use and a stated period of time. The marketing objective, however, is not necessarily to lease the space to whomever has the purchasing power. Rather, the leasing agent has an obligation to the building's ownership to admit only stable and desirable rent-paying tenants. Criteria must be established on which to base the selection of commercial tenants. On the other hand, a prospective tenant also has certain criteria that must be met by the building. Specifically, the building must provide a sufficient amount of space and offer the flexibility to use that space as the prospect's business operations dictate.

The process of determining whether a prospective office user would be an acceptable, stable tenant and whether the product would fulfill that user's requirements is referred to as qualification. To qualify a prospect, it is necessarry to determine the company's financial status and business reputation and ascertain its office space needs. These needs can be categorized as operational requirements, aesthetic requirements, and financial limitations. It is from this data concerning space needs that office plans will evolve.

In a practical sense, qualifying is an ongoing process that begins even before the prospect is contacted and continues through negotiation of lease terms. When the names of potential tenants are first obtained, available information enables the agent to qualify or disqualify some of them. By analyzing the data gathered, companies whose needs the building cannot accommodate can be eliminated from the prospect list, and those who warrant further research can be noted.

For instance, a referral source may tell the agent that XYZ Company is planning to expand and needs space that its current building cannot provide. If it is known that the XYZ Company needs at least 50,000 square feet and only 25,000 square feet are available to lease, the agent automatically can disqualify the XYZ Company for the building being marketed. The ongoing purpose of qualifying is to determine if the leasing agent should continue to invest marketing dollars in the prospect.

Business Reputation and Stability

To a certain extent, the acceptability of a commercial tenant is based on the company's business reputation. This can be determined by investigating the type and stability of the prospect's company operation. Not only must the leasing agent be sure that the tenant is capable of performing under the conditions of the lease, but the firm must be able to bear the expense of tenant improvements, which can be quite costly. Consequently, credit information must be obtained that will allow the leasing agent to verify the prospect's capabilities to perform under pending credit terms and conditions. To facilitate the credit verification, a credit information sheet (sampled in figure 9.1) may be used. If the prospect is a large, reputable national or international firm, or even a respected local establishment, financial stability may be assumed to be secure and a credit check is unwarranted.

Generally speaking, corporate growth and expansion create a picture of a financially stable prospect. For instance, if a national insurance company is opening a new regional office, this indicates that the firm feels it is strong enough to actively penetrate that market and signals that the company is a strong potential tenant and could assume the expense of establishing a new office. However, this is not always the situation.

If information reveals that the credibility of a prospect is questionable, the agent has certain alternatives. Upon receiving the necessary permission, the prospect's banker or accountant may be interviewed to gather more information on the firm's financial status. Likewise, the company's financial statement may be requested and audited. Should the agent find the search favorable to the

Qualification of Prospective Tenants 115

Figure 9.1

Credit Information

Individual or Firm_____

If Corporation, When and Where Incorporated_____

_____

Present Address_____

_____

Name, Address and Telephone Number of Present Landlord_____

_____

Previous Address (if present address less than one year old)_____

_____

Name, Address and Telephone Number of Previous Landlord_____

_____

Credit References (except bank):

1._____
2._____
3._____

Name of Bank_____
Address of Branch_____
Checking Account Number_____
Financial Statement Attached_____Yes _____No
Involved in Any Litigation_____Yes _____No
If Yes, Explain_____
Individual Only:
Social Security Number_____
Employer _____
How Long_____

prospect, a memo to the files to augment the credit report would be in order. When poor market conditions exist, a landlord may be willing to accept a weaker tenant than would otherwise be acceptable. Furthermore, additional security deposit money from a weaker tenant or a guarantee from a stronger individual or entity could offset the landlord's risk and lead to acceptance of the questionable tenant.

In addition to its financial status, the prospective tenant's business image also must be investigated. Every office building embraces a certain image; hopefully, it is one of high standards, a good reputation, and a professional atmosphere. The image of the tenants must be compatible with that of the building. Only if a firm's respectability matches that of the building should it be considered a likely prospect.

Sometimes it is difficult to determine a company's image. The agent can gain some insight by meeting with the prospect to discuss the company's background, future, and operations. By taking notice of the work environment and the employees, the observant leasing agent should be able to draw an accurate picture of the firm's image.

Operational Requirements

The most basic of the prospective tenant's space needs are its operational requirements. The leasing agent must determine what the prospect must have in order to operate. To ascertain these requirements, questions must be asked that elicit complete, objective answers. These answers form the foundation on which accurate and precise office designs later can be created. Fully aware of the prospect's operational requirements, the agent can effectively convert its two-dimensional organizational chart into a functional, three-dimensional office setting.

As the prospect describes the envisioned company office space, the agent must translate what is heard in terms of: (1) How accommodating is the office space in its present state? Can it easily be adapted to this potential tenant? (2) If the present space must be altered or remodeling done, how long would it take to complete the job? How long would the space be vacant before the tenant would be able to move in and pay rent? and (3) What will it cost to make alterations required to accommodate operational needs, and who will absorb these expenditures? The landlord often makes certain

Qualification of Prospective Tenants

provisions for tenant improvements, but the total cost may exceed the landlord's allowance. If this is the case, further consideration must be given: If the cost is in excess of the allowance, will the tenant willingly pay the difference? If the excess cost is the result of elaborate or unusual decorating and remodeling, will the landlord grant approval for such improvements?

In order to place the prospect's business in the appropriate amount of space and adequately fulfill its functional needs, the company's entire operation must be examined. Gaining a thorough understanding of the prospect's operational requirements calls for two steps to be taken. First, details of the prospect's existing situation should be secured. Specifically, the leasing agent should pursue information about:

1. The Present Lease Situation
    a. Firm name, address, and telephone number
    b. Personal contact and title
    c. Square feet occupied
    d. Rate and monthly rate
    e. Term and expiration date
    f. Miscellaneous details, such as options to cancel, renew, or expand, if any
2. Product Information (As compared to the agent's product. The perceptive agent has toured, studied, and made mental notes about the prospect's product before the interview to increase the understanding of the prospect's situation and judge how the agent's product will be of greater benefit to the prospect.)
    a. The building
        (1) Parking availability, charges, and convenience
        (2) Curb appeal, landscaping, and exterior aesthetics
        (3) Entrance, main lobby, and directory
        (4) Elevators
        (5) Upper elevator lobbies
        (6) Public restrooms
        (7) General appearance
        (8) Management services and policies
    b. The leased premises
        (1) Location within the building
        (2) Reception room approach
        (3) Wasted or overcrowded space
        (4) Special tenant improvements

3. Tenant Attitude
   a. Details of present lease
   b. Product deficiencies

The agent who is able to obtain these details can competently judge whether the prospect qualifies for tenancy and a continuation of the leasing efforts is warranted. The more complete the prospect profile, the more effectively the subject property's features can be translated into desirable benefits.

The second step in uncovering operational requirements is to take a tour of the existing space. During this tour, questions should be asked and data gathered about the work that is accomplished in the office. This information will form the groundwork for an office plan that makes maximum utilization of leased space.

As the agent listens to a company representative, observations generally will focus on key office areas. Common to most offices are reception areas, executive areas, departmental areas, and special-purpose areas. The agent must determine the space needs of each area and each individual within that area, confirm observations by talking to the office staff, press for criticism about the existing office layout, and make detailed written notations about what is seen and learned.

Reception Area

The reception area should not be neglected by the leasing agent, because it plays a critical role in creating a good impression upon visitors to the prospect's office. The size of the reception area will depend on a number of factors. For instance, how much seating should be available for visitors? Except for those firms that have an excessive number of vendors and certain professional offices, seldom will many visitors be waiting in the reception area at any one time. Likewise, conveniences for visitors, such as cloakroom facilities or a telephone, should be noted. Does the receptionist have duties that require privacy, such as typing, filing, handling mail, and answering in-coming telephone calls? If so, it might be preferable to have the receptionist seated in an inner office space rather than within the reception room itself. Is a special display area for brochures, periodicals, or products manufactured or sold by the company necessary? If the reception area is to act as a showroom and contain exhibit material, its size will be dictated in part by the display. Is there an alarm or closed circuit television system to be installed, and, if so, what are its specifications? Such security measures often are necessary in metropolitan or high-crime areas.

Executive Areas

Similarly, a detailed study of the executive areas is necessary. Included within this category of space are suites for the senior officers of the company, such as the chairman of the board, president, executive vice president, treasurer, and others depending on the nature of the business. These members of top management hold prestige positions and are given large private offices to add influence and respect in the eyes of employees and visitors to the office.

In analyzing the space requirements of the executive area, the leasing agent certainly should find out how many executive offices are needed and their sizes. In addition, such questions as these should be raised: What are the special requirements for the executive offices with respect to furniture, lighting, telephones, etc.? Do the executives have secretaries? If so, what are the requirements for their stations? Are there needs for dining space, private baths, kitchens, or informal seating? The list of questions can be long, but it is the agent's responsibility to elicit all of the details considered necessary to determine if the building can accommodate the prospect's needs and, subsequently, create the appropriate office designs.

Departmental Areas

From the executive areas, the tour continues through the various departmental areas. Included might be public relations, accounting, marketing, finance, legal, and other specific departments depending upon the business operation. Each department should be analyzed for its own unique operational characteristics as well as its space needs. In all cases, the agent should be seeking an answer to the question: What does this department need in terms of space and design in order to operate efficiently and effectively?

There are two types of space needs within the departmental areas: private or semiprivate offices and general office areas. While it is widely recognized that top management members are in positions to demand private and sometimes luxurious offices, there is some disagreement as to the need for private and semiprivate offices among lower-echelon personnel. Usually, however, department managers or supervisors are given private offices. The exception would be those companies whose management believes supervisors should be physically closer to their subordinates. Likewise, professional staff members and those whose work either is of a confidential nature or requires a high degree of concentration generally are given private work places. Often, there will be a company policy concerning private office assignments. In all cases, this is the decision to be made by the prospective tenant, not the leasing agent.

Once it has been determined how many private or semiprivate offices are needed and what their space requirements are, it is necessary to turn attention toward secretarial and clerical workers and other support staff. The types of questions to be raised will depend on the nature of the department. For instance, in the purchasing department, do clerks require adjacent filing space? Would an employee in the credit department need a chair for visitors? Do any workers need special office equipment, and, if so, how much space is required for it? In short, not only the number of general office workers but their ancillary requirements should be determined. Throughout this functional analysis, the leasing agent also should be attuned to telephone, electrical wiring, and plumbing that may become necessary.

Special-Purpose Areas

Special-purpose areas also must undergo scrutiny by the agent. As businesses vary, so do these areas and their needs. The astute agent realizes the importance of any special-purpose areas to the prospective tenant and sharpens observation skills while touring these areas. For instance, the proper allowance of space is important to designing effective special-purpose areas. Total area per number of employees can range from 100 square feet for a very tight layout to 250 square feet for an average layout. The agent must know what each area requires and be able to accommodate it accordingly.

The following list of special-purpose office areas is by no means complete, but, it does include most of those found in the typical office. The more experienced a leasing agent becomes in the space planning process, the more evident certain requirements become.

Telephone/Communications Room. If a complex telephone system is required, assistance from the telephone company should be obtained early in the design stage. Telephone experts can offer advice on the specific designs that must be executed for proper telephone installation and maintenance. Costly space changes, alterations in electrical wiring, and the like may be avoided if precautions are taken in the planning stage. Likewise, it is important that the specific tenant equipment space requirements are included in the tenant's area and not in the building telephone closet. This precaution is necessary as over a period of time the building telephone closet may become overloaded with individual tenant equipment and other tenants may not have room to be accommodated.

Communication needs vary and often encompass more than a telephone system. Areas might be needed for sending and receiving mail, wrapping and stamping packages, handling heavy interoffice correspondence, or maintaining telecopiers or telex systems. Some firms, such as banks, find pneumatic tubes a necessity for interoffice deliveries. The leasing agent must determine all of the prospect's communication needs in order to evaluate how they will fit into the office plans.

Electronic Data Processing (EDP) Center. Should a prospect be establishing or maintaining an EDP center, the leasing agent must take into account its total impact. Not only do computers demand excessive electrical power, but EDP equipment requires stabilized temperatures and a raised floor to accommodate the expanded electrical requirements.

A building's HVAC system may not be able to maintain temperature control in a specific area. This can become a problem if the building's management adopts a policy of discontinuing air conditioning after regular office hours. If this is so, the leasing agent must know if 24-hour service can be provided through other means, possibly by the installation of package air conditioners.

Also worthy of special attention is the weight of EDP equipment, which often is immense. The agent must know if the building is designed to support the equipment. If the tenant is committed during the development of a building, engineers can be alerted to the tenant's structural requirement and adaptations may be made. If the building already exists, a qualified engineer should be called upon to evaluate the structure in terms of its ability to handle the heavier floor load anticipated. What is placed upon a floor, including people, furniture, and equipment, is referred to as "live load," and the agent must know the product's live load factor. Most office buildings are designed with a load-bearing capacity of 50 pounds per square foot. Many buildings, because of structural beams, can support heavy loads only at certain areas of each floor. Given the specific circumstances, the agent must consider the limitations imposed by the building as they affect the prospect's EDP center and offer possible solutions.

Storage Area. An office tenant will have various storage requirements, one of the most important being the storage of records. Company policy, government regulations, and possible legal ramifications are key reasons that companies retain records. While current records generally are kept in individual departments for easy access, infrequently used records often are maintained in a centralized storage area. If the prospect has such record-storage requirements, the agent must ask accordingly: Are the files floor-to-ceiling? Are they legal size, letter size, or both? Is necessary space being allotted both for current and future files? Can the building's floor bear the weight of the storage areas? As with the EDP equipment, a qualified engineer should be consulted before the plans can be drawn. Would the prospect consider alternate storage possibilities for seldom-used records, such as other floors, the basement, or "dead corners" of an attached parking facility?

In addition to storing records, the prospective tenant also may have other storage requirements. The leasing agent must determine what is to be stored and where it would be most conveniently located. For instance, nearly all companies still need easily accessible storage areas for often-used office supplies. Other storage requirements will depend on the nature of the business activity. A publisher, for example, may need to store copies of its books, while the administrative office of a toy manufacturer may want to have samples of its toys. In any event, all storage requirements should be taken into consideration.

Copy Center. Copy machines often require special electrical outlets for operation. The amount and type of duplicating done by a company dictate the size and number of machines required as well as the amount, size, and color of paper used and, therefore, stored. Since collating and arranging copies also may be done in the center, space should be allotted for this activity as well. The agent must consider all possible functions associated with the copy center and what must be done to accommodate them.

Lunch Room or Kitchen. Depending upon the size and character of the company, employee dining facilities may be provided. In this respect, the agent must determine the nature and scope of the facilities: Will the building's electrical system accommodate the required appliances, such as a microwave oven, refrigerator, or beverage machine? Is there adequate space for comfortable seating? Is the area ventilated? Is the area designed to accommodate installation of a sink if one is not in existence?

Often an employee dining facility doubles as a lounge area. If this is the case, the space needed for additional furnishings should be taken into consideration. Sometimes, for example, an employee lounge has a couch to serve as a resting area for employees who become ill while at the office. The leasing agent should ask if management wishes to provide such an amenity.

Conference Room. Conference rooms are used for a variety of purposes and, therefore, can demand a variety of special equipment. At the outset, the leasing agent must ascertain how many conference rooms will be needed. In the case of very large companies, there may be the need for a conference room for every department. In other situations, one conference room may suffice for everything from sales meetings to meetings of the board of directors to company workshops.

As the leasing agent develops an understanding of the prospect's operation, the requirements for conference areas can be determined. Questions that may be raised regarding each conference room include these: What is the maximum number of people that the room will need to accommodate? What is adequate space for required seating? Is the room to be used for audio-visual presentations? If so, can it be darkened adequately? Can audio-visual equipment be installed without difficulty? Regardless of whether the equipment is temporarily or permanently installed, can the building's electrical system accommodate it? Is the seating designed so all parties can easily view presentations? Are demonstration areas, chalkboards, or other wall-mounted writing surfaces necessary? Should a public address system be installed? Will a telephone be needed in the conference room? Is special air conditioning or ventilation required for a room that may contain a large number of people for long periods of time?

Library. Many firms house their own reference facilities and, regardless of their size, they require special attention: How much and what type of shelving is necessary? How much expansion can be anticipated? How extensive are storage areas for periodicals, microfilm, newspapers, etc.? Are there display cases or bulletin boards? Are there study areas? What type of lighting is required? How extensive is the filing system? Where are library personnel stationed? Does the library have its own copy machine? Is it necessary that the library area be soundproof? Will walls or ceiling have to be changed for sound-absorption purposes? How much traffic does the library bear over a week, a month, a year?

Laboratory. Perhaps a leasing agent will find that the prospect has a photography dark room or a laboratory for testing processes. If flammable or toxic chemicals are used, the building's insurance premiums can go up. Furthermore, some communities restrict laboratories to specific areas through zoning ordinances. The agent must be aware of such effects. If laboratories are allowed in the office building, the agent will need to inquire about such things as: Are the proper plumbing and sinks available, or can they be readily installed? What special lighting fixtures are necessary? What type of ventilation is required? What temperature controls must be maintained? What appliances will be installed? Is special cleaning required? What are inherent dangers posed by the use of chemicals, light, heat, etc., and what safety precautions should be considered in the space planning efforts?

Other special-purpose office areas might include classrooms, display rooms, galleries, private baths, and the like. Whatever purpose the area is to serve, the agent must investigate and thoroughly understand its operation as well as understand and perceive its unique requirements and relationship to the office building.

Work Flow Allocations

As the existing office space is toured, the agent not only should note the space requirements but also analyze the flows of communication, including paper as well as people. This calls for the agent to identify interpersonal relationships on the basis of job title and function. Are supervisors near their subordinates? Can employees who work with one another get from desk to desk or department to department without difficulty? Are secretaries contiguous to their supervisors? The organization must be viewed from the perspectives of job responsibility, supervision, and accountability. While a study of how these relationships are established in the prospect's existing space is necessary, consideration also should be given to how, if possible, improvements could be effected in the new office space. An office should be planned to meet the established productivity of a firm. However, special recognition is earned by increasing a company's efficiency through carefully designed space plans.

One of the best ways of noting space requirements and the location of supervisors with respect to their subordinates is to draw a bubble schematic while the tour is being taken. A bubble schematic, such as the example shown in figure 9.2, is a rough drawing that assists in the formal planning of office space. It enables both agent

Qualification of Prospective Tenants 125

Figure 9.2

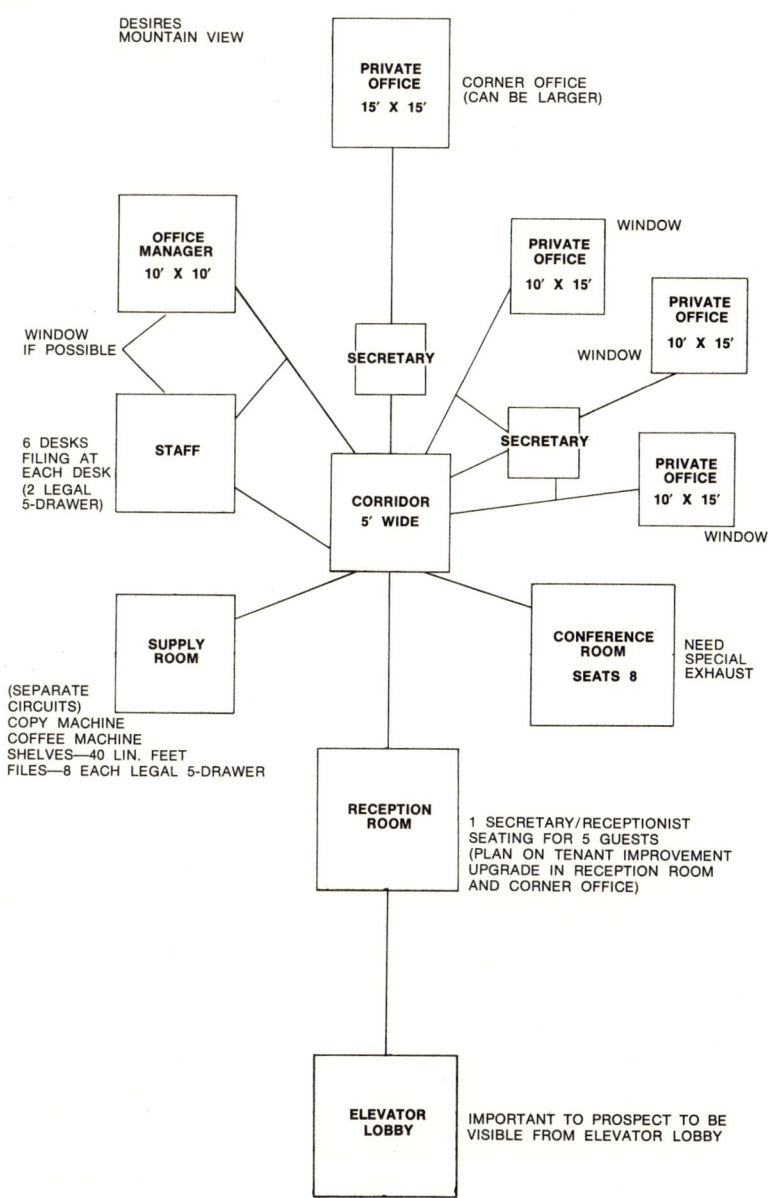

and prospect to visually review activity centers, personnel interaction, and people circulation without preparing a formal layout. The schematic does not attempt to place the activity centers in an exact location within the overall space; rather, bubbles are drawn to establish the need for the centers. The lines drawn from one activity center to another stipulate required access or people flow. The schematic, accompanied by detailed notes about each center, provides the space planner with the information necessary to complete acceptable designs and layouts for the office space.

Expansion Possibilities

A common problem in planning office space and understanding a company's operational requirements is overlooking its probability of expansion. If plans for expansion are taken into consideration during the initial stages of the space planning process, future problems, especially in terms of cost, can be eliminated. If the initial office plan includes areas that will allow for expansion, company growth can be handled in a logical and inexpensive manner.

In order to plan for expansion, it is necessary for the prospective tenant to forecast future company growth and additions to the staff over the term of the lease. While an often difficult process, the leasing agent should insist that it be done. Once the forecast is prepared, an estimate can be made of additional square footage that will be needed. If the forecast is made on a department-by-department basis, a more accurate expansion-oriented office plan can be created.

Landlords often are reluctant to provide options for expansion in leases, inasmuch as they reduce the ability to lease option space. Nonetheless, tenants often negotiate for expansion options, especially with long-term leases, because they know that over a given time period and without this allowance, they will be overcrowded. The agent should be prepared to deal with all possibilities in expansion situations.

Aesthetic Requirements

In addition to having the proper amount of space, the prospect will want to occupy an office whose appearance is pleasing. In this respect, certain aesthetic requirements will come to light. As a rule, a company will desire an office that reflects the theme or image it hopes to project. For example, a book publisher may want to relay a scholarly image, while a financial firm may want to portray a conservative worldly image.

An office mood can be created in a variety of ways. Furniture, for instance, can be used to reflect a certain period, such as contemporary, antique, or traditional. Color also plays an important role in office aesthetics. Unless the agent has experience in the specialized field of interior design, a professional designer should be employed if the prospective tenant proposes unique or extraordinary aesthetic ideas. Often a tenant will hire its own designer, especially if an unusual, individualized office environment is sought.

Although the agent is primarily concerned with physical space requirements, foresight in determining how the space will look influences spatial arrangements and suite design. For example, the operational analysis of the reception area may reveal that the firm has numerous visitors whose introduction to the company is projected by this area. Consequently, the reception area should be designed to reflect the company's image. If this image is to be progressive and modern and will require special track lighting, modular furnishings, and sleek wall and floor coverings, the agent must self-impose the question, "Can the building accommodate this?" Similarly, if the executive area is to convey a subdued, traditional, successful image, perhaps softer or controlled lighting, built-in wooden cabinetry, and expensive artwork may be required. If so, the leasing agent will need to determine if the electrical system can be adapted to special light fixtures and a security alarm system. Will custom carpentry fit into the executive areas, or must the agent make provisions to build the cabinets on the site?

Throughout the analysis of aesthetic requirements, the building's structural similarities and possibilities must be kept in mind. Fulfilling aesthetic preference can require special electrical wiring, telephone systems, plumbing, and climate control adaptations. It is erroneous to assume that the interior design of an office bears no relationship to technical space planning efforts. The ideal office interior is one that meshes operational efficiency and economy with aesthetic attractiveness.

Financial Limitations

As the prospect divulges operational and aesthetic requirements, the leasing agent must be mindful of the associated costs of meeting these requirements. Several considerations regarding financial limitations are necessary. If the prospect has defined the financial situation, the agent must work within the constraints of the alloted funds. On the other hand, should the prospect expound upon the requirements, out of touch with the expense such fantasies might incur, it is the agent's responsibility to appraise the requests and keep a tight rein on excessive costs. Diplomatically, the prospect must be made aware of the cost involved in meeting outlandish demands.

At this stage of space planning, the agent is not in a position to quote exact prices for construction, remodeling, and redecorating. At a later date, when the final suite presentation is made, these details will be thoroughly discussed. However, as a prospect relays the company's requirements, experience and knowledge will enable the agent to detect those impractical requests that are cost prohibitive as well as realistic needs that must be met. Should a prospect appear unaware of the extraordinary expenditure of fulfilling a specific request, it might be advantageous for the agent to tactfully hint at its cost.

This is preferable to misleading the prospect to believe that an attempt will be made to meet the request. Such a remark—handled well—can assure the prospect that the agent is genuinely interested in working within the established financial framework as well as maintaining balance with the operational and aesthetic requirements. Part of the leasing effort is meeting a prospect's real office space needs. Every prospect's desires are different, and many may be difficult to fill. It is the agent's responsibility to meet those wants that the product and the budget allow or, in lieu of this, diplomatically present viable alternatives.

The degree to which prospective tenants are aware of tenant improvement costs varies widely. Large national firms with many offices in different cities generally are informed about these expenses. The agent, therefore, in dealing with these prospects, need not be concerned about emphasizing cost factors. However, smaller local firms often are inexperienced about the costs of improvements that must be made to satisfy both operational and aesthetic needs. If costs are in excess of a local firm's budget, this may cause the proposed lease to flounder. The agent, in such a case, should advise that certain desires could place improvement expenses outside stated limits. For example, the prospect may want an executive office complete with built-in bar, customized wooden cabinetry, a sink, and a refrigerator. On the other hand, the prospect's true needs and budget allow for a less elaborate design. The agent could suggest keeping the bar but eliminating the extra, costly frills and indicate the estimated difference in cost. The choice, of course, remains with the prospect. If the desire for the more costly improvement is strong enough, the agent must avoid antagonizing the prospect by pushing the cost factor too far.

The cost of tenant improvements has been stressed as a potential negative factor in attracting a new tenant to an office building. However, the experienced leasing agent knows that, although initially concerned about these costs, the prospect often will upgrade materials beyond building standards and increase costs dramatically after the lease is signed and while working drawings are being prepared. If the prospect chooses to do this and funds are available, the agent should not discourage the improvements.

Summary

Qualifying a prospective office tenant requires research into its business reputation and an in-depth questioning session and tour of existing facilities to judge its spatial requirements.

In order to determine if the building can accommodate the tenant, and subsequently, to draw up proposed plans for the space to be leased, the leasing agent must gain total knowledge of the prospect's three types of needs: Operational, aesthetic, and financial. Essentially, the agent pursues a detailed answer to the question: "What does the company need and what can it afford in order for its office to both be attractive and function effectively and efficiently?

As the prospect's realistic needs and less practical desires come to the fore, the agent must analyze alternate approaches to solving the prospect's office space problem, compare the financial aspects of each option, and investigate space utilization for the present as well as the future.

By taking into account the owner's policy with respect to allowable tenant improvements and their costs and the building's structural capabilities and limitations, the agent can realistically weigh those factors that will have an impact on changing the status of the prospect to that of tenant.

10 Space Planning

During the early 1900s, one major goal of property managers was to improve the quality of the office building, especially in interior design and layout. Efficiency in space planning was beneficial to business operations, but it also was an important means of attracting new prospects and keeping present tenants. The property manager and the space planners of the early twentieth century raised the corporate consciousness about the importance and benefits of a well-designed working environment.

Proper office surroundings were becoming a key issue. For example, on the subject of lighting: "It is generally conceded that uncomfortable working conditions induce unnecessary fatigue and that fatigue reduces the potential capacity of the individual and causes increased number of mistakes. . . . It is, therefore, desirable for us to direct our attention to the matter of providing proper lighting conditions for the desk worker." (P. J. Norton, "Artificial Lighting for Offices," *Skyscraper Management,* May 1931, p. 9). Likewise, another author remarked on the use and positive effect of conditioned air in the office setting: "Studies have revealed that there is a noticeable increase in efficiency of workers having conditioned air. . . . It is expected that studies will be available to prove conclusively the actual psychological benefits of air conditioning." (Paul E. Holcombe, "Air Conditioning," *Skyscraper Management,* May 1931, p. 32).

As the importance of efficient office design and layout gained recognition, the demand for "a new field for the application of specialized knowledge—that of office planning" increased. The reasons for which this profession evolved included "the general speeding up of business, the advent of high rents, and the realization that a man spends more of his waking hours in his office than in his home." (Warren D. Brunner, "The Office Layout Specialist and the Building Manager," *Skyscraper Management,* September 1931, p. 28). Indeed, it became apparent that not only was the American office worker concerned about *what* job was being performed but *where* it was performed as well. Space planning was becoming an integral part of the leasing efforts.

The demand for pleasant working conditions continued and increased dramatically during World War II. As military needs depleted the labor supply, there suddenly were too few employees for too many jobs. Companies became highly competitive for employees and began to recognize that one means of luring workers was to offer attractive, comfortable offices. The pleasant, favorable office setting became commonplace and very much the expectation of yesterday's employee and today's as well. At the same time, the need for greater efficiency of space, equipment, and people had been and still is recognized by the business world. Consequently, the leasing agent has found that successful marketing of office space is contingent on being able to plan coordinated office interiors that economically combine functional efficiency and effectiveness with a pleasing appearance.

The Space-Planning Process

The leasing agent must be equipped to translate a prospective tenant's operational and aesthetic requirements into a comfortable and functional work place within any financial restrictions that may be imposed. To do this, office space plans must be prepared.

The size of the prospect's company operation affects the procedure followed in space planning. A large company may have or employ its own space planner. However, the leasing agent will want to be a part of any meeting between the prospect and space planner to maintain control of the situation. For instance, how much time will the space planner require to complete the office design? Is the time frame compatible with the agent's leasing efforts? Are the space planner's ideas so elaborate and exorbitant that cost will cause the prospect to reconsider the office space? Will the space planner create designs the building cannot accommodate? Many national firms

Space Planning

have office criteria. For example, a large national accounting firm may dictate all division managers, staff accountants, and executive assistants in every regional office must receive a certain number of square feet for office space. Likewise, the General Services Administration has specified space allocation standards. Every government agency has uniform office space allocations regardless of regional location. The agent should be fully aware of such requirements and their relationship to the office leasing effort. In any event, if a space planner is brought in as a third party, clear lines of communication must be maintained to ensure realistic planning.

A smaller firm, on the other hand, might rely strictly on the leasing agent to plan the new office. This requires a great deal of trust in the agent on the part of the prospect and provides the opportunity for the agent to demonstrate additional expertise. Occasionally, leasing agents act as space planners and personally design office interiors. In other instances, leasing and management companies have in-house space planners trained for this task or employ outside space planners. In both cases, the agent must establish a good working relationship with the person assigned to the job. For the purpose of simplicity, this chapter assumes that the leasing agent is working with a chosen space planner. However, the concepts set forth are applicable regardless of who is responsible for the space planning.

To initiate the space planning process, exact data concerning operational and aesthetic requirements and financial limitations must be obtained. This is done throughout the qualifying interviews and tours of the prospect's current space. Based on an objective analysis of these factors, the space planner can translate the information into formal plans.

The relationship between the space planner and the leasing agent is a crucial one in moving closer to a suite design that is accepted by the prospect. ("Suite" is the term used to refer to the tenant's entire premise.) Communication between these two parties must be constant and clear, as each one's interpretation of information affects the development of the suite design. Communication also should be maintained with the prospect, who periodically is brought back into the process of suite design for further input and ongoing acceptance or rejection. Cost estimates also may be discussed.

The cost of creating space plans usually is assumed by the landlord, because it is incurred before the lease is signed and is part of the merchandising effort. However, this should be delineated under leasing policy set down by the landlord to the agency. In some instances, if the landlord will not provide space planning services, the agency will risk the expense, knowing that it is essential if it is to earn the leasing commission. In other cases, the tenant will be required to pay for the planning. Some landlords will pay for space planning, but, if a lease is consummated, the cost of the planning is deducted from the landlord's tenant improvement allowance. Even when the landlord pays for space planning, redrawing and expenses beyond the preliminary plan often are charged to the tenant. Before proceeding with the actual space planning, the expenditure to carry out the task must be approved. Thus, the agent must request authorization (see figure 10.1) for the planning. The importance of the authorization is twofold: (1) It alerts the property manager of possible tenancy, and (2) it helps the agent's supervisor manage subordinates more effectively and evaluate the performance of the agent. In an office building, space planning is followed by preparation of working drawings and construction specifications and interior design services are provided. Who is to cover these additional expenses also must be a function of ownership policy; however, since these activities occur after the lease is signed, the expense usually must be borne by the tenant.

Developing the Preliminary Plans

When the leasing agent is thoroughly informed as to what the prospect must have for an efficient and effective office setting, detailed notes are given to the space planner. During the meeting between the lease agent and planner, the following should transpire:

1. The operational and aesthetic needs should be made clear. The bubble schematic is a useful tool in this discussion. Likewise, the prospect's image should be given particular attention so that it is successfully handled in the design process.
2. The space planner must know what funds have been allocated for the potential tenant's new office space. Budget guidelines enable planners to meet design requirements while simultaneously avoiding unnecessary extravagance in the choice of materials and workmanship.
3. The prospect's current office situation must be understood so that its efficiencies can be maintained or upgraded and its problems can be remedied.
4. The interrelationships of the various departments and person-

Space Planning 135

Figure 10.1

Authorization for Services

Building Name_____
Owner Name_____
Tenant Name_____
Tenant Floor Level_____
Approximate Square Footage Rentable Area_____
Actual Square Footage Rentable Area_____
                      (To be calculated at completion of job)

Services to be Performed
_____Space Study
_____Architectural Working Drawings
_____Engineering Working Drawings
_____Supervision
_____Interior Design Work
_____Consultations
_____Other Services_____

Fees
Cost Per Square Foot for Space Study_____
Cost Per Square Foot for Working Drawings_____
Hourly Rate or Lump Sum for Fee of All Other Services_____

AUTHORIZATION SIGNATURES:
Date Authorized_____
Accepted by_____Leasing_____
Date_____Development_____
Date Promised_____Other_____

nel should be clear. Again, the bubble schematic can be an insight into the flow of work.
5. The leasing agent must discuss the necessary circulation factor, that is, the amount of space that must be allowed for office traffic. The circulation factor typically is 10 to 15 percent of the total square footage otherwise needed to fulfill all operational needs. (This average percentage was arrived at after an analysis of the circulation figures used in many planning projects.)

The space planner takes all the data that has been gathered and draws a rough draft of the potential tenant's space. In incorporating prospect requirements into space plans, some space allocation guidelines may be set. Although larger national firms may impose guidelines on the space planning process, other situations call for the space planner's input.

The actual space required for the needs of specific office workers varies. However, the following figures represent suggested space allotment per employee:

1. General office worker: 65 to 80 square feet.
2. Supervisor: 100 to 120 square feet.
3. Administrative Assistant or Secretary: 150 square feet.
4. Administrative Executive: 300 square feet.
5. Executive Assistant or Secretary: 200 to 250 square feet.
6. Executive (private office): 400 to 500 square feet.

If corridors are adjacent to these offices, another 50 to 100 square feet per office must be added.

A word of caution on these suggested space allotments: They are guidelines only. Density plays an important role in making space allotments so as to avoid maintenance problems, difficulties in elevator operations, and the like. For example, if a major company wanted to use 40,000 square feet for general office workers and allot each only 65 to 80 square feet in a building of only 50,000 square feet, many problems would arise from such a high population density. Elevators would be overworked, parking facilities would be insufficient, and cleaning services would need to be increased, to name a few. Furthermore, overall appearance of the office would be overcrowded. If the same company with the same requirements were placed in a building with 400,000 square feet, the population and the situation would be more balanced by the other tenants with less density and fewer problems would arise.

Space Planning

Upon completion of the first set of plans, the leasing agent meets with the planner to study them and verify that they reflect the prospect's needs and wants.

If the resultant plan appears to have created excessive improvement costs, alternatives must be considered. If costs can be cut, this is the stage at which it should happen. If the agent and the space planner choose viable alternatives in the design process, confrontation with the prospect may be avoided. A plan calling for an unanticipated expenditure may cause the prospect to grow uncertain about relocating to the building or force complete withdrawal from the situation. Hence, by anticipating and solving problems on the drawing board, the agent and planner can contribute to a successful leasing effort while demonstrating a genuine interest in the prospect's requirements.

Another by-product of the agent-space planner relationship is development of an understanding of each other's efforts. As the design develops and the time for the final presentation comes closer, the planner becomes the agent's ally in selling the plans to the prospect. During lease negotiations, the planner may act as an intermediary between agent and prospect and assist the latter in understanding and accepting the proposed design.

Prospect's Review of Preliminary Plans

Upon converting operational and aesthetic needs and financial limitations into preliminary plans, a conference with the prospect is necessary. (Figure 10.2 is a reduced copy of a preliminary plan, which would be used at such a conference.)

While the prospect studies the office space plans, the leasing agent should call attention to the various ways in which they meet the established requirements. The prospect should be encouraged to ask questions about the plans at any time and be allowed to keep the plans for a time to study them closely. The actual time alloted for in-depth review of space plans will vary according to the situation. A small office space user may need just a few days to review plans, whereas a user of 20,000 square feet may need longer to study them. Experience and common sense will tell the agent how much time to allow. It would be advisable, in all circumstances, to call several days after the plans had been given to the prospect and encourage review. Thus, the prospect is made aware of the agent's interest, and, perhaps, procrastination of the review will be dis-

Figure 10.2

Space Planning

couraged. The preliminary plans are to be persuasive and should bear certain characteristics:

1. The plans should be neat, organized, and accurate.
2. Room dimensions should be shown clearly and the scale should be indicated. (Many designers use $\frac{1}{8}$ inch = 1 foot; however, if suites are small, $\frac{1}{4}$ inch = 1 foot may be more appropriate.)
3. Each of the work areas should be defined, and room delineations clearly marked.
4. A legend should be provided to aid the prospect in reading the plans.
5. The prospect should be able to see that the necessary furniture and equipment will fit into the space allotted, inclusive of the circulation factor.
6. Doors and windows should be shown on the plans.
7. Plans should show the premises in relationship to the core and elevator lobby.

By giving the prospect time to examine the plans and suggesting that changes are best made at this early stage, the agent involves the prospect in the process, thereby increasing commitment and interest.

The earlier that ideas and changes can be implemented, the less involved and expensive they are. The agent should not be surprised if the prospect requests items not discussed previously that would require additional space. Typical of such requests are those for special doors or electrical wiring. To reiterate, the leasing agent's experience will detect whether or not requests are cost prohibitive. If they are, the prospect should be cautioned about the expense. The agent should not promise that a request will be honored, nor should it be totally rejected. Before making any response, the actual cost should be determined. If excessive, satisfactory alternatives should be suggested to the prospect. Again, a perceptive agent understands the prospect's motivation and can make suggestions tactfully while moving closer to the signing of a lease.

Estimating Improvement Costs

Up to this point in the space planning process, the leasing agent has:

1. Qualified the prospect by determining the requirements and limitations for office space.

2. Conveyed this data to a space planner who has incorporated them into preliminary plans.
3. Reviewed the preliminary plans with the planner and made any necessary alterations.
4. Shown the plans to the prospect and discussed content and possible additions or changes.

The fifth step is to respond to the most logical and likely question the prospect will pose: What will it cost to make the plans a reality? What is the bottom line? The agent should be prepared to answer this question when the preliminary plans are discussed.

If the leasing agent researches the costs involved in constructing or remodeling of office space, the estimates can be confidently discussed with the prospect. However, the agent should emphasize that they are estimates only. Experts must provide actual cost figures, which can be relayed as such to the prospect.

Methods of Securing Estimate

To reach the point at which the agent can talk knowledgeably about tenant improvement costs, a detailed analysis must be provided by someone fully familiar with applicable expenses. The estimate may be provided by a general contractor or by the owner or property manager acting as a general contractor.

If the construction or remodeling of office space is to be done by a general contractor when the lease is signed, the responsibility of estimating the costs often lies with the company that will perform the work. Several methods are used by contractors in providing estimates:

1. The cost-plus method, also referred to as the time-and-material method. Using this approach, the contractor quotes the price of costs, labor (time), and materials. Management usually will accept an estimate based on this method from a contractor with whom it is familiar and feel confident about prices being quoted.
2. The cost-plus basis with a "not to exceed" limit. This method of estimating construction cost places a ceiling on the maximum that can be spent. If the costs are less than the estimated maximum, the final contracting bill also reflects this.
3. The fixed-bid basis. Quite simply, this method of cost estimating requires the contractor to state that the project will cost a stated amount based on the plans and specifications provided.

Space Planning

The method used is determined by the nature of the work to be performed, the time limits imposed by occupancy dates, and the degree of completeness of the plans and specifications. The contractor provides estimates without charge, as it is generally considered to be an overhead expense. By keeping informed of costs and trends in construction and management, the leasing agent will be attuned to whether or not the contractor's estimates are competitive.

Rather than using a general contractor, many owners or managers act as their own contractors, subcontracting the various construction functions. In such a case, the manager or owner provides the estimate.

Data may be obtained from price lists, catalogs, subcontractors' estimates, and general knowledge of the market. This method of making tenant improvements usually is competitive with general contracting. For example, the property manager acting for the owner often can cut costs of certain materials by purchasing them in large quantities and making them available to subcontractors for installation. The owner or manager will also supervise the construction groups. The usual general contractor's overhead (about 15 percent) and profit (from five to 15 percent) can be reduced substantially or eliminated altogether. Furthermore, if the property manager supervises the construction, control of the project is greatly increased.

Sources of Cost Data

Regardless of the approach taken to secure an estimate, the agent should be familiar with the process in order to evaluate the estimate's accuracy and deal with the prospect as a knowledgeable spokesman. Two items will further this understanding—the cost or price book and the job estimate form.

A cost book is a listing prepared by the leasing agent of unit costs of labor, materials, and service. These unit prices are obtained from trade subcontractors or materials suppliers and as such are based on local markets. The more detailed the listing, the greater will be the book's value.

A job estimate form is used in conjunction with a cost book to provide a quick, well-organized means of computing an estimate of tenant improvement costs. Figure 10.3 is a sample job estimate form. The accuracy of the estimate depends on the accuracy of the cost book and the care taken during the take-off, or the estimate of the number of units for each item of construction—e.g., lineal feet of partitions, square feet of ceiling tile, square yards of carpet, single

Figure 10.3
Confidential: Estimate of Approximate Construction Cost
Based Upon Estimated Quantities

Requested by_____   Date_____
Prospective Tenant_____   Rentable Area_____
Drawing_____   Usable Area_____
Floor_____

1. Partitions (Furnish and Install)
   A. Demising—½ of ____ Lineal Feet = ____ Lineal Feet @ $____ = $____
   B. Interior   ____ Lineal Feet @ $____ = $____
2. Doors, Frames, Hardware (Furnish and Install)
   A. Interior: Single   ____ @ $____ = ____
           Pair   ____ @ $____ = ____
   B. Entrance: Single   ____ @ $____ = ____
           Pair   ____ @ $____ = ____
3. Acoustic Ceiling (Install)   ____ @ $____ = ____
4. HVAC (Install)
   A. Individual Ceiling Unit   ____ @ $____ = ____
   B. Thermostats   ____ @ $____ = ____
5. Exhausts (Furnish and Install)   ____ @ $____ = ____
6. Lighting (Install)
   A. 2 x 4s   ____ @ $____ = ____
   B. Switches   ____ @ $____ = ____
7. Telephone, Electric (Furnish and Install)
   A. Duplex, Wall   ____ @ $____ = ____
   B. Telephone, Wall   ____ @ $____ = ____
   C. Tel-Electric, Floor   ____ @ $____ = ____
   D. Separate Circuits   ____ @ $____ = ____
   E. Other   ____ @ $____ = ____
8. Sprinklers (Furnish and Install)   ____ @ $____ = ____
9. Plumbing (Furnish and Install)   ____ @ $____ = ____
10. Carpet (Furnish and Install)   ____ @ $____ = ____
11. Paint Bulkhead and Window Soffit   ____ @ $____ = ____
12. Share of Public Corridor   ____ @ $____ = ____
13. Building Department Filing and
    Permit Expense   ____ @ $____ = ____
14. Exit Lights (Furnish and Install)   ____ @ $____ = ____
15. Fire Horns (Furnish and Install)   ____ @ $____ = ____
16. Other Special Items   ____ @ $____ = ____
                                        ____ @ $____ = ____

                                        4 percent
                                           Contingency $____
                                        15 percent
                                           Contractor Fee $____
                                        Subtotal $____
                                        Service Charge $____
                                        TOTAL $____

Space Planning 143

rolls of wall covering. If the agent is unfamiliar with the take-off process, experienced subcontractors are usually cooperative in explaining take-off methods they use.

In the latter part of the job estimate form is a space for the service charge. This is an estimate of the cost of administering the construction job, usually expressed as a percentage of the total cost of the work performed. Most owners or managers, even if the job is placed with a general contractor, perform certain administrative functions and should be reimbursed for this time.

Contingencies should be taken into consideration during the estimating process. A contingency expense is added on as a protective device for the general contractor or manager/owner as contractor. Consequently, if errors are made in take-off of unit quantities or costs increase, the contractor will not be held liable for the result of a mistake. The contingency estimate is a percentage of the total cost of the work to be performed, usually no more than 10 percent and often as low as three or four percent.

Prior to discussing costs of construction with the prospect, the agent must confer with the landlord for approval of the design. Most importantly, the landlord's allowance for tenant improvements must be ascertained, from which the charge to the tenant will be established. The leasing agent is cognizant of all allowances ownership will make, costs to be assumed by the tenant, and all other expense factors that can affect the suite design process.

Special Suite Design Considerations

The previous chapter and this chapter offer one general sense of direction for the suite design process. However, any experienced leasing agent knows that although certain procedures always do apply, unique situations can require special approaches to be adopted. As a rule, the status of the tenant will have an impact on the process of designing space and assigning costs. Specifically, unique considerations must be given to the tenant renewing a lease, the expanding tenant, the contracting tenant, the relocating tenant, the tenant leasing previously occupied premises, and the tenant in a new building. In each of these instances, the suite design and cost assignment process may run the gamut from simple to complex. Nonetheless, the astute leasing agent is able to impose the principles of space planning on the individual situation.

The Renewing Tenant

Often when the tenant renews a lease, the size and layout of the office is not changed and the suite-design process is bypassed. On the other hand, some tenants upon renewal request the landlord to refurbish the suite or redesign it.

Initially, the agent will seek approval from the landlord for the requested refurbishments and discuss who will be absorbing the costs. In some cases, the landlord may have budgeted for the entire expense; in others, ownership may agree to pay for a certain percentage of the cost; in still others, the tenant will be responsible for all costs. Market conditions often dictate who assumes the financial responsibility. If the renewal occurs in a tenant's market (extensive vacant space), the landlord probably will assume improvement costs in order to keep the tenant, especially if it has been a good tenant. In a landlord's market (little vacant space), the landlord may not consider it necessary to pay for improvements. In addition to market conditions, size and importance of the tenant are important considerations. The greater the space that is occupied, the more likely the owner will be to absorb improvement costs in order to keep the tenant in the building.

The Expanding Tenant

Expansion is a costly and difficult undertaking. It represents not only an increase in the overall rental but also construction costs and expenditure of executive time. The tenant who intends to expand must be handled expertly, and the expenses must be minimized. For almost every existing tenant that needs to increase its office size, space planning is necessary. The space planning process for the expanding tenant is critical to the continuation of the lease not only at the time of expansion but also in future years. One reason office users seek space elsewhere is because their existing layouts have, over a period of years, become inefficient. If plans for expansion are made at the outset, moving can be avoided.

The cost of planning space for an expanding tenant usually is charged to the tenant. Again, however, current local market conditions may dictate that the landlord must make a contribution in order to keep the tenant.

As with planning an office for a new tenant, expansion plans must be designed with the user's operational and aesthetic requirements and financial limitations in mind. In addition, certain other factors must be incorporated so that the expansion area does not

Space Planning

appear as an appendage to the original space. First, the space should be used wisely. Second, the logical flow of people and paper should be analyzed and planned for. Third, the existing space may have to be modified to accommodate efficient use of the total office area and ensure that the expansion area is consistent with and complimentary to the original space.

With an expansion prior to the termination of a lease, either the landlord or the tenant may require an extension of the lease. Especially if the remaining term is short and the tenant pays for a majority of or all of the improvement costs, the tenant will want an extension as a guarantee of recouping construction costs. On the other hand, the landlord will want an extension if the improvement costs are charged against the building.

When an existing tenant expands into additional space, the rental rate will be affected. Either two rates will be charged—the rate for the existing space until the term of the lease for that space expires and the rate for the expanded space which usually runs with the existing lease—or a single rate will be imposed for all of the space during the expanded term. The leasing agent has an opportunity at this juncture to increase current cash flow to the landlord by homogenizing or averaging the two rates into a single rate. Consider the hypothetical case of a tenant occupying 4,000 square feet, one year left on the lease, and an immediate need for an additional 1,000 square feet. The current rate is $8 per square foot; the expanded rate, $9 per square foot.

Rental on Existing Space = 4,000 square feet @ $8.00 per square foot = $32,000 per year or $2,666.67 per month

Rental on Expansion Space = 1,000 square feet @ $9.00 per square foot = $9,000 per year or $750 per month

Total Rental = $32,000 + $9,000 = $41,000 per year or $3,416.67 per month

Assume further that the owner will permit an expansion only if the tenant agrees to extend the lease term by five additional years. The rental rate for that five-year extension period (exclusive of escalation factors) is established at $9.50, based on analysis of the office rental market. The tenant's annual rental consequently increases from $41,000, as calculated above, to $47,500, which is computed in this way:

Rental on Total Space = 5,000 square feet @ $9.50 per square foot = $47,500 per year or $3,958.33 per month

Rather than increasing the annual rental from $41,000 to $47,500 when the lease extension becomes effective, the leasing agent might suggest that the rental rate be homogenized, or averaged, over the full six years of the agreement (one year of the original lease plus five years of the extended term). The homogenized rental is computed as follows:

Rental for First Year of Expansion	$ 41,000
Rental for Five Years of Extended Term	237,500
($47,500 per year × 5 years)	
Total Rental during Six-Year Period	$278,500

Average Annual Rental = $278,500 ÷ 6 years = $46,416.67 per year or $3,868.50 per month

The homogenized rental provides an increase to landlord's cash flow of $451.38 ($3,868.05 − $3,416.67) per month during the first year.

The Contracting Tenant

The contracting tenant is one whose space requirement is reduced for one of many reasons—the company is reorganizing, a subsidiary or department is being relocated, financial cutbacks are necessary. Usually the tenant will make space reductions at the end of the lease term; however, if the request comes before the lease expires, problems are bound to arise.

The landlord will react in one of several ways to this request. If the tenant has been a good one and it is obvious the current space is too large, the landlord may be accommodating, possibly by relocating the tenant or by reducing the existing space. If the tenant is having financial problems, the landlord may permit the space reduction in order to lower the monthly rental rather than run the risk of being faced with a tenant who defaults. If the market is strong, the landlord may refuse the reduction but agree to terminate the lease, especially if there is a strong possibility that the space can be leased to another tenant at a higher rate. On the other hand, the landlord may disallow the request altogether, forcing the tenant to

Space Planning

remain liable for all of the space under the terms of the lease. If the lease contains no subleasing provision, the tenant would have little recourse.

Space planning for a contracting tenant can be quite complicated. Unless an entire department or division has been eliminated, the tenant will be attempting to compress the original space into a smaller area. A tight rein must be held on space planning, keeping in mind that efficiency is critical for this type of tenant. Creating a smaller working space necessitates considerable tenant improvement costs. If the tenant is reducing space in order to cut back on expenses, making improvements may pose problems. While the space planner must thoroughly understand the tenant's operational and aesthetic requirements, specific attention should be turned to the limitations.

The Relocating Tenant

Oftentimes, a tenant will want to expand but all adjoining areas are occupied. Occasionally, one of these contiguous tenants will be relocated to another suite within the building to permit the expansion. To avoid antagonism, the leasing agent should approach the tenant with a positive attitude. Space planning, which likely will be needed for the relocating tenant, can go far toward dispelling hard feelings. No relocation cost should be charged against a tenant who is forced to relocate. Usually the landlord absorbs it then is reimbursed by the expanding tenant. Relocation expenses may include space planning costs, moving expenses, additional rent, and tenant improvement expenses including over-standard building improvements. Possibly the relocating tenant may lose a special location on a floor, a view, or certain amenities unique to the floor (storage areas, lounges, etc.). Appeasing substitutions can be made available in the design of the new space.

The advantages that a relocating tenant can gain are numerous. However, a perceptive leasing agent also can capitalize. For example, does the relocating tenant's needs suggest that, when the company moves, space should be added? If so, though the tenant may be required to pay for the tenant improvements allowable to the additional space, the agent can further satisfy the tenant and, in doing so, satisfy the landlord as well.

The New Tenant in Previously Occupied Space

If a new tenant's needs correspond with previously occupied space and the tenant is satisfied with the space as it exists, the space planning task may be altogether unnecessary or at least uncomplicated. However, such a near-perfect situation is uncommon.

While the area may be acceptable, it is unlikely that the layout will be. Perhaps a special-purpose area demands new electrical wiring, new telephone systems, new ceiling, or new partitions. If so, expensive construction as well as demolition may be necessary. The landlord must be involved, inasmuch as fewer dollars usually are allocated for tenant improvements in an existing building than in a new building. Estimates must be obtained to determine the economic feasibility of the plans. If the new tenant fails to see advantages in the existing space or the agent fails to convince the new tenant of the advantages, it may be preferable to disqualify the tenant rather than incur excessive alteration expenses that may not be cost effective.

The Tenant in a New Office Building

As preleasing becomes more commonplace, the space planning process for tenants in a new building often is finished before the building is. The agent is forced to sell the building as an intangible idea. Doing this usually requires the use of plans and specifications, color renderings, photographs, models, and any other visual aids that are available. Depending on the degree of completion of the building, a tour may aid in convincing a prospect about the office suite's view.

Space planning in a preleasing situation is an opportunity to create a perfect space: The only limitations are windows and walls and the building core.

The landlord may stipulate a fixed tenant improvement allowance based on square footage leased or provide a quantity allowance for various items, as shown in figure 2.1. Often the two types of allowances are combined. Sometimes, the landlord provides some items as a base building expense and does not include them as an expense in the tenant improvement allowance. The methods of allocating improvement costs are as diverse as the imaginations of creative developers. As a rule, however, tenant improvement allowances are inadequate and excess costs must be absorbed by the tenant.

Summary

Developing preliminary plans requires, first and foremost, the agent's complete understanding of the prospect's operational and aesthetic requirements and financial limitations. This is the foundation for creating office space designs that further the marketing effort.

The agent relays the prospect's needs to a space planner, who prepares the plans. By attempting to foresee problem areas and make the necessary alterations, rejection by the prospect or changes that become more costly with each subsequent step are avoided.

In addition to overseeing the preparation of attractive and efficient office plans, the agent must be able to estimate accurately the construction costs and, more specifically, the tenant's share of those costs. By mixing personal knowledge, data from contractors and ownership, and an understanding of the prospect, it should be possible to meet all the established criteria.

The status of a tenant has an effect on the space planning procedure. Whether a tenant is renewing a lease, expanding, reducing, relocating, moving into existing space, or preleasing in a new office building will have an impact on the space planning process.

Each step in the space-planning process, from gathering prospect information to making final suite presentation, is critical to securing a signed lease. The agent must be diplomatic and creative in working within the criteria set by the prospect, the leasing situation, the product's capabilities, and ownership's guidelines. The reason for the haste is obvious: Until there is a tenant-landlord agreement (a signed lease), the prospect is open to solicitation of other office building leasing agents.

11 The Formal Presentation

When the suite design plans have been as refined as possible, the knowledgeable leasing agent is prepared to make a formal sales presentation to the prospect that is tailored to the individual situation and is in language that is easily understood.

The formal proposal to the prospect usually requires five steps: (1) the presentation of the suite design; (2) a tour of the office building and its environs; (3) preparation of the finish schedule; (4) discussion of tenant improvement costs and allocations; and (5) the proposal of the lease terms and conditions.

Throughout the leasing effort, interim commitments have been sought as signals to continue. Upon completion of the formal presentation, the leasing agent will be seeking a final commitment, an answer from the company's key decision-maker. The effective agent is prepared to give accurate answers to any questions that are raised throughout the presentation, fully understand the prospect's objections or doubts and be able to dispel them, and, finally, obtain a favorable decision. The more polished the presentation, the greater the likelihood of satisfying the prospect and leasing the office space.

Formal Suite Design Presentation

The preliminary office space plans, described in the previous chapter, are designed to indicate that the prospect's functional needs can be met by the building. They further provide an opportunity for the prospect to verify at an early stage that the space planner's interpretation of the office requirements is correct. In short, they are a starting point for sophisticated refinements that are necessary to accurately translate the prospect's needs into efficient space. Once these refinements have been made, formal plans (sampled in figure 11.1) are prepared to more graphically depict the office suite. (Figure 10.2 represents the preliminary space plans while figure 11.1 represents the formalized plans of the same company. The refinements are evident when the figures are compared.) When attractively prepared and persuasively presented, the formal space plans are the ultimate marketing tool.

The presentation of the suite design may be either simple or elaborate, the marketing budget allotment and the size and importance of the prospect dictating the format. The simplest of formal suite design presentations consists of showing and explaining floor plans. A more elaborate presentation may call for customized color perspective renderings of each office area and detailed design plans that indicate where desks, plants, filing cabinets, and so forth may be located. If mounted on boards for easel presentation, these visual aids will be especially effective. The purpose of these visual aids is to show the prospect as closely as possible what the space would look like.

Regardless of the extensiveness of the presentation, certain principles should prevail. The leasing agent should:

1. Point out those elements of the plan which meet basic requirements.
2. Call attention to those elements that offer unexpected advantages or create efficiency not provided in the prospect's present office space.
3. Indicate, in square feet, the space to be provided and areas designed for expansion.
4. Describe the special view or design results that meet the prospect's aesthetic needs and wants.
5. Ask questions designed to elicit positive answers about the suite design.
6. Remind the prospect that changes are still possible without actually encouraging such changes.
7. Encourage careful examination of and questions about the plans.
8. Above all, indicate genuine interest to accommodate all of the prospect's desires for the office space.

This presentation should be made in the agent's office, not the prospect's, or some other advantageous location. If held in the agent's

The Formal Presentation

Figure 11.1

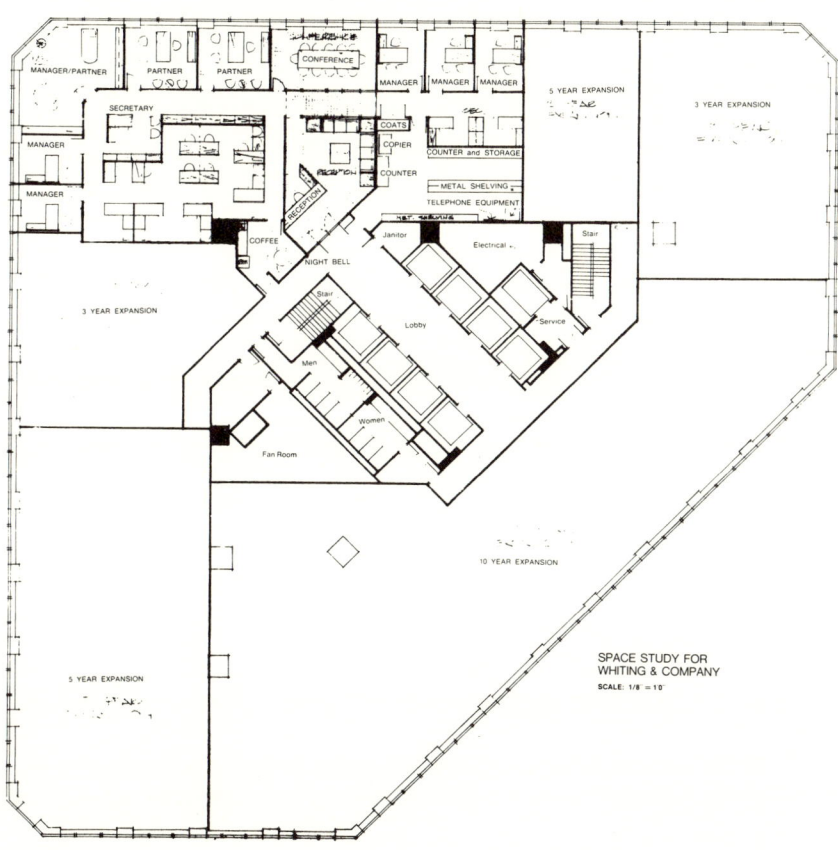

office, the secretary should be given explicit directions to permit no interruptions. If the agent's office is in the building under consideration, it provides an excellent opportunity to conduct a detailed building tour. If the agent's office is located elsewhere, possibly arrangements can be made to hold the meeting in the subject building. A sense of belonging to the building is suggested subtly by this situation and furthers the prospect's image as a building tenant. If the building is under construction, either the agent's office should be used or a suitable substitute found. Often a presentation will be made to a group of executives from the company considering office space. If so, a site for the presentation should be found that provides adequate seating.

Building Tour

A tour of the office building conceivably could take place at any time during the leasing process. However, after having seen the suite design, the prospect will be better prepared to visualize itself in the building. Consequently, a tour is usually more profitable if it is conducted immediately after and in conjunction with the presentation of the space plans. A premature tour can be damaging. If a prospect is unfamiliar with office improvements and cannot yet visualize the firm in a vacant space as it is toured, the building may be dismissed totally. This is especially true if extensive alterations are required to meet the prospect's needs. Having explained the suite design, on the other hand, the agent can demonstrate the dramatic change that will occur. Prospects can tour buildings under construction as well as existing buildings. Most people are intrigued by the construction process; if the agent provides a convincing explanation of how the prospect would fit into the building, the tour can heighten interest.

If the presentation of the suite design is held somewhere other than in the office building, and the tour follows, a route should be taken that provides the best view of neighborhood amenities, such as restaurants, banks, and highway access. Travel time can be used as an opportunity to mention the benefits of the building. Upon arrival at the building, these features should be explained further. Attention should be called to the building's curb appeal, the appearance of the main lobby, the accessibility of the elevators, retail facilities within the building, and any other advantages that come to immediate attention. The strong points of the building should be

The Formal Presentation

amplified, and committing questions should be asked that test the prospect's reaction. For instance: "As you can see, we have both a quick-service, inexpensive restaurant here on the main floor as well as a fine dining facility on our top floor. Such a combination is convenient for both you and your employees, isn't it?" Similar questions should be asked about the location of the prospective tenant's suite in the building, management services, parking, and building and neighborhood amenities. If positive feedback is received, the prospect's interest in the office building is reinforced. If the reaction is negative, more creative salesmanship is called for.

The tour also provides an opportunity for the agent to discuss the building's tenant mix as an advantage. For example, the prospect can be told of respected businesses that are tenants, thereby enhancing the image of the building and the prospect.

Arriving at the prospect's proposed suite, its benefits should be pointed out. For instance, if the reception area is near the elevator banks, this should be noted. Likewise, restroom facilities, freight elevators, storage areas, and other features on the floor must be highlighted.

Plans of the prospect's office should be available when the space is toured. This helps the prospect envision the architectural drawings as a three-dimensional office.

While moving through the area that will become an office suite, all benefits should be pointed out. In an older building, attention should be called to existing improvements that will enhance tenancy in that suite, such as expensive paneling, special shelving, or lunch room appliances. It should be mentioned that these improvements are extended at no cost. Items that will be moved or demolished should be pointed out and an explanation given of replacement items. It is helpful to point out these alterations as they appear on the plans. Committing questions should continue: "Mr. Prospect, by removing this wall we can create a larger conference room for you. Isn't this the size that you find most accommodating?" Throughout the tour, the plans' ability to accommodate people circulation, interrelationships in the work process, and the like should be reinforced through questioning. Again, the prospect should be asked if further changes are necessary.

Many agents find it worthwhile to take the prospect on a tour through a highly developed suite after having obtained permission of the tenant. This demonstrates the potentiality for improvement that may not be apparent in the proposed suite and is especially valuable in dealing with a businessman who has never before been involved in office space selection. If properly planned and executed, the tour becomes a powerful selling tool that convinces the potential tenant of the value of the building.

Finish Schedule

A finish schedule is a list of items that will be used to "finish off" the suite design. The completed schedule represents the prospect's final decision about wall and floor coverings, ceiling materials, and the like that best reflect the desired company image.

The prospect's size affects the development of the finish schedule. A large firm may rely on a committee or company-hired interior designer to make decisions, while in a small firm decisions may be made by staff or family members, such as the president's wife. In any case, all decisions must be made by the prospect, not the leasing agent.

Samples for all items included in the finish schedule, such as paneling, wall coverings, paint chips, and carpeting, should be made available to the prospect. The leasing agent should then bring samples of the building standard materials to the meeting with the prospect. These are necessary in this decision-making process, and the prospect should be given sufficient time to study them.

With plans unrolled, the placement of furniture, telephones, electrical outlets, and other items can be confirmed, and the prospect should have no doubts about the future appearance of the proposed suite. One further thought: In some cases, the tenant's representative may have to show the plans to company associates and superiors for their approval. The agent may not be present at this type of meeting. It is essential that the plans are self-explanatory and that the tenant's representative understands them fully enough so as not to confuse company associates and possibly destroy the accomplishments the agent has made thus far.

Payment Structure

The agent must be able to answer the question, "What is all of this going to cost?" At any stage of the space planning process, if alterations are requested, costs will be affected. Yet once all changes have been made, estimates become actual costs and are apportioned: The tenant improvement allowance is deducted from the total cost of construction, and the balance is the responsibility of the tenant. In practice, improvement costs often remain estimates until construction is complete. At that time, any costs over the owner's allowance are charged against the tenant. If a tenant requires a firm figure, a contingency will be added to protect the owner against possible changes in costs.

Payment of the tenant's portion of the construction cost generally is handled in one of two ways: (1) It is paid in cash upon occupancy, or (2) the landlord amortizes the tenant's expense over the term of the lease. The approach taken depends on market conditions, local custom, the landlord's financial situation, and the desirability of the tenant. If the latter method is used, the landlord may charge interest based on current market rates. Other payment possibilities may be adopted. The tenant may wish to negotiate not only the amount of money to be paid but also the method of payment.

Lease Proposal

If a prospect accepts the suite design and layout and the estimates for improvements, the time is right to initiate discussion of the general terms and conditions of the lease and present the document itself. This is the lease proposal.

In some instances, a prospect may be so positive about the building that a lease proposal is not necessary and a lease immediately can be submitted to the prospect for consideration. Certainly, whenever a prospect requests a lease, the agent should oblige. In other cases, a lease is proposed prior to planning the space, many firms signing leases without seeing suite designs. Experience, providing the range of tenant improvement costs, and a workletter, dividing construction obligations between landlord and tenant, remove the necessity of a plan and estimate.

The lease proposal can be as simple as a one-page letter or as formal as a custom-made book. Its extensiveness is dictated by the prospect's size and importance, the apparent closeness to signing a lease, and the agent's familiarity with the prospect. If, for example, the prospect's representative is a personal friend of the agent or owner, the letter will be less formal than would be necessary for a strictly business acquaintance. The lease proposal can be regarded as the conclusion of a successful suite design presentation or a further tool for convincing the prospect to become a tenant.

The lease proposal can be presented in one of several places: (1) At the prospect's office or board room if such a presentation is requested, (2) at the agent's office (if, for example, the product is under construction), or (3) at a neutral facility, such as a restaurant. This would be especially appropriate if the agent wishes to host a luncheon as part of the presentation.

The lease proposal reiterates the facts about the working environment and lists the general terms and conditions of the lease. It should be made available for the prospect to take back to the office to study. Since the lease proposal can be critical to the success of a transaction, care should be given to its preparation. The following outline is offered as a format of a comprehensive proposal:

Cover. The cover of the presentation book should display a photo of the building, its logo, or some illustration that represents the building, the management company, and the leasing agency. Illustrations elsewhere in the book can further sell the product. The book should be bound sturdily.

Title Page. The title page should be customized to include the name of the prospect, the project, the leasing agent, and the date of the proposal.

Table of Contents. If the book is subdivided with tabs, this section can be omitted. If not, and if the presentation is lengthy, a table of contents is needed.

Letter of Introduction. The letter of introduction may be one of the most important parts of the book. It is addressed to the prospect and signed by the landlord (not the leasing agent). Its purpose is to make the prospect feel important and encourage reading of the presentation. If the proposal contains a special incentive or concession designed especially for the prospect, it should be mentioned here.

Lease Proposal. Another important part of the presentation book is that which describes the general terms and conditions of the proposed lease and discusses the following: suite number and floor, square feet, term of the lease and occupancy date, rate, monthly and annual rental, recovery or escalator provisions, parking tenant improvements, options (e.g., expansions, renewal), and any other special provisions. The termination date of the proposal also must be stated. That is, a time limit is set for the prospect to study and accept or reject the proposal.

Proposal Addenda. To further clarify or expand the lease terms and conditions, additional information may be included: definition of net rentable area, expanded recovery provision data, tenant improvement description and cost estimates, tenant improvement outline specifications, and design and construction criteria.

Location and Site. At this point, the prospect is reminded of the locational benefits to be received by moving into the building. Regional information and neighborhood information may be provided, and detailed data given about view and neighborhood amenities.

The Product and the Premises. All features of the building and its environment and how they can benefit the prospect should be noted.

Access and Public Transportation. Vehicular access to the building and peak-hour travel times from important selected outlying areas should be indicated, as should access from the building to necessary facilities, such as an airport, government centers, post office. If the building is serviced by public transportation, the facilities, routes, and transfer connections should be described. Maps can support this presentation.

Parking. Parking is often critical in the selection of office space. The parking facility of the product should be described, as should other nearby parking facilities. It is also worthwhile to discuss access to parking facilities and the walking time from these facilities to the office building.

Miscellaneous. Any special features that the product may have (i.e., heliport, hotel facilities) should be explained.

The Developer/Owner/Management Team. The expertise and financial stability of the developer and owner (if they are separate entities) are important to the prospect and should be cited. Likewise, a statement of the philosophy of the management agent can be effective. The management team is responsible for providing tenant services, and the capabilities of the team should be reinforced.

Conclusion. A succinct summary of the product's benefits is a viable way to close the presentation. This section also should ask the prospect's permission to allow preparation of the lease documents.

Exhibits. Such items as building outline specifications, tenant improvement outline specifications, suite design plans, standard form lease, design and construction criteria, and janitorial specifications may be included as an appendix.

The cost to develop such an extensive proposal book can be high. The size and importance of the prospect will have to be weighed against the effectiveness of the presentation and the budget relating to this expense. If the presentation is being made to a board of directors, a number of the books may be needed. In other instances, even if several individuals make up the selection committee, only one book is required, although a modified presentation folder containing the cover letter, lease proposal, and conclusion may be prepared for each person.

Summary

The formal presentation of the suite design and lease proposal must be regarded as a carefully planned, diplomatically executed step in the leasing process. At any time during this presentation, the agent may meet with objections or rejections. By being prepared, these difficulties can be met and overcome.

Space plans should be explained thoroughly to the prospect and the strengths and efficiencies pointed out. By encouraging ongoing confirmation, the agent moves the prospect closer to complete acceptance.

A tour through the building can enable the prospect to see itself as a tenant. If effectively conducted, the tour can be one of the agent's most valuable marketing tools.

Upon approval of the office design, the agent discusses those items which will finish off the suite—carpeting, paints, other wall coverings. The list of items is the finish schedule. Once costs for these and all other tenant improvements are determined, the portions to be paid by the landlord and the tenant respectively and the method by which the tenant will pay its share must be determined.

Should the decision dictate further merchandising tactics on the part of the leasing agent, a lease proposal may be necessary. If so, this calls for the development of a lease presentation book that the prospect can study while evaluating the building as a possible office site.

It cannot be overemphasized that an ill-prepared, unknowledgeable agent can damage or even sever the leasing efforts. Thus, at every stage, the leasing agent must be equipped to deal with any kind of setback.

12 The Lease Document

It is impossible to be effective in any sector of the real estate management business without a familiarity with leases. The office leasing sector is no exception. The objective of all marketing activities undertaken by a leasing agent is to transform a prospect into a tenant by obtaining a signature on a lease. Consequently, the leasing agent's span of knowledge must encompass more than the techniques of marketing space. An understanding of office leases and lease terminology is equally essential.

A lease is a contract that transfers the right to use and enjoy a given piece of real estate from the owner to a tenant for a definite period of time and under specified conditions. Under the typical office lease, the tenant, referred to as the lessee, is conveyed the right to use and occupy an area of space, customarily expressed in square feet, by assuming a legal obligation to pay rent to the landlord, or lessor.

Most leases designed for the rental of space, including office leases, are similar in content yet follow no predetermined formula. Much depends on the nature of the office building involved and the negotiations between the owner and the tenant. Nonetheless, a leasing agency generally has what it considers to be a standard form lease, which it uses as a starting point for negotiating lease terms with tenants. With a standard form lease, it becomes unnecessary for a new lease to be prepared with each new tenant. This increases efficiency and standardizes rental arrangements and operations throughout a given building. Even more important, if it has been prepared with care, a standard lease helps to eliminate possible omissions from a lease that later might work to the detriment of either party to the agreement.

Despite the recognized importance of an agency having a standard form lease, it generally is conceded that no such document exists. Depending upon legal stipulations and local leasing customs, leases vary from state to state. Leases may even vary within a given state as a result of local zoning regulations and unique leasing practices. Furthermore, real estate agencies and property owners adopt lease forms that are standard only to their operations. Consequently, many leases exist and become standard for the people who use them.

Lack of uniformity among so-called standard form leases, however, does not detract from their usefulness. The value of a standard form lease is as a starting point for negotiation between the landlord—the lessor—and the prospective tenant—the lessee. It is during the negotiation process that the standard form lease evolves into a contract that is specifically tailored to a given rental arrangement.

Types of Leases

There are three basic types of leases with which the leasing agent should be familiar. One of these is the gross lease, under which the tenant pays a fixed rental and the owner pays all other operating expenses related to the property. The gross lease, although generally reserved for residential rentals, is used for office space as well.

In office leasing, the net lease is much more common. Under a net lease, the tenant assumes the obligation to pay for certain operating costs specified within the lease document. Three variations on the net lease are utilized. Under the net lease, the tenant is obligated to pay utilities, real estate taxes, and other special assessments associated with the leased premises. The net-net lease requires to the tenant to pay the same costs plus ordinary repairs and maintenance. Under the triple-net, or net-net-net, lease, the tenant pays all of this plus some capital improvements.

Also worthy of note is the percentage lease, used for the rental of retail space. The percentage lease provides for the payment of a fixed minimum rental plus a percentage of the tenant's gross income. In this way, the landlord shares in the locational benefits of the property. If an agent is responsible for leasing ground-floor retail space in a large office building, knowledge of the percentage lease is essential.

Lease Characteristics

Despite the possible dissimilarities between standard form leases, there is one characteristic all should have in common: They should be in writing. Most states operate under the statute of frauds, which requires all leases for terms of more than one year to be in writing. Consequently, an oral lease between an office tenant and landlord for more than one year—and most office leases are for long terms—would not be valid. It is recommended that even month-to-month leases be in writing to avoid conflict and clearly describe the rights and obligations of both parties to the agreement.

The actual preparation of a standard form lease initially must be delegated to an attorney. If the management function and the leasing function are being performed by two distinct entities, responsibility for insuring that the lease is prepared sometimes falls within the scope of duties of the managing agent. After all, management will be providing the services called for in the lease and will desire input and control over the lease terms, covenants, and conditions. On the other hand, sometimes the leasing agent is charged with preparing the lease and thus must be aware of all the lease's components. In any event, the leasing agent and the managing agent should regard the standard form lease as an adaptable instrument designed to facilitate—not hinder—the signing of a mutually fair and beneficial rental agreement.

While recognizing that there are variations among office leases, it is possible to cite six primary elements that appear in every valid lease:

1. The correct names and signatures of the legally competent parties to the agreement.
2. A description of the leased premises.
3. The term of the lease.
4. The consideration that supports the agreement; i.e., the rental payment.
5. The purpose for which the premises are to be used.
6. All rights and obligations of the parties to the contract.

Within the broad framework created by these six elements, numerous specific clauses are necessary and possible. Descriptions of the most common clauses follow. It is worth noting, however, that not all of the clauses described herein are applicable to all leasing circumstances, nor do they necessarily constitute universally accepted legal practice. Rather, the comments are directed to general leasing customs. Leases are, after all, prepared by legal counsel, not the agent. The agent's role is to negotiate the specific terms of the agreement on behalf of the owner. Nonetheless, the agent will be an effective negotiator only if there is familiarity with the terms encountered in leases.

Parties

The first section of the lease is necessary to identify the the parties to the agreement as well as indicate the date on which the lease is drawn. Typically, this introductory clause states something to this effect: "This lease, made and entered into this _____ day of _____, 19__, between _____, (hereinafter referred to as 'Lessor') and _____, (hereinafter referred to as 'Lessee')." This introductory section of the lease usually notes as well as the city, county, and state in which it is to be in effect.

 The complete and correct names of the lessor and the lessee and the nature of their entities are needed in completing this section of the standard lease form. If a party to a lease is an individual, the full legal name followed by this identification should be noted: "John Doe, an individual." If the individual does business under another name, the individual's name should be followed by the other name: "John Doe, an individual, d/b/a The XYZ Company." If a party to the lease is a partnership, the company should be so identified: "The XYZ Company, a partnership." If the party is a corporation, the corporate name should be followed by the state of incorporation: "The XYZ Company, a Delaware corporation."

 In identifying the parties to the lease, the competency of the tenant must be determined. Competency, which is controlled by law, may vary from state to state. However, all jurisdictions consider minors and insane and senile parties to be legally incompetent to enter into a lease. If such persons were to become parties to a lease, the instrument would be unenforceable.

 Inasmuch as all jurisdictions consider corporations as individual entities, corporations are competent parties. Obviously, however, a corporation must act through an agent, who generally is a director or officer of the corporation. When leasing to a corporation, the leasing agent must be aware that an agent will be acting for that corporation. An agent of a corporation is competent to enter into a lease only if granted the proper authority to do so. This authority occasionally is given by the corporate charter, but the more common means is by a resolution of the board of directors that authorizes the corporate agent to execute the lease. As a means of verifying that a corporate representative has the power necessary to act, a certified copy of the resolution may be requested.

Having ascertained the competency of the parties to the agreement, their signatures will appear at the end of the lease.

If the tenant is a partnership, the signature of any two of the partners generally is considered sufficient to bind the partnership. However, obtaining the signatures of all general partners—or at least verifying that the partner who executed the lease is given the authority to do so via the partnership agreement—is preferable. While obtaining signatures of all general partners might be a simple process in the case of a limited partnership, in which the number of general partners usually is few, with general partnerships, the process may be more complicated. Such a matter is worthy of counsel with an attorney.

If the tenant is a corporation, two agents, usually officers of the corporation and one of whom preferably is the corporate secretary, should sign the lease.

Naturally, signatures representing both of the parties are required to make the lease valid. With respect to the building ownership, the actual owner or, if the owner is a corporation, one of its agents, may sign the lease. However, a lease is usually executed by a duly authorized agent acting on behalf of the property owner. A lease executed by an agent in behalf of an owner should be signed as follows: "Robert James, by Pam Harwood, Agent."

Leased Premises

The leased property must be identified precisely, particularly in the case of multitenanted buildings. Without an accurate description, the lease could be invalid. Generally, the description of the leased premises, often referred to as the "demised premises," includes, when applicable, these elements: street address, name of the building, suite number, and the number of square feet being leased by the tenant. The more precise the description, the greater will be the protection afforded to both parties.

To further clarify and describe the leased premises, a lease should have attached as an exhibit a floor plan or key map of the given floor or floors with the leased premises clearly marked. This should be done whether the tenant occupies a partial floor, an entire floor, or more than one floor.

Similarly, the importance of noting the number of square feet being leased cannot be overlooked. For instance, under some escalation clauses, a tenant is liable for a share of increased operating expenses based on the ratio of leased space to the total area of the entire building; the number of square feet occupied is important in determining this ratio.

Term

A valid lease states specifically when the lease term is to begin and end. Preferably, exact commencement and termination dates are given, as is the period for which the lease is to run.

Sometimes, however, precise commencement dates are impossible to determine at the time a lease is drawn. This is often the case when a building under construction is being preleased. In such an instance, the commencement date of the lease may be tied to the occurrence of some event. On a lease for office space that previously was occupied and requires tenant improvements, for example, the commencement date may be tied to the completion of interior construction. In such an instance, a construction rider might be added that lists the obligations of the tenant for the improvements and stipulates acceleration of the commencement date without occupancy if the tenant fails to perform as agreed.

While the commencement date will not necessarily be specific, the term or number of months the lease runs must be. A lease of an indefinite term probably may be ruled invalid if taken to court.

Rental

A lease must contain a statement of the consideration (i.e., rental) which supports the agreement between the tenant and landlord. From a legal standpoint, consideration is the price demanded and received in exchange for a promise. Without consideration, a contract may not be enforceable. In the case of an office lease, the periodic payment of rent over the term of the lease is the consideration for the promise by the landlord of the use and occupancy of the premises.

The Lease Document

The rental clause in an office lease states the amount of rental to be paid, the method of payment, and to whom the payment is to be made. As a rule, it is advisable to recite the total rental to be paid over the entire lease term, providing that the method of payment shall be in terms of dollars per month, quarter, or year. This is done for several reasons: First, it may be necessary should a lawsuit involving the lease arise; second, it may be required by a mortgagee; and third, the total amount of the rental provides the basis of the commission payable to the leasing agent.

Depending on the nature of a management firm's operations, invoices may or may not be sent to office building tenants. Those that send invoices do so because tenants demand them and because of the necessity to charge tenants for utilities, extra cleaning service, parking costs, and the like. Invoices also are necessary to keep tenants aware of any increases in rent attributable to escalation factors. If management prefers not to send rental notices, the lease should state that rental payments are due without prior notice on demand.

The lease also should state when rent is due. It is customary to provide for rent to be payable in advance on the first day of each month during the term of the lease.

If an office building is to operate successfully, a steady flow of income is necessary. Consequently, rentals must be paid on time by all tenants. The lease may be used to encourage prompt payment.

Security Deposit

As a means of guaranteeing that a tenant will comply with the conditions of the lease, a security deposit may be required. The typical deposit is equal to one month's rent. A security deposit is held by an owner for a variety of purposes, the most common of which are compensation for damage to the space being leased beyond normal wear and tear and failure to pay rent.

Rather than providing for a security deposit as a clause within the standard lease, many firms provide this item by addendum.

Rental Adjustments

In periods of rapidly rising costs and spiraling inflation, owners of income property have found it necessary to include clauses in long-term leases that enable them to adjust rents in accordance with changes in economic conditions. Without a means of adjusting rents, costs may climb while rental income remains the same. The result is that the landlord suffers financially, the services provided to the property are curtailed, and the overall value of the building to the tenant and owner declines.

With inflation causing landlords to seek a variety of ways to protect themselves, there are as many rental adjustment clauses as the imagination can develop. The most common of these clauses—commonly referred to as escalation clauses—base rental adjustments on changes in operating costs and cost-of-living indices.

Operating-cost escalation clauses are the most widely used means of adjusting rents. Under such a clause, increases in operating expenses are passed on to tenants on a pro-rata basis. To do this, it is necessary to define which costs are considered to be operating costs and explain how changes in these costs are to be passed on to tenants of the office building. As a rule, the percentage of the increased costs to be paid by the tenant is based upon the ratio of the rentable square footage occupied by the tenant to the total rentable area of the building, or:

$$\frac{\text{Tenant Area (Square Feet)}}{\text{Building Rentable Area (Square Feet)}} = \frac{\text{Tenant's Percentage of}}{\text{Increased Operating Costs}}$$

One means of recovering costs via an escalation clause is to stipulate in the lease that operating expenses beyond a certain stated amount will result in an adjustment in the rent. Other leases provide for rental adjustments in relationship to a base year, the total operating costs associated with this base year becoming the amount by which increases or decreases in rent are measured.

The other frequently used rent adjustment clause, the index escalation clause, calls for a rental adjustment in an amount equal to the relative index change from year to year. The most commonly used index is the Consumer Price Index. The theory behind the use of an index for rental adjustment is that an index fairly measures the economic value of the dollar, and, in consequence, rent escalation based on it upholds the landlord's income in terms of actual spendable dollars. An index escalation clause should state the index to be used and establish the base year index against which future indices are to be compared and, again, note how the adjustment is to be passed on to tenants.

Other types of escalation clauses also are utilized. For example, rental may be based on changes in wage levels or utility costs. While the items of comparison are different, the concept behind and implementation of these escalation clauses are the same as those previously described.

The Lease Document

Similarly, all of the clauses may contain recovery clauses that allow periodic estimates of increases and consequent monthly collections of the adjustments. This is considered preferable to many owners who, without such clauses, must wait until the end of the year to collect the adjustment in a lump sum and thus run into major cash flow problems throughout the year. Anticipated budgets with year-end adjustments obviously alleviate this problem.

(The Institute of Real Estate Management has prepared a monograph, *Lease Escalators and Other Pass-Through Clauses,* which provides sample clauses for consideration. Its explanations and sample documents can help the agent and landlord make a business decision about the kind of escalation clauses to develop.)

Use

The standard form lease must contain a clause that indicates the purpose for which the leased office space is to be used. This is necessary to ensure that the tenant does not put the space to unlawful use—for instance, use the office to conduct an illegal gambling operation—or use the premises in such a way that might physically damage the property or detract from its image.

Rights and Obligations

The bulk of the typical office space lease consists of the rights and obligations of the two contracting parties. The purpose here is to indicate who is to do what and hopefully eliminate the possibility of misunderstandings between the landlord and tenant. The clauses outlining the rights and obligations may vary.

Utilities and Services

Any and all services that the owner is to provide for the tenant—and that the tenant expects to receive—should be detailed in the lease. The usual services that are provided include air conditioning and heating, water, janitorial service, elevator service in the case of high-rises, building directory listings, and electricity. The document should indicate which party is to bear the cost of the stated services. With the rising costs of utilities and services, landlords have expanded this section of the lease.

If the landlord is to provide heating and air conditioning only during stated hours, this should be noted. A tenant who might need air conditioning after regular business must be sure that such service can be obtained. With computers entering the operations of many businesses, tenants often need longer hours of air conditioning to cool them. During lease negotiation, this concern very well may arise.

Office space generally is cleaned by the landlord; if so, this should be noted in the lease. Many tenants will demand that janitorial cleaning specifications be attached to the lease as an exhibit. These specifications should detail the general cleaning and trash removal that is to be done nightly and note how frequently other, more thorough work is to be performed. If any janitorial costs are to be borne by the tenant, this should be noted.

A provisison for elevator service is necessary. Some office leases might be quite specific in this regard, stating that, for example, four elevators are to be in operation during ordinary business hours and at least one during other times.

If the office building lobby has a building directory and the owner provides the service of listing the tenant on it, the lease should indicate this arrangement.

With rapidly increasing utility costs, it becomes important to the owner to maintain a control on all such costs, especially electricity and heat. The lease should stipulate the amount and kind of service the landlord is to provide for the tenant and also delineate the methods the landlord can use to determine any excessive use that is to go to the tenant's account. This item often is the object of negotiation.

No landlord who provides necessary services to the occupants of an office buildinng will want to enter into a lease that does not contain a clause that allows services and utilities to be interrupted due to repairs, inspection, or reasons beyond management's control without liability or abatement of rent. This often is called a "breakdown" clause. Needless to say, most tenants will attempt to negotiate a reduction in the landlord's rights under this article or at least some form of compromise arrangement. After all, were elevator service in a high-rise to be halted for a day, the activities of a law firm on the 30th floor, for example, would be seriously interrupted.

Also as a result of the accelerating costs of utilities, owners may try to demand that energy conservation be practiced by tenants. A clause under which the tenant agrees to conserve energy and notify the landlord of excessive use expands the owner's rights in this respect. An energy conservation clause may even stipulate that instal-

The Lease Document

lation of special equipment designed to minimize utility use would be at the tenant's expense. The leasing agent should not be surprised if prospects question this clause and request its deletion or, at the minimum, alteration.

As fossil fuels become more scarce, government regulations are being imposed on heating and air conditioning of public buildings and government may force landlords to install special equipment or cause other capital expenditures to be made for energy conservation. Pursuant to this, unless a landlord can be reimbursed for voluntary capital expenditures designed to conserve energy, the landlord is not likely to expend these resources. Similarly, the landlord may wish to install separate utility meters if the utility company were to impose a penalty for a master meter. The agent should explain that changing to individual meters is to the potential benefit of the tenant, who should have no objection. However, the tenant may wish to place a dollar limit to its liability in the conversion to individual metering.

Quiet Enjoyment

Common to most standard leases is a clause of quiet enjoyment or quiet possession, a legal term which means that the owner is obligated to protect the tenant against the claim of another firm that it is really the tenant of the specified space. Essentially, this clause provides that, assuming all obligations under the lease are fulfilled, the tenant is granted quiet and peaceful use of the leased premises.

Maintenance and Repairs

As a rule, the tenant is responsible for repairs to the leased premises. Thus, the repair clause is designed with the idea that the tenant should take good care of the leased premises and neither misuse or damage it nor permit misuse or damage by others. In addition to this general concept, specific areas of concern might be noted. For instance, responsibility for the replacement of bulbs and ballasts in light fixtures might be given to either the tenant or the landlord.

The lease also should state how and by whom repairs are to be performed and stipulate who is financially responsible for such repairs. Normally in an office building, the owner takes care of exterior walls and the roof, and the tenant is charged with the care of interior office areas. To ensure that the leased premises are maintained and repairs are made when necessary, a clause might provide that the tenant has a stated number of days to perform them. Failure to do so could result in the landlord, at its option, assuming the responsibility and subsequently charging the tenant for those repairs in the form of additional rent.

It is worth noting that a repair clause excludes "normal wear and tear" from the tenant's obligation. This phrase, defined as the deterioration of the premises based on normal business operations, is not to be considered as an excuse for poor maintenance.

Alterations

A lease should include exact language as to when, under what circumstances, and to what extent a tenant may alter the leased premises. Usually, an alteration provision prohibits a tenant from making any alteration of or improvement to the leased premises without the express consent of the landlord. There are numerous reasons for such a provision. For one thing, tenant leasehold improvements could damage the building, adversely affecting its value, or violate local building codes. A requirement of prior approval can see that this does not occur. Further, the landlord will want to determine the impact an improvement might have upon the real estate tax assessed against the property. Obviously, a substantial improvement could increase real estate taxes—a situation the owner wants to avoid. This problem can be met by including in the lease a provision that all additional taxes assessed because of improvements are to be the responsibility of the lessee.

Hold Harmless

The hold harmless, or indemnification, lease clause is sometimes attacked by prospective office tenants. The standard provision says that the owner will not be liable for damages or injury sustained in, on, or about the leased premises. Further, it provides that if an injury or damage is caused by negligence on the part of the tenant in the common areas of a building, the tenant likewise agrees to hold the landlord harmless.

Although the language of the typical hold harmless clause would appear to excuse the landlord of almost any liability whatsoever, general principles of law tend to dispute this. In some jurisdictions, provisions that a landlord is not responsible for damages due to its own negligence are determined invalid.

Insurance

The lease should contain a clause that requires the tenant to obtain a certain amount of public liability insurance which names the landlord as a co-insured. The naming of an additional insured does not

The Lease Document

increase the tenant's premium. The reasoning for such a provision is that if a person is injured in the leased premises and a suit is filed as a result, the plaintiff usually will sue both the tenant and landlord.

In some instances, the tenant also is responsible for carrying fire and extended coverage insurance. Further, some tenants will try to require an express provision to the effect that the landlord will maintain fire and extended coverage for the full replacement value of the improvements.

Destruction

A lease should contain a provision stating the applicable procedures and rights in the event that the leased premises are damaged or destroyed by fire or other casualty. As a rule, the lessee will be held financially liable if deemed responsible.

Still, the most important role of the clause is to prevent termination of the lease by the tenant by virtue of partial destruction of the leased office space or prevent holding the landlord in breach of the lease because the premises are untenantable. It is not uncommon for a clause to state that the lease does not terminate if the landlord makes the repairs within a given time and provides for an abatement in rent for the period during which the repairs are made. The clause also may provide that if damage is extensive, the landlord has the option of terminating the lease, without liability for damages to the tenant, rather than make repairs. In the case of total destruction, the lease generally is terminated.

In conjunction with this provision, most leases stipulate that the landlord is to provide insurance for the building and the tenant is to provide insurance for personal property. Likewise, a clause under which both parties waive claims against the other for damages caused by insurable casualties is common. This generally is followed by a provision that the insurance carriers of both parties are to recognize this waiver.

Eminent Domain

As more and more real estate is condemned by local, state, and federal governments for urban renewal projects, new highways, and the like, it has become increasingly important for office leases to contain a condemnation clause, or clause of eminent domain. Such a clause describes the rights of the parties should a governmental authority exercise its right of complete, partial, or temporary eminent domain.

The typical lease states that the agreement is terminated and all tenant improvements and fixtures revert to the landlord upon condemnation. The purpose of the clause is to eliminate sharing with the tenant an award received in an eminent domain proceeding and remove any liability connected with the inability of the owner to meet obligations as a result of the condemnation. Tenants often want to expand their rights under this clause. For instance, a tenant may want the right to any award for moving expenses or loss of business caused by the condemnation, or the right to join in the landlord's condemnation proceedings at the tenant's expense so as to recover such tenant costs.

Substitution of Premises

The owner of an office building will want a lease that reserves the right to relocate various tenants to comparable offices within the building. Without this right, should a larger tenant desire to expand into a contiguous area occupied by a smaller tenant, the larger tenant might move from the building in order to obtain the needed additional space. This customarily occurs in new buildings, in which the space leased to a small tenant early in the leasing program may bar the leasing of an entire floor to an even more desirable tenant. If the office is part of a larger complex or if the landlord owns other comparable buildings in the neighborhood, the clause might provide that such relocation be extended to a comparable building. The owner, however, should not be capricious or arbitrary in exercising this right.

In addition, the owner generally agrees to pay for the expenses incurred to relocate the other tenant. In practice, the tenant who will occupy that space in the future usually compensates the landlord for these expenses.

Tenants probably will attack this provision during negotiation. They may want to delete the paragraph altogether, have the right to cancel if they do not consider the substitute premises comparable, or specify certain portions of the building that would be considered as acceptable substitutes. A compromise usually can be reached.

Subordination

Most mortgagees require a subordination clause which makes the lease subject and subordinate to any first mortgage. The effect on a tenant of subordination to a mortgage can be great. If there is a foreclosure of the mortgage on the building, this could terminate the lease and result in the tenant's eviction by the mortgagee. Most tenants will object to the subordination clause, but few will be able to do anything about it.

A tenant may attempt to secure a provision that the mortgagee will not disturb the tenant following foreclosure if the tenant is not in default. This is especially likely with a major tenant, since the rental paid by this tenant will be a major portion of the rental income stream. In the event of foreclosure, this income stream may be extremely critical to the mortgagee.

Sale or Assignment

The lease should provide that the landlord may sell the building and assign the lease to the purchaser and thereafter be relieved of all obligations under the lease. The purchaser then becomes liable as landlord by virtue of the sale.

Change of Building Name

From time to time, the landlord may want to change the name of the office building. Without a clause that expressly allows this to be done, the owner may be held liable for applicable damages to tenants. Such damages could include the cost to reprint stationery or loss of business. Although smaller tenants may agree to this clause, large users, to whom identification with a building is important, seldom will accept it.

Access to Premises

The lease should give the landlord the right to enter to inspect the leased premises without violating the "quiet enjoyment" clause. The lease nevertheless should contain a provision that the landlord may inspect the premises at reasonable times with a minimum disturbance to the tenant, except in emergency situations.

Default

Every lease should clearly define default, or the conditions under which the office tenant fails to fulfill its obligations and the lease may not be in full force and effect. Tenants often will require in the lease that the landlord must provide them with written notice of default. Further, most leases provide for a grace period for the situation to be corrected. Ten days commonly is allowed to remedy delinquent rental payments, and 30 days is allowed for default on other terms or conditions.

Strict Performance

An office lease generally contains a strict performance clause. Essentially, it is a provision to the effect that a waiver by the landlord of one default does not constitute a waiver of any other default either of the same nature at a later date or of a different nature.

Surrender of Possession of Premises

The rights of the landlord and the obligations of the tenant upon termination of the lease need to be expressed. Essentially, this clause indicates that the tenant is to return the premises in substantially the same condition as it was received, normal wear and tear and insurable casualty damages excepted. It further stipulates that all improvements made to the premises become the property of the landlord; however, the landlord may be able to demand that certain improvements erected by the tenant be removed upon vacancy. Difficulty will be encountered upon termination of a lease that does not contemplate the ownership of improvements. All personal property also should be removed and debris cleared away, and a program for dealing with the tenant who fails to remove personal property should be outlined. The lease further should provide for damages if the tenant does not surrender the premises on the date of termination.

Oftentimes a lease includes a clause for holding over, which means that the tenant can continue to occupy the premises after the lease has expired and subject to obtaining the owner's permission. Usually this clause states that if the tenant holds over after the lease has expired, it will be under the same terms and conditions on a month-to-month basis. However, it is not unusual for office leases to state that any extensions are at rates fixed by the lessor. The holdover clause avoids what may be an otherwise automatic renewal of the lease, something the owner may not desire.

Compliance with Laws

Ordinarily, the obligation to comply with legal requirements affecting real property is on the owner; it is not shifted to the tenant when a lease is signed. In reaction to this, a lease may provide for compliance by a tenant, at the tenant's expense, with all laws, ordinances, and regulations of federal, state, county, and municipal authorities and directions of public officials with respect to the leased premises.

Upon seeing this clause in a standard form lease, many tenants will wish to alter the language so that the landlord is always responsible for the structure and the tenant is responsible for the interior of the leased premises. Thus, for instance, if a fire alarm system were required to be installed throughout an office building, the tenant would not be held liable for the installation. The rule of thumb usually is that if the tenant causes the cost, the tenant pays, and if the owner causes the cost, the owner pays.

Compliance with Rules and Regulations

Many office buildings have a set of rules and regulations that govern the activities within the building. When such rules and regulations are in effect, that should be attached as an exhibit to the lease and a covenant that the tenant will abide by them included. The standard clause states that the landlord has the option of changing the rules and regulations, although tenants may negotiate to limit the changes so that the rights contained in the lease are neither reduced or eliminated during the rental term or any extension thereof.

Assignment and Subletting

An office tenant with a long-term lease may have numerous reasons for seeking to assign or sublet the leased space: The decision may be made to sell the business, larger or smaller quarters may be needed, a merger may be effected, or the business may encounter financial difficulties. Consequently, the right to sublet is important to a tenant. However, the landlord must have control over who occupies the premises. The lease generally states that the tenant cannot sublease or assign the lease without the prior written consent of the owner. Usually the lease further states that such consent may not be unreasonably withheld. Although the tenant would remain liable as a guarantor under any sublease or assignment, there is at least a provision for escaping major financial loss.

Insurance Rates

Many leases contain a clause providing that the tenant shall do nothing that would increase the premium of the fire insurance. If this clause were to be violated, the tenant would be obligated to pay the increase in the form of additional rent.

Attorneys' Fees

A clause requiring the tenant to pay all attorneys' fees and related expenses necessitated by actions of the tenant is not uncommon. The tenant often will negotiate for reciprocal rights for these expenses should the tenant, through no personal fault, become involved in any litigation because of the lease.

Additional Rent

A clause that authorizes the landlord to consider any charges against the tenant as additional rent is considered critical to most owners. Filing a civil suit to collect payments (other than rental) due from a tenant is costly and often takes a long time to resolve. Rental payments, on the other hand, generally can be recovered more quickly and with less expense. Furthermore, if a tenant refused to pay construction costs owed but were to pay the rent, eviction would not be possible if the lease did not contain the additional rent clause.

Air, Light, and View Rights

A lease may indicate that the owner grants no rights to air, light, or view.

Notice

Because formal communication between the two parties may be necessary from time to time, a provision describing what constitutes legal notice is called for.

State Law

Inasmuch as rental agreements must be based on state laws, the standard form lease should reference itself to the appropriate jurisdictional guidelines. The required language will vary from state to state.

Heirs and Successors

A lease should provide that the successors of both landlord and tenant are to be bound to the terms and conditions of the contract. In other words, death does not terminate a lease.

Reasonable Consent

A tenant is forbidden from taking certain actions, such as building improvements or subletting the space, without the express approval of the owner. A clause to the effect that the owner will not unreasonably withhold this approval is appropriate. This eliminates the need to insert reference to reasonable consent throughout the lease.

Mortgage Protection

Many mortgages require leases to include a clause that protects the mortgagee by requiring the landlord to keep it informed of any tenant defaults and subsequent actions.

Addenda

If addenda are attached to the lease, they should be referenced in the body of the contract. (See chapter 13.)

Summary

A lease, which must be written if the rental arrangement is for more than one year, gives the office tenant the right to use and occupy a specified area of a building in exchange for periodic payments to the landlord.

Most leasing agencies have a standard form lease; however, this is somewhat a misnomer, in that one standard form lease may be quite different from another. Nevertheless, in order to be valid, a lease should contain six elements: (1) the correct names and signatures of the legally competent parties to the agreement; (2) a description of the leased premises; (3) the term of the lease; (4) the amount of the rent; (5) the purpose for which the tenant is to use the premises; and (6) all rights and obligations of both parties to the contract. Within the framework established by these six elements, various specific clauses are possible and usually necessary. The astute leasing agent is aware that the standard form lease is subject to change based upon negotiation.

13 Exhibits and Other Lease Documents

A standard form lease alone seldom will be complete enough to express the legal arrangement between the office building tenant and the building's owner. Attachments to the lease will be needed. They generally will fall within two categories: (1) Those designed to clarify or define an agreement within the lease, and (2) those whose purpose is to alter the agreement either specified or implied within the standard form lease.

Supportive Exhibits

Those attachments that elaborate on points agreed to within the standard form lease generally are referred to as exhibits. Included here are any supplementary documents that more clearly define, for the benefit of both the tenant and the landlord, that to which they already have agreed within the lease itself. These documents are referenced in the lease and legally are considered part of it.

The three most common exhibits to leases are these: (1) a floor plan and complete description of that portion of the office building to be leased by the tenant showing all demising partitions; (2) a workletter or construction rider improvement schedule to the lease that provides the design and construction criteria for the leased premises; and (3) rules and regulations. In certain circumstances, additional exhibits may become necessary. Typically, for identification purposes, each exhibit is assigned a successive letter according to its reference in the lease. The first exhibit to which reference is made would be Exhibit A, the second would be Exhibit B, and so forth.

To emphasize a point made previously that is applicable to lease attachments as well: The forms and exhibits shown within this text are not necessarily standard within the industry, although they are representative. Many variables, such as legal, ownership, tenant requirements, and local custom come into play when lease exhibits are being prepared.

Office Floor Plan

The legal relationship between a landlord and a tenant is one in which the latter pays the former for the use and occupancy of a specific area. Although the lease itself will refer to the building name and address, the floor and suite number, and other identifying information, a floor plan showing the demised premises (the actual office space being leased by the tenant) is necessary to complete the legal requirement that calls for a full and exact description of the premises. By appending to the lease a floor plan which clearly delineates the floor and area being rented, the possibility of confusion or misunderstanding is eliminated, and the two parties are assured that they have the same space in mind.

If a tenant will be occupying space on a multitenanted floor, the floor plan becomes especially worthwhile. Typically, the area to be leased will be shaded or otherwise highlighted and all demising partitions indicated. An exhibit of a floor plan is equally important with respect to a tenant occupying a complete floor. Inasmuch as the tenant would not be leasing elevator shafts, stairways, and possibly other common areas, a floor plan could show clearly which of those areas within a full-tenant floor are to be considered tenant space and which will remain within the jurisdiction of the owner. If a tenant will occupy more than one floor, an exhibit of each floor should be included. Further, if an expansion provision is part of the lease, the area of expansion should be indicated and so titled.

Figure 13.1, which shows the space a tenant will occupy, is an example of the type of document that may be added to a lease. Oftentimes, space plans are substituted for this drawing. Either one is acceptable.

To demonstrate the acceptance of this attachment, the lessor and the lessee must sign it.

Exhibits and Other Lease Documents 183

Figure 13.1

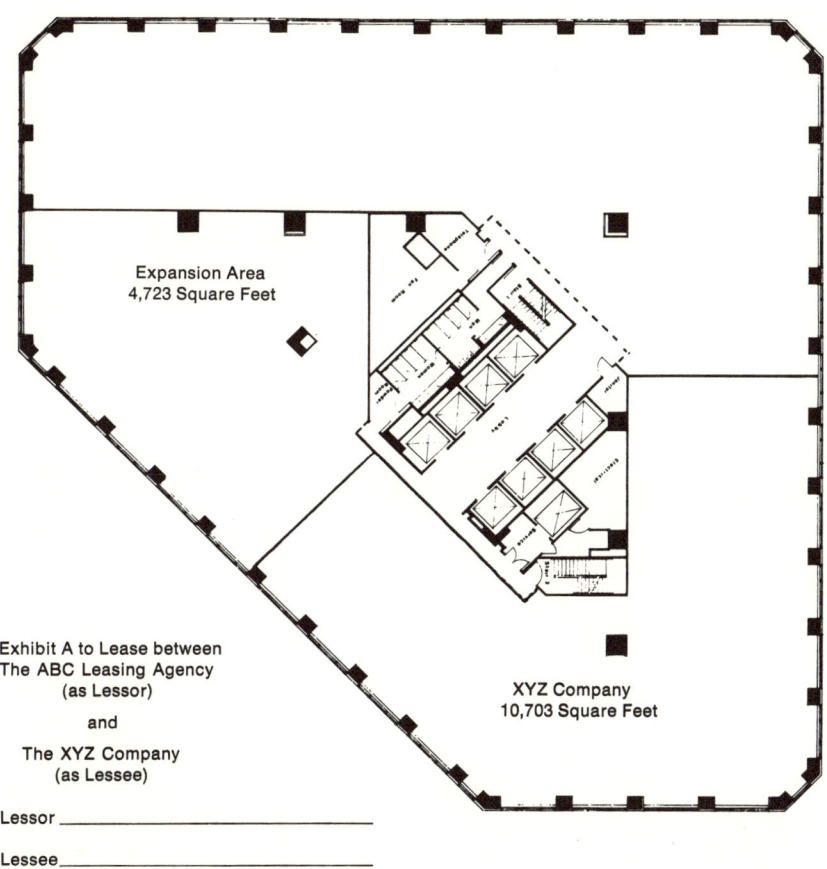

Typical Highrise Floor Plan:
25th Floor

Figure 13.2

Exhibit B
To (name of building) Lease
Construction Rider to Agreement

THIS RIDER, is attached to and forms a part of a certain lease dated _____, between (name of building), herein represented by its (name of agency), hereinafter referred to as Lessor, and _____, hereinafter referred to as Lessee.

1. Construction and Completion of Building.
   (a) The Base Building will be constructed by Lessor substantially in accordance with the plans and specifications for (name of building) prepared by (name of building architect), dated _____. Lessor, however, reserves the right to make such changes in and to the original Plans and Specifications as Lessor, in its sole discretion, shall deem necessary or desirable so long as the size, appearance and quality of the building are not substantially altered.
   (b) All other design and construction work with respect to the improvements of the Leased Premises shall be referred to as "Tenant Improvements", and shall be at the sole cost and expense of Lessee, except to the extent of the contribution by Lessor, as provided below.
2. Lessee's Plans and Specifications.
   (a) Lessee agrees to furnish complete information respecting Lessee's program and space planning requirements for Tenant Improvements to Lessor's Architect not later than _____.
   (b) Upon submission to Lessor's Architect of the requirements as described above in subparagraph (a), Lessor's Architect will prepare, at the sole cost and expense of Lessee, all architectural, mechanical and electrical engineering plans and the specifications required for the performance of the work, and all amendments or supplements thereto, including complete detailed working drawings and specifications for Lessee's partition layout, entrances, ceilings, fire protection, heating and air conditioning, lighting and electrical outlets. Lessee agrees to review and approve or "approve as noted" these plans and specifications within ten (10) days upon submission by Lessor's Architect.
   (c) It is understood and agreed that all plans, drawings and specifications are subject to Lessor's approval, which the Lessor agrees shall not be unreasonably withheld.
3. Tenant Improvements Construction.
   (a) The Lessor will construct Building Standard Tenant Improvements in and to the premises in accordance with final architectural construction drawings as described in Paragraph 2.(b) above. Building Standard construction is defined as typical design and construction finishes, details, materials, cross-sections, performance ratings, and average quantity allowances, which have been developed by the Lessor and Lessor's architects as representing the optimum aesthetic, functional and operational balance with the Base Building. These Building Standard Improvements are fully described in the document "Design and Construction Criteria for Office Premises", which is available from the Lessor and included in this Construction Rider by reference.
   (b) The Lessor shall execute a contract with such persons, firms or corporations as it, in its sole discretion, deems advisable for the completion of said Building Standard Improvements. Lessor will provide and install Building Standard Tenant Improvements for which Lessor's

Workletter

In the past, office buildings were designed with individual offices ready for use. Although certain minor alterations might be performed for a tenant—especially a large tenant—seldom was tenant construction a major consideration. New office buildings, on the other hand, are little more than empty shells. Each interior is custom planned and built for the tenant who will occupy the space,

Figure 13.2 (continued)

sole construction obligation is to pay to Lessor's contractor the cost of construction thereof for a total contribution amount not to exceed $_____.

(c) If Lessee requests Lessor to perform any Building Standard Tenant Improvement work or custom or special Tenant Improvement work over and above the Lessor's contribution listed in Paragraph 3.(a) above, this work will be performed by the Lessor's Contractor as a "Tenant Reimbursable". The Lessee shall approve the written estimate of such cost of the work prior to commencement by the Lessor's Contractor, which approval not to be unreasonably withheld. If Lessee shall fail to approve any such estimate within ten (10) days, the same shall be deemed disapproved in all respects by Lessee, and Lessor's Contractor shall not be authorized to proceed thereon.

(d) The Lessee will pay the actual cost of the improvements, based on final installed work, upon final determination of the actual cost by the Lessor's Contractor, less Landlord's contribution listed in Paragraph 3.(b) above, with no mark up by the Lessor. The sums due by Lessee to Lessor under the provisions of this paragraph shall be billed from time to time and shall be paid within ten (10) days after demand by Lessor or its agent, but in no event later than the date of occupancy of the demised premises by Lessee.

4. Commencement of Rent.

It is agreed that notwithstanding the date provided in the Lease for the commencement of the term thereof, such term shall not commence until the substantial completion of all Tenant Improvements as hereinabove defined, and the termination date shall be extended for a period of time equal to the period of any such delay in commencement of the term thereof; provided, however, that if Lessor shall be delayed in substantially completing said work as a result of:

(a) Lessee's failure to furnish information with respect to Lessee's requirements for the Tenant Improvements within the time limits provided in paragraph 2.(a) above;

(b) Lessee's failure to approve detailed working drawings as provided in paragraph 2.(b) above;

(c) Lessee's failure to approve written cost estimate as provided in paragraph 3.(c) above;

(d) Changes by Lessee in the final plans and specifications prepared pursuant to paragraph 2.(b) above;

(e) The performance by any person, firm or corporation (other than Lessor's contractor) employed at Lessee's request and the completion of work by said person, firm or corporation;

(f) Delay of delivery of materials, finishes or installations requested by Lessee other than materials, finishes and installations used as Building Standard items by Lessor's contractors in the Building; and

(g) Any other delay (including, without limitation, delay in providing necessary approvals or disapprovals required of Lessee) caused by the action or inaction of Lessee;

then, in that event, the commencement of the term of said Lease and the Lessee's obligation for the payment of rental thereunder shall be accelerated by the number of days of such delay.

Witnesses:

_____ By _____
                                                          Lessor
_____

_____ By _____
                                                          Lessee

---

with certain building standard materials, equipment, and methods used to maintain a degree of consistency in the building. Often office space that has been custom built for one tenant will be demolished and a new office be custom designed and built for the next. Consequently, construction of tenant areas has become critical to the leasing of office space in existing buildings as well as new ones. Concomitant to this, the document that reflects the agreement between the tenant and landlord concerning construction has become important. Usually this exhibit, commonly referred to as a workletter or construction rider, has two parts: a section that relates specifically to the construction of the office space in question, and a section that sets forth the construction criteria imposed upon the building as a whole. (A sample construction rider, written for an actual building under construction, appears in figure 13.2. It should be studied for its format, not its content, inasmuch as a workletter must reflect details of the given circumstances and building.)

The primary function of the first section of the workletter is to establish who will pay for tenant improvements and who will arrange for the work. The amount a landlord will contribute toward tenant improvement costs depends on market conditions. In a highly competitive atmosphere, for instance, the landlord may assume a much greater responsibility than at other times. Often, the cost of tenant improvements exceeds the amount contributed by the landlord; consequently, most workletters contain a clause that assigns responsibility for these additional costs to the tenant.

The workletter also may contain requirements for preparation of the architect's plans for tenant improvements, a provision concerning the date on which rent is to commence, and, in the case of a new building, a provision concerning its construction and completion.

The second portion of the workletter outlines the criteria for the design and construction of tenant improvements. (Design and construction criteria are sampled in the appendix, A.5. The specifications listed reflect an actual building and are not necessarily applicable to any other building.) Included here will be general information related to tenant improvements as well as building standards and building standard allowances. The rider stipulates the policy and procedure for planning, designing, and constructing the office space and brings to the tenant's attention at the earliest opportunity those building conditions that must be accommodated.

Included in the workletter may be specifications for such items as partitions, doors, hardware, flooring, ceiling, electrical and HVAC systems, fire protection, window coverings and windows, and office graphics. The design and construction criteria relating to these improvements usually are decided upon early by the building's architect and interior designer. Not always included in these specifications are the materials provided in the building's public areas, such as furnishings in elevator lobbies and equipment in restrooms. If the tenant is

Exhibits and Other Lease Documents

to pay a pro-rata portion of the improvement of these public areas, the specifications pertaining to them should be included.

The construction rider is part of the lease and clearly must be explained to the prospect when the lease is proposed. The criteria are designed for the benefit of both the lessee and the lessor. However, some points of the construction rider could be considered objectionable by prospects, and attempts may be made to negotiate them during the leasing process.

Rules and Regulations

In order to maintain the integrity of an office building, rules and regulations may be imposed upon its tenants by ownership or management or both. Such rules and regulations should be made a part of the lease and accepted by the tenant. An example set of regulations, imposed on tenants of an actual office building, appears as figure 13.3. Not only do rules and regulations touch upon legal matters as set by local, state, and federal statutes but also upon items that maintain the aesthetic appeal of the building, demonstrate a concern for tenant safety and welfare, and protect the rights of the tenant and landlord.

Rules and regulations must be designed to coincide with the characteristics and use of a given office building; thus, they will vary from building to building. For example, item 14 in the sample rules and regulations forbids the opening of windows; obviously, such a rule would be inappropriate in a high-rise building that is constructed with windows that do not open.

Lease Alterations

It is unusual for a leasing agent to secure a signature on a lease without any changes to the standard form lease. If a tenant makes requests for alterations to the standard form lease, the problem of whether the landlord will accept them is introduced. Therefore, as changes are requested, the agent must exercise caution in promising that these changes can be accepted. The landlord's requirements and objectives must be taken into consideration before the agent, all too enthusiastic to secure a signed lease, grants requests made by the prospective tenant. The standard lease form represents the arrangement ideally sought by the building's ownership goals and approved by ownership.

Figure 13.3

Rules and Regulations
Exhibit C

    1. The sidewalks, entrances, passages, courts, elevators, vestibules, stairways, corridors, or halls shall not be obstructed or encumbered by any Lessee or used for any purpose other than ingress and egress to and from the leased premises.
    2. No awnings or other projections shall be attached to the outside walls of the building without the prior written consent of the Lessor. No curtains, blinds, shades, or screens shall be attached to, hung in, or used in connection with any window or door of the leased premises without the prior written consent of the Lessor. Such awnings, projections, curtains, blinds, shades, screens, or other fixtures must be of a quality, type, design and color, and attached in the manner approved by the Lessor.
    3. No sign, advertisement, notice or other lettering shall be exhibited, inscribed, painted, or affixed by any Lessee on any part of the outside or inside of the leased premises or building without the prior written consent of the Lessor. In the event of the violation of the foregoing by any Lessee, the Lessor may remove the same without any liability, and may charge the expense incurred by such removal to the Lessee or Lessees violating this rule. Interior signs on doors shall be inscribed, painted, or affixed for each Lessee by the Lessor at the expense of such Lessee, and shall be of a size, color and style acceptable to the Lessor. Lessor reserves the right to install and maintain a sign or signs on the exterior and on the roof of the building.
    4. The sashes, sash doors, skylights, windows, and doors that reflect or admit light and air into the halls, passageways, or other public places in the building shall not be covered or obstructed by any Lessee, nor shall any bottles, parcels, or other articles be placed on the window ledges.
    5. No showcase or other articles shall be put in front of or affixed on any part of the exterior of the building nor placed in the halls, corridors, or vestibules, without prior written consent of the Lessor.
    6. The water, wash closets, and other plumbing fixtures shall not be used for any purpose other than those for which they were constructed, and no sweepings, rubbish, rags, or other substance shall be thrown therein. All damages resulting from any misuse of the fixtures shall be borne by the Lessee who, or whose servants, employees, or agents, shall have caused the same.
    7. No Lessee shall mark, paint, drill into, or in any way deface any part of the leased premises or the building of which they form a part. No boring, cutting, or stringing of wires shall be permitted except with the prior written consent of Lessor and as it may direct. No Lessee shall lay linoleum, or other similar floor covering, so that the same shall come in direct contact with the floor of the leased premises, and if linoleum or other similar floor covering is desired to be used, an interlining of builder's deadening felt shall be first affixed to the floor by a paste or other similar material soluble in water, the use of cement or other similar adhesive material being expressly prohibited.
    8. No bicycles, baby carriages, vehicles, birds, or animals of any kind shall be brought into or kept in or about the premises, and no cooking shall be done or permitted by any Lessee on the said premises. However, this does not prevent Lessee from having coffee, soft drinks, candy and other items for use of Lessee's employees, servants, agents or visitors. Lessee shall not cause or permit any unusual or objectionable odors to be produced upon or permeate from the leased premises.
    9. No space in the building shall be used for manufacturing, or for the sale of property of any kind at auction.

Changes can be written as marginal notes directly on the standard form lease, or they can be made in an addendum or rider to the lease. Should a change be made by means of a note in the margin, the lessor and lessee must initial the notation to acknowledge its acceptance. Oftentimes, however, additions, deletions, or changes of

Figure 13.3 (continued)

10. No Lessee shall make, or permit to be made, any unseemly or disturbing noises or disturb or interfere with occupants of this or neighboring buildings or premises or those having business with them. No Lessee shall throw anything out of the doors, windows, or skylights, or down the passageways.

11. No additional locks or bolts of any kind shall be placed upon any of the doors or windows by any Lessee, nor shall any changes be made in existing locks or the mechanism thereof, without the prior written approval of Lessor, which approval shall not be unreasonably withheld. Lessee will be supplied, free of charge, with two keys for each door on the leased premises. Each Lessee must, upon the termination of his tenancy, restore to the Lessor all keys of stores, offices, and toilet rooms, either furnished to or otherwise procured by such Lessee.

12. All removals or the carrying in or out of any safes, freight, furniture, or bulky matter of any description must take place during the hours which the Lessor or its agent may reasonably determine from time to time. The Lessor reserves the right to prescribe the weight and position of all safes, which must be placed upon two-inch thick plank strips to distribute the weight. The moving of safes or other fixtures or bulky matter of any kind must be made upon previous notice to the superintendent of the building and under his supervision. Lessee agrees not to place a load upon any floor of the leased premises exceeding the floor load per square foot area which such floor was (and is) designed to carry and which is allowed by law. Business machines and mechanical equipment shall be placed and maintained by Lessee at Lessee's expense in settings sufficient, in Lessor's judgment, to absorb and prevent vibration, noise and annoyance.

13. No Lessee shall occupy or permit any portion of the premises leased to him to be occupied as an office for a public stenographer or a public typist, for the manufacture or sale of liquor, narcotics, dope or tobacco in any form, as a barber or manicure shop, or as an employment bureau. No Lessee shall advertise for laborers giving an address at the said premises, without prior written consent of Lessor, which consent shall not be unreasonably withheld.

14. No Lessee shall open, or permit windows in the leased premises to be opened at any time.

15. The premises shall not be used for lodging or sleeping, or for any immoral or illegal purpose.

16. The requirements of Lessees will be attended to only upon application at the office of the building. Employees shall not perform any work or do anything outside of their regular duties unless under special instructions from the office of the Lessor.

17. Canvassing, soliciting, and peddling in the building are prohibited, and each Lessee shall cooperate to prevent the same.

18. The Lessor specifically reserves the right to refuse admittance to the building after 7:00 P.M. and before 7:00 A.M. daily, or on Sundays or on legal holidays, to any person or persons who cannot furnish satisfactory identification, or to any person or persons who, for any other reason in Lessor's reasonable judgment, should be denied access to the premises.

Accepted:

_____

_____
Lessee

words or phrases become excessive and marginal space is inadequate to accommodate them. In these instances, an addendum or rider is attached to the lease, and the marginal note alerts the parties to the fact with a statement such as this: "An addendum is attached hereto and made a part of the lease." With this, the document that modifies the original lease becomes part of the final rental agreement.

An addendum or rider to a lease is a legal document that adds to, clarifies, or amends the terms of a standard form lease and should explicitly identify the lease of which it is a part, name the tenant and landlord, and provide the necessary language to change the lease form. An example of an addendum format is shown in figure 13.4.

Figure 13.4

Addendum to Lease

    The attached lease made and entered into this _____ day of _____, 19____, by and between _____, as Lessor, and _____, as Lessee, of which lease this Addendum to Lease is made a part is hereby amended and supplemented as follows:

                    WITNESSETH:

    1. The following is added to Article _____:
                (title of article)

(Insert here the additions to the article, e.g., Adjustments to Rent, being altered. The insertion should begin and end with quotation marks.)

    2. The following is added as new Article _____:
                (title of article)

(Article Number.) (Inserted here are the subjects not covered in the standard form lease. The insertion should begin and end with quotation marks.)

    IN WITNESS WHEREOF, the parties hereto have executed this Addendum to Lease by proper persons there unto duly authorized so to do on the day and upon first herein written:

Witness   Lessor

_____   _____

Witness   Lessee

_____   _____

Options

An option, when granted by the lessor, provides a tenant a right or privilege not otherwise granted within the standard rental agreement. With few exceptions, options work to the benefit of the tenant and result from specific tenant requests. As with the original lease terms, options, and even the details within a specific option, are always subject to negotiation.

A thought must be kept in mind when options are being negotiated: The types of options that will be requested and those the landlord should consider granting depend on the competitive environment and other conditions within the marketplace. The three most common options that will be sought by office tenants deal with expansion rights, renewal rights, and lease cancellation rights.

Option To Expand

A tenant who has an eye to the future and whose long-range plan anticipates growth will look for office space that lends itself to expansion. Consequently, such a tenant will want a lease that gives the firm the right to lease additional space within the building at some time in the future. The typical option to expand obligates ownership to offer the tenant a specified area of additional space at some time in the future and at some specified rent. Within this broad description, however, various expansion options can be structured.

One form of expansion option gives the tenant the right of first refusal over a specified area of office space when it becomes available. Depending on the wording agreed to within the option, this may be either a one-time right or a continuing right. If it is a one-time right, the tenant would be offered the specified space only once. Obviously, if it is accepted, the space would become the tenant's under a leasehold. Were he to refuse the space, the option would no longer apply. If the option provides for a continuing right, the tenant must be given the opportunity to rent the space any time it becomes available. Because of the problems that often arise with the continuing right of first refusal, this type of option rarely is granted, the one-time right of first refusal option being used more commonly. In either case the option may state that the tenant must either accept or refuse the space that is offered within a specified period of time.

A second form of expansion option imposes a limitation on the time period during which a tenant may exercise this right. For example, if a tenant negotiates for a one-year option to expand into a specified area, the landlord must make that space available to the tenant at any time during the one year. However, should the tenant not exercise this option within the stated period, the option would no longer apply. This type of option to expand generally is looked upon with disfavor by a landlord. Obviously, any lease with another tenant to fill that potential expansion space would have to be on a short-term basis; finding such a tenant could be difficult and, in consequence, the space could stand vacant throughout the option period.

A more acceptable way to structure this type of expansion option would be to allow the tenant the option to take the space only on a specified date in the future (typically three or five years from the date of the commencement of the lease) and to require the tenant to provide the landlord ample notice (typically 90 or 120 days for small expansion areas and up to a year for larger areas) should the tenant plan to exercise the option. If the tenant were to fail to notify the landlord pursuant to the terms of the lease, the option would expire and become null and void.

A similar type of expansion option, but one that is more advantageous to the landlord, allows the landlord to lease the expansion space for a specified period of time (three to five years is common) but requires that the landlord offer it to the tenant who has the option to expand upon expiration of that lease. This type of expansion option is especially common in leases for space in new buildings.

As with the general format of the expansion option, the details within it likewise are subject to negotiation. One of the key factors of negotiation is the rental that would be charged on the additional space were the option to be exercised. For instance, the option may set the rental as the same base rent the tenant is paying under the original lease plus an appropriate agreed to escalation, or it may reference it to the market rental at the time the option is exercised, or it may tie it to a cost of living index.

Likewise, the area that is specified as expansion space may be subject to negotiation. For instance, the tenant may demand space that is contiguous to the original space, or may agree to have the option on space elsewhere within the building. Indeed, some large tenants may even want the right to be offered any space within the building that becomes available during its tenancy.

Another factor of negotiation revolves around tenant improvements that might be required when the additional space is taken by the tenant. The option may be negotiated so that the tenant will

Exhibits and Other Lease Documents

accept the space in its existing condition at the time it becomes available, or it may require the landlord to assume either all or some percentage of tenant improvement construction costs.

As indicated, any option to expand will be more advantageous to the tenant than to the landlord. The decision to exercise the option is entirely in the tenant's hands, whereas the landlord must tailor the rental program around the awareness that an option space must be available at the time specified. On the other hand, an astute leasing agent can be creative in making the most of such an option. For instance, one creative approach to providing expansion space while eliminating landlord concern is to provide for it in the original lease so that the space automatically becomes a part of the tenant's premises on a specified date and the rent is payable on the additional space at that time. Further, with short-term expansions in new buildings, some leases include an expansion area in the lease with some abatement in rent for a number of months for the expansion area. While expansion options generally are seen in a negative light by building owners, there are hidden advantages that should not be overlooked. For one thing, granting an option to expand helps guarantee that the tenant will renew the original lease inasmuch as the tenant will not be crowded for space. Furthermore, rights usually imply responsibilities, and depending on the circumstances, if a particular type of option is especially important to a tenant, that tenant may be forced to pay a higher rental in exchange for being granted the right being demanded.

Option To Renew

Another right that a tenant may negotiate for is an option to renew the lease upon its expiration. Although there are variations, the typical renewal option specifies that the tenant may renew the original lease for an additional term determined by both parties, under the same conditions, and for the same basic rental rate plus escalation increases paid under the original lease.

For ownership, an option to renew usually is considered quite a disadvantage, in that it may limit the income that could be realized from that space in the future. For instance, consider the tenant with an option to renew who leases space at $12 per square foot plus escalation for a five-year term. For the sake of discussion, assume that the escalation computes to 25¢ per square foot per year. At the end of the five-year term when the lease expires, the tenant would be paying $13.25 per square foot and could exercise the option to renew at this rental. However, if market conditions have changed, $13.25 could be considered below market value. Nonetheless, ownership would be tied to another five-year lease at only $13.25.

On the other hand, if the tenant is desirable and the option specifies that the rental rate for the renewal period shall be the prevailing market rate at the time of the renewal plus applicable increased costs in operating expenses and taxes, the landlord is more likely to grant the renewal option. This approach assures the tenant of continuing occupancy and the landlord of a fair rental rate.

Any option to renew should state clearly that the tenant has a certain time period in which to notify ownership of a decision to renew or not renew. Failure to heed notification requirements would negate the tenant's option.

Option To Cancel

In certain markets or for certain tenants, a landlord may agree to an option that would permit the tenant to cancel the lease prior to the expiration. A main concern of the landlord, however, is being faced with a vacancy; depending upon the market, the space may or may not be leased within a reasonable period of time.

Various cancellation options are possible. Under one type of cancellation option, a landlord allows the tenant to cancel the lease at any time. If office space is in high demand, this may be feasible. However, any other situation could be disastrous. Secondly, a landlord may allow a tenant to cancel as long as certain notification requirements are met. Thirdly, a landlord may allow a tenant to cancel subject to a penalty. Penalties range from negligible to quite severe and minimally should reflect a loss of security deposit and the recapture of the unamortized tenant improvement costs originally paid by the landlord. Any penalty would be negotiated when the option is being added to the lease.

Fourthly, an option to cancel may be applicable only to tenants that are expanding and then only if additional space could not be provided when needed. If a tenant is unsure about expansion at the time of signing the lease, the tenant may resist this type option to cancel, thus giving the opportunity to move and be free of the leasehold should it become necessary.

An option to cancel often is included in a lease with a tenant whose organization is dependent on a single individual. It is sought out of a concern for the future of the company should this person die or become disabled. Such an option becomes a protective measure on the part of the tenant as well as the landlord. For instance, this option would avoid the need for the landlord to file suit against the estate of a deceased tenant and allow the agent to lease the space to others once it is vacated.

Special Provisions

Special provisions, like options and other changes to the standard form lease, generally reduce the landlord's rights and should, therefore, be approached with caution. The kinds of special provisions that can be added to a lease are innumerable. The following list of special provisions includes those that appear quite frequently.

Parking

If an office building has its own parking facility, restrictions on tenant use of such a facility are often stipulated in the lease. Considerations that must be made when parking regulations are added as part of the lease include: (1) How many spaces will be guaranteed for the tenant? (2) Will the spaces be provided at no cost? Even if the parking provided to the tenants by the landlord is free at the time of a lease, the agent should be cautious about how the parking article is written in the lease. On some future date, the landlord may want to charge for parking and the free parking clause in the lease would disallow this. If not, what will the cost be? It is best not to quote a fixed rate for parking as parking rates can be frequently increased. The best language would be: "at the rates from time to time in effect" or "at building standard rates." (3) Will each space be marked with the names of individuals in the tenant's employ? Will the areas be marked "reserved" or with company name or both? Reserved parking creates real problems if there is high demand for parking spaces. Many parking stalls will be empty as individuals will not always be parked in their reserved spaces. Parking lots and garages can be oversold; that is, if a parking garage has 200 spaces, the parking manager can sell 220 or more spaces because of absenteeism on any given day. This of course cannot occur if all the spaces are reserved for individuals and must not be occupied by others. What costs are involved to identify the spaces? Every consideration that could lead to a misunderstanding should be clarified in the lease addendum.

Directory Board

The amount of space and responsibility for the cost of putting a company's name on the directory board is usually stipulated in the lease.

Many tenants place a high degree of importance on the accessibility of and ease with which their names appear on the directory board: It leads business to them. Thus, many tenants desire more names on the directory than allowed by the lease. Law firms typically want all the lawyers in the firm listed on the directory board. This is not normally allowed in the standard form lease, and law firms will want to alter the lease to allow it. Further, they will negotiate that the landlord should pay for this and any changes that occur from time to time.

Painting, Floor Coverings, and Other Refurbishment Items
A tenant whose lease exceeds five years usually is going to be concerned with the general condition of the office space in the later years of the term. A tenant often will attempt to negotiate for replacement of worn floor coverings, cleaning of building standard draperies, painting or replacement of wall coverings, or refurbishment of other items in the premises. Negotiations will determine who is to absorb this expense.

Services and Utilities
If a tenant is to provide and pay for a service or utility, it should be articulated in a special provision in the lease. Some standard form leases require the landlord to provide and pay for all utilities and services. In others, janitorial services, utilities, and security fall into an area of tenant responsibility. Similarly, if the landlord is to assume the cost for any additional utility expense (extended hours of operation for HVAC) or a special maintenance staff, these responsibilities should be clarified. Every service extended to and every utility used by the tenant must, quite obviously, be paid for, and this provision must cover who is responsible for the cost of each service or utility.

Rental
If there is a negotiated deviation from the rental clause provided in the standard form lease, it must be added as a special provision in an addendum to the lease. Such elements that may affect the rental schedule include whether or not the rent is based on percentage rent, if a different or altered escalator clause is provided, or if rent is based on the Consumer Price Index. Often a lease is negotiated wherein the first year's rent is lower than other years or rent is increased each year. Again, ownership and tenant must fully understand the rental rate for the office space being fully occupied and the lease should precisely state that rate.

Exhibits and Other Lease Documents

Miscellaneous

Other special provisions often requested or needed by the tenant are those dealing with free rent, alterations to the assignment, subleasing, signage, replacement of glass, altered subordination, eminent domain, and other situations that may occur. The special provisions added to the lease are restricted only by the limited creativity of the parties involved; the uniqueness or specialty of the tenant, the product, or both will prove this.

However, the astute leasing agent must be cognizant of ownership goals and objectives so as not to accept and allow special provisions that are unreasonable or not feasible to the operation and maintenance of the building. The content of special provisions is negotiable, and the agent's responsibility to ownership should be a priority as these kinds of provisions are negotiated with the prospective tenant.

Other Lease Documents

In addition to supportive exhibits, alterations to the lease, options, and special provisions, the leasing agent must be familiar with other lease documents as well. These include the guaranty, amendments to lease, the sublease, the assignment, and termination of lease.

Guaranty

Occasionally, the leasing agent will have a prospect who desires to lease office space but whose credit is insufficient to be acceptable to the landlord. For instance, a new or small corporation might provide insufficient credit. In such an instance, another person or entity can guaranty the lease thereby allowing the landlord to accept it. In the instance of a new or small corporation whose assets are questionable, the officers of the company, if their personal assets are sufficient, can guaranty the lease making it strong enough to accept.

Thus, a guaranty is used to insure the landlord that the rent will be paid by someone other than the tenant in the event of default and all other terms, covenants, and conditions of the lease will be met. Credit reports, financial statements, interviews with bankers, and other financial references of the individual or entity making the guaranty are imperative. In any instance in which the credit worthiness of a prospect is questionable, caution is warranted. Business failure reflects on the office building in which the tenant is located as well as the leasing agent who recommended the lease. Most importantly, such an unfortunate occurrence can be damaging to an office building's income stream.

An example of a guaranty, which would be attached to and become part of the lease, appears in figure 13.5.

Figure 13.5

Guaranty

In consideration of making the Lease by and between _____ _____ as Lessor and _____ as Lessee dated the _____ day of _____, 19_____, at the request of the undersigned and in reliance on this Guaranty, the undersigned hereby guarantees the payment of the rent to be paid by the Lessee and the performance by the Lessee of all the terms, covenants and conditions of the Lease, and the undersigned promises to pay all the Lessor's expenses, including reasonable attorney's fees, incurred by the Lessor in enforcing all obligations of the Lessee under the Lease or incurred by the Lessor in enforcing this Guaranty. The Lessor's consent to any assignment or assignments, and successive assignments by the Lessee and Lessee's assigns, of this Lease, made either with or without notice to the undersigned, or a changed or different use of the demised premises, or Lessor's forebearance, delays, extensions of time or any other reason whether similar to or different from the foregoing shall in no way or manner release the undersigned from liability as guarantor.

IN WITNESS WHEREOF, the undersigned has executed this Guaranty in the presence of competent witnesses on the date first above written.

Witnesses: (Individual or Entity Providing Guaranty)

_____   _____
                                (Title or Individual)

_____

Amendments to Lease

It is sometimes necessary to alter a lease during its term. The tenant might expand or contract or exercise an option or the term may be

Exhibits and Other Lease Documents

extended, options or special provisions may be fully satisfied and thereby require deletion, security deposits may be reduced or eliminated, rental rates could change, and so forth. An amendment to lease is the document used to delineate a change after the lease has been executed.

The first time a lease is amended, the document is entitled "Amendment to Lease." The second time the amendment is called "Second Amendment to Lease"; the third time, "Third Amendment to Lease"; and so forth.

The typical amendment to a lease includes: (1) title of amendment (Amendment to Lease, Second Amendment to Lease, etc.); (2) date of the amendment; (3) name of landlord; (4) name of tenant; (5) a clause that recites the premises, the lease being amended (date), and any previous amendments (and dates); (6) a clause that stipulates what the parties to the lease wish to accomplish with the amendment; (7) the effective date of the amendment; (8) the various changes, deletions, or additions to the lease; (9) the signature blocks.

A sample format that can be used in writing a second amendment to lease appears in figure 13.6.

The Sublease

Most standard office leases prohibit subletting without prior consent of the lessor. If the lessor approves, this consent should be obtained in writing via a consent to sublease document, prepared by the landlord. A sample consent to sublease appears in figure 13.7.

The sublease itself is a lease between a tenant and a subtenant. Usually arrangements for rental payment and services are handled between the lessor and sublessee, although the lessee is often liable if the sublessee defaults in any way. Because of the details involved in a subleasing situation, both the sublease and the consent to sublease documents should be familiar to the leasing agent.

The terms of the sublease should not conflict with those in the original lease, and the leasing agent should verify this. Further, the sublease should expire at least one day prior to the expiration of the lease. This is required to avoid confusion regarding the actual responsibility of the tenant (rather than the subtenant) to the landlord.

Usually the tenant's attorney prepares the sublease. However, the building owner will not consent to the sublease without seeing the document and will request a copy for the files. From time to time,

Figure 13.6

Second Amendment to Lease

    This Second Amendment to Lease made and entered into this _____ day of _____, _____, by and between _____ _____, hereinafter referred to as "Lessor" and _____, hereinafter referred to as "Lessee."

WITNESSETH:

    Whereas, Lessor leased certain premises in _____, located at _____,_____,_____, to Lessee pursuant to that certain lease dated the _____ day of _____, _____, as amended by Amendment to Lease dated the _____, day of _____, _____, hereinafter referred to as the "Lease," the premises being more particularly described therein; and

    Whereas, Lessor wishes to (This section describes the applicable situation being amended, e.g. expand the premises or extend the lease), and Lessee wishes to (Identical circumstances as above); and

    Whereas, Lessor and Lessee therefore wish to amend said Lease;

    Now Therefore, in consideration of these present and the agreement of each other, Lessor and Lessee agree that the said Lease shall be and the same is hereby amended as of the _____ day of _____, _____.

1. (In this section of the amendment, the various articles of the lease are altered or deleted or new articles are added.)
2. (If more than one article is being changed, deleted or added, each item is numbered consecutively. Words, numbers or figures, phrases or sentences can be deleted or replaced to reflect the desired amendment. Additions can be made to an article, or a new article can be added.)
3. (The last consecutive number used always should state: "All other terms, covenants and conditions of this Lease, as amended, remain in full force and effect as heretofore.")

    In Witness Whereof, Lessor and Lessee have executed this agreement in the presence of the undersigned competent witnesses on the date first above written.

Witnesses:

_____ Name of Lessor

_____ By: _____
                                                           (Lessor)

_____ Name of Lessee

                                                        By: _____
                                                                  (Lessee)

Exhibits and Other Lease Documents

the leasing agent will assist in the preparation of the sublease, especially if the agent procured the tenant.

The lease form used for the prime lease should be the same one used for the sublease. When the same form is used, the word "lease" at the top of the page should be altered to read "sublease" with the words "herein referred to as the 'lease' " in parentheses so the entire document, when it refers to the lease, does not have to be altered. The lease will list the prime tenant as lessor and the subtenant as lessee, and the lease should be signed accordingly. All other portions of the sublease are completed in the same manner as the lease. If the subtenant should sublease the space to another, it is possible to have a sub-sublease. To create such an arrangement, similar procedures should be followed.

Assignment of Lease

A lease may be assigned to someone other than the party named in the document through an assignment. Unlike the sublease, wherein the tenant remains responsible to the landlord, when a lease is assigned to another party, the tenant relationship is transferred to the assignee. However, most landlords require that the tenant (assignor) remain as a guarantor to the lease to further protect the landlord. Like the sublease, an assignment of lease requires the written consent of the landlord. Consequently, the leasing agent must also be knowledgeable about the consent to assignment, a sample of which appears in figure 13.8, as well as the assignment itself. (See figure 13.9.)

Termination of Lease

If the parties have agreed to a termination of the lease prior to its expiration date, a termination of lease should be drafted and executed by both the landlord and the tenant. The basic parts of a termination of lease include: (1) date of termination of lease agreement; (2) the name of the landlord; (3) the name of the tenant; (4) clause reciting the lease being terminated and its date and any amendment or amendments thereto and their dates; (5) clause stipulating the reason for the termination of the lease; (6) the effective date of termination; and (7) the signature blocks. Other clauses may be inserted if the landlord and tenant are contemplating a new lease or considering other terms and conditions. An example of a termination of lease appears in figure 13.10.

Figure 13.7

Consent to Sublease

This Agreement, made and entered into this _____ day of _____, _____, between _____, hereinafter referred to as "Lessor," and _____, hereinafter referred to as "Lessee," and _____, hereinafter referred to as "Sublessee."

WITNESSETH:

Whereas, by a written lease between Lessor and Lessee herein, dated the _____ day of _____, _____, (add the amendments and dates in this area, if applicable), hereafter referred to as the "prime lease," Lessor leased to Lessee certain premises known as Suite _____ situated on the _____ floor of the _____, more particularly designated on the floor plan attached to said lease as Exhibit "(use applicable letter according to the lease, e.g. A)," and made a part of said lease, and hereinafter referred to as the "premises," and,

Whereas, Lessee now desires to sublease to Sublessee said premises for a term commencing on the _____ day of _____, _____ (this date should not exceed one day less than the expiration date provided in the prime lease), to be used as general offices for the conduct of Sublessee's business and for no other purpose, and

Whereas, Lessor is willing to consent to such sublease;

Now Therefore, Lessor, in consideration of the foregoing, does hereby consent to the subleasing of the premises to Sublessee for the purpose above mentioned, provided, however, that such consent is conditioned upon Lessee and Sublessee executing a Sublease not inconsistent with the provisions of the prime lease and this Consent to Sublease.

And, Lessee, in consideration of the foregoing, does hereby covenant and agree that Lessee shall remain liable to Lessor for all the obligations of Lessee set forth in said prime lease.

And, Sublessee, in consideration of the foregoing, hereby agrees with respect to the premises covered by the sublease to perform and be bound by all of the provisions of the said prime lease as if the Sublessee were the Lessee named herein (except the covenant pertaining to payment of rent and adjustments to rent, it being understood that payments under said provisions shall be made by Lessee to Lessor). (Note the phrase in parentheses can be omitted if Sublessee is to make payments directly to Lessor.)

It is further understood and agreed by the parties hereto that Lessee and Sublessee shall not after execution of said Sublease alter or modify their respective rights and obligation thereunder in any manner inconsistent with or in violation of the terms of said prime lease or the Consent to Sublease, and any such purported alteration or modification shall, at the option of Lessor, be considered a default under the prime lease.

In Witness Whereof, the parties hereto have executed this instrument in the presence of the undersigned competent witnesses on the date first above written.

Witnesses:

Name of Lessor

_____

(Lessor)

Name of Lessee

_____

(Lessee)

Name of Sublessee

_____

(Sublessee)

Figure 13.8

Consent to Assignment and Guaranty by Assignor

This Agreement, made and entered into this _____, day of _____, _____, between _____, hereinafter referred to as "Lessor," and _____, hereinafter referred to as "Lessee,"

WITNESSETH:

Whereas, Lessor and Lessee, entered into a Lease dated the _____ day of _____, _____, (Add in this area any amendments with their dates, if applicable), hereinafter referred to as the "Lease," for certain premises in the _____, _____, more particularly described therein; and

Whereas, under article ____(Number of Article re: Assignment and Subletting)____, thereof, Lessee cannot assign said lease without the prior written consent of the Lessor; and

Whereas, Lessee has agreed to assign said Lease to _(Name of New Lessee)_, herein known as Assignee, pursuant to an agreement in the form attached hereto and requests Lessor to consent thereto; and

Whereas, Lessor is willing to consent to said Assignment provided that Lessee will guarantee performance of the Lease by its Assignee.

Now Therefore, Lessor hereby consents and does agree to the assignment of said Lease by Lessee as of the effective date of said Assignment, as stated herein, and as conditioned and limited herein and Lessee agrees to guarantee the performance of all obligations of Assignee.

In Witness Whereof, the parties hereto have executed this instrument in the presence of the undersigned competent witnesses on date first above written.

Witnesses: Name of Lessor

_____   _____
                                                      (Lessor)
_____   Name of Lessee

_____   _____
                                                      (Lessee)

Figure 13.9

Assignment of Lease

    This Assignment, made this _____ day of _____, _____, between <u>(Name of Old Lessee)</u> hereby known as "Assignor," and <u>(Name of New Lessee)</u>, herein known as "Assignee,"

WITNESSETH:

    That for and in consideration of the sum of one dollar ($1.00), receipt of which is hereby acknowledged, and other good and valuable considerations, Assignor hereby assigns to Assignee, and Assignee accepts and takes from Assignor, all of Assignor's rights, title and interest in and to that certain lease between _____, as Lessor, and _____, as Lessee dated the _____, _____ of, _____ (Add in this area any amendments with their dates, if applicable), hereinafter referred to as the "Lease," for premises located in _____, _____, more particularly described in said Lease.

    Assignee accepts this assignment and agrees to pay the rents therein provided and to perform and keep all terms, covenants and conditions therein contained to be performed and kept by the Lease.

    This Assignment, if consented to by Lessor, shall be effective as of the _____ day of _____, _____.

    In Witness Whereof, the parties hereto have executed this agreement in the presence of the undersigned competent witnesses on the date first above written.

Witnesses: Name of Assignor

_____

_____   _____
                                                                              (Assignor)

                                                            Name of Assignee

_____   _____
                                                                              (Assignee)

Summary

Alterations to the standard form lease are commonplace. They can be as simple as a brief marginal note approved by both parties, or

Figure 13.10

Termination of Lease

This Termination of Lease, made and entered into the _____ day of _____, _____, by and between _____, hereinafter referred to as "Lessor," and _____, hereinafter referred to as "Lessee."

WITNESSETH:

Whereas, Lessor leased certain premises to Lessee in _____, at _____, _____, _____, pursuant to that certain Lease dated the _____ day of _____, _____, as amended by _____, dated the _____ day of _____, _____, hereinafter referred to as "Lease," in which Lease the premises are more particularly described therein; and

Whereas, (this clause stipulates the reason for the termination; e.g. landlord and tenant entering into a new lease, the space being leased to others, etc. If no special reason for termination exists, this clause is omitted.)

Whereas, Lessor and Lessee wish to terminate the Lease on the conditions hereinafter stated;

Now Therefore, in consideration of these present and agreement of each other, Lessor and Lessee hereby agree that the Lease and the term thereof shall terminate on the _____ day of _____, _____. (If there are additional contingencies to the termination, they would be listed at this point; e.g., tenant paying penalty monies to affect termination, listing the new tenant taking the space, etc.)

In Witness Whereof, Lessor and Lessee have executed this agreement in the presence of the undersigned competent witnesses on the date first above written.

Witnesses: Name of Lessor

_____

_____   _____
                                              (Lessor)

_____   Name of Lessee

_____   _____
                                              (Lessee)

they can be sufficiently complex to require an addendum to the lease. Similarly, options that give the tenant certain rights may be negotiated, options to expand, renew, and cancel being most common.

Special provisions that deal with such considerations as parking, directory boards, services and utilities, rental structures, signage, and subleasing also may be needed. Just as with options, the content of special provisions are negotiable.

Other lease documents of which leasing agents must be knowledgeable include the guaranty, amendment to lease, the sublease, the assignment of lease, and the termination of lease.

Whatever alterations to the lease document are made, the agent assumes responsibility of not only leasing the office space but leasing it under provisions acceptable to and permitted by ownership.

14 Negotiation

Negotiation is the art of reaching mutually profitable agreements. Satisfaction is sought by each party involved in the negotiating process. Negotiation is a transaction of business aimed at reaching a meeting of the minds among the parties involved. Negotiation becomes successful when a positive environment is created. Thus, the leasing agent, acting for the building owner, and the prospect work together to achieve mutual satisfaction, as evidenced by the signing of a lease.

Prospects almost always will attempt to negotiate at least one clause in a lease. In fact, almost every lease clause is subject to at least some degree of negotiation. For example, escalation and recovery provisions, designed to periodically raise rental rates as operating costs increase, are nearly always brought to the negotiating table by the prospect. If the lease calls for a security deposit, the prospect may try to negotiate to have the requirement deleted or reduced or the deposit placed in an interest-bearing account with the interest accruing to the prospect. The prospect may try to bargain with the agent to have the building's hours of operation extended at no additional charge. If the lease permits a building service to be stopped for just cause, the prospect may require either a right-to-cancel clause that may be imposed if services have not been resumed after a reasonable time or a clause that requires an abatement of rent until the services are restored. Numerous other provisions also may be brought to the negotiation table. The agent must anticipate those lease clauses that will be challenged. Equally important, the leasing agent, in order to be professional and successful, must understand the techniques of artful negotiation and the benefits derived from them.

The Conceptual Basis for Negotiation

Before embarking on the negotiation process, the motivation behind both the agent and the prospect should be rationalized. In order to direct the discussion toward a positive conclusion, the concepts of human behavior, perception, and leadership and their impact on negotiations should be understood.

Human Behavior

During lease negotiations, prospects often run the gamut of emotions from livid to content. The level of reaction depends on the significance the prospect places on the various points that are raised.

Generally, a knowledgeable potential tenant will not randomly question lease clauses but rather seek to negotiate only those points that are important to the company and its operations. The prospect's goal is to satisfactorily fulfill needs and possibly avoid being deprived of services or amenities currently enjoyed or desired. Inasmuch as only requests that are considered vital to the prospect will be raised, the leasing agent must be receptive and treat them with genuine concern. If they are tampered with or ignored, dissatisfaction will arise; if responded to favorably, gratification will dominate.

It is imperative that the agent remain sensitive to the prospect's needs and wants throughout each meeting. Constant attentiveness gains support and acceptance and moves the parties closer to a signed lease. Inattentiveness is an alienating force.

An important part of successful negotiation is interpreting not only what is expressed but also what is implied through behavioral patterns. Consequently, these patterns must be constantly and accurately judged. The successful agent must develop many useful techniques in reacting to the behavior of prospects. For instance, if the prospect makes an impossible request, the agent must interpret the reality of the request based on an awareness of the tenant's personality and respond accordingly. One approach that may be taken in such a situation is the black hat-white hat approach. This approach is a common method used by leasing agents to respond to impossible requests. The prospect may demand an addition to a lease or the removal of something in a clause that goes beyond the limits of what the agent can grant without express approval from the agent's supervisor, i.e., the building owner or director of leasing. Or, the request may be something the agent knows will not be agreed to regardless of the situation. Thus, the agent—the white hat—reacts, for example, by stating, "Mr. Prospect, I just can't remove that clause from the lease. The director of leasing of our agency would never allow it, and he is definitely unmovable on this matter." The director of leasing (or it may be the owner or the mortgage company) is the black hat—a lever to be pressed when the negotiation is demanding. Thus, the agent firmly takes a stand, with reason, and usually is able to negotiate in favor of ownership.

Perception

The role in which a prospect sees the leasing agent influences the direction taken during lease negotiation. While it should be made clear that the agent is acting on behalf of the building's owner, it should be made equally clear that the agent is genuinely interested in satisfying the prospect.

Because personalities are unique and can be further affected by daily activities, perceptions can vary. For example, a prospect who is having a bad day may perceive that the company is "being taken" for excess expenses when the agent is firm on tenant improvements. The sensitive agent, aware of the prospect's rebellious or defensive mood, shifts the negotiation to a less taxing matter and plans to rediscuss tenant improvement costs at a more appropriate time. Thus, successful negotiation of lease conditions hinges on the agent's ability to perceive prospects accurately and inspire them to perceive the agent in a preferred light.

Leadership

The agent as the catalyst in prompting the prospect's commitment must be in control of the situation at all times rather than be controlled. It is the agent's leadership qualities that secure tenants for an office building. Skills in leading the prospect to make desired responses and reinforcing correct decisions are essential to the successful culmination of lease negotiations.

Benefits of Negotiation

Negotiation must be looked upon as a worthwhile exercise exempt from nonsense and aggravation. Negotiation, professionally and carefully conducted, is profitable to both the prospect and agent.

The benefits are not only of a short-term nature (i.e., a commission for the agent and a new location for the prospect) but also can be measured over the long run (i.e, the agent earns a possible referral source, and the tenant is satisfied throughout the term of the lease). The benefits of skillful negotiation are many. First, the process of negotiating emphasizes to the prospect that the agent is willing and even eager to satisfy reasonable requests. The very fact that the two parties meet at the negotiating table indicates mutual trust and interest.

Second, the willingness of the agent to negotiate with the prospect lends itself to the establishment of a long-term relationship. If the agent proves to be reliable, capable, and dependable in meeting realistic demands, the prospect will look to the agent for future needs.

Next, as the agent deals with the representative of the prospective tenant, the negotiating process responds to that individual's personal and professional needs for recognition.

Fourth, information is exchanged through negotiation. The agent conveys knowledge about the product and the leasing agency, while the prospect reveals data about the business, its organization, and the problems to be solved within a given time frame. Give-and-take conversation educates the parties involved about each other. The more that is known about the other's expectations, the more progressive communication can be.

Finally, negotiation is an opportunity for the agent not only to refine and display expertise in the profession but also act as an advisor and counselor. A prospect may make unrealistic demands because of inexperience in renting space and negotiating lease conditions. By diplomatically explaining the reasons for certain terms, the agent can offer sound advice while encouraging harmonious discussion.

Techniques for Negotiation

The author of *Fundamentals of Negotiating*, Gerard I. Nirenberg (New York: Hawthorn Books, 1973), discusses many techniques useful in the negotiating process and further subdivides them into two categories—"when" strategy and "how and where" strategy. These tactics are readily adaptable to the office situation and are worthy of any leasing agent's consideration.

Both types of strategy will be used at one time or another by the leasing agent in negotiating office leases. Conversely, prospects may

Negotiation

use them as well. However, the leasing agent, eager to secure a signed lease, must control the process. An understanding of negotiating techniques facilitates this control.

The "When" Strategy

The "when" strategy revolves around timing. The agent's perception is called upon to judge when to move ahead in negotiations or further clarify the subject at hand. The "when" strategy is subdivided into forbearance, surprise, fait accompli, bland withdrawal, apparent withdrawal, reversal, limits, and feinting.

Forbearance. Forbearance, or intentionally detaining an answer to a question, is applicable throughout the negotiation of a lease. For instance, it would be unwise to point out a highly demanding lease clause, such as an equity adjustment provision in the recovery clause, during the early state of the negotiation process. The timing is not right; the prospect's interest level is not high enough. To mention such a restrictive provision so early might discourage the prospect altogether. Rather, the discussion should be postponed until just prior to the development of the lease. Even at the final negotiation meeting, the leasing agent could forbear a discussion that might lead to a dangerous objection until all other negotiable items have been resolved. In this way, both sides are permitted the chance to mentally resolve the conflict and avoid confrontation.

Becoming the listener as opposed to the talker is a form of forbearance. If a point has been made clear, further discussion may confuse or negate what was already established. For example, assume an agent has been given a firm commitment but continues to "sell" the building; the prospect may be talked out of the decision because an all-too-persistent leasing agent did not know when to stop.

Surprise. A sudden shift in an argument or approach can cause surprise and force a specific type of response. For instance, negotiations may be progressing with ease when suddenly the agent expresses dissatisfaction with a talent request, such as a demand for a renewal option without an increase in rent at the time of renewal. Shocked by the turn of events, the prospect may retreat, knowing that the request was unreasonable.

The surprise, however, must be used cautiously and exercised to telegraph a stopping point to certain requests, not introduce confrontation. The prospect in the previous situation, for example, may have responded angrily to the agent's dissatisfaction if it was felt that the request was reasonable. In this case, the surprise would have done more harm than good.

Fait Accompli. This strategy involves high risk and is used more often by the prospect than the agent. The leasing agent often is looked upon as a consultant to the prospect, who consequently feels secure enough to make unreasonable demands and expect no counteraction. For example, the prospect may make changes to the lease before signing and returning it, confident that the landlord will accept the alterations. Having made the changes and signed the lease, the prospect considers it an accomplished fact.

Such a move should not be intimidating or threatening to the agent. While this technique is an attempt by the prospect to dominate or control the situation, it is highly probable that the lease will be rewritten at least one more time before it is mutually acceptable.

Bland Withdrawal. The bland withdrawal relies on a "Who me?" attitude. The strategy could be applied, for example, if a prospect appears to be immediately dissatisfied with a certain lease clause: "Mr. Prospect, I can see that this clause is disturbing to you. I also know that the work we've both done to move this far, as well as the many things you like about your new offices, is very important to you. I know that the landlord wants you as a tenant. But his hands and mine are tied! This clause must remain as written. When you consider the whole deal, I think you'll understand. Do you have any other problem with the lease?"

This tactic, like all others, may not work. The bland withdrawal is, at best, a weak strategy. If unsuccessful, the agent can resort to forbearance, trying to satisfy other negotiable clauses while leaving the non-negotiable one until later, possibly when a trade-off can be bargained.

Apparent Withdrawal. This strategy is best illustrated by the leasing agent who, at an apparent impasse, rises from the negotiating table, walks to the door, closes it behind him but keeps a hand on the doorknob. The prospect must be convinced that the agent has withdrawn, unaware that the intent is to reopen on a more positive tone.

Before using this negotiating technique, the leasing agent must become proficient to be sure that such a demonstration will not have a detrimental effect.

Many prospects want to negotiate the rental rate; usually, however, this is not subject to change. If the agent cannot convince the prospect that the rental rate is not negotiable, an apparent withdrawal may be effective. The leasing agent then can reopen the negotiation by demonstrating a reduction in the effective rate through an offer of a few months' free rent or an increased tenant improvement allowance. The apparent withdrawal often is used by the prospect as well as the agent in negotiating leases. An astute agent is not to be deterred by the prospect who employs the strategy.

Reversal. If rental rates for competitive space are being reduced because of slow market conditions, success may be found by increasing the product's rates. This is an example of reversal strategy, which calls for the opposite action to be taken than would seem appropriate. The adage, "If it costs more, it must be better," is applied to the reversal. However, caution must be exercised. Only if the product offers unique benefits that warrant the increase can the strategy be used effectively. Otherwise, it can easily become a misrepresentation of the building.

Limits. The leasing agent can impose various types of limits on the negotiating process. A time limit can and should be placed upon the final acceptance of the lease. The agent also can limit the clauses in the lease that are negotiable. For example, it may be determined that the rate and escalation provisions are not negotiable, but expansion and renewal provisions are. What restrictions to impose and when becomes critical in the application of this tactic. If the agent knows that the prospect wants to alter the escalation provision but the landlord will allow no changes, the agent should express this limit at the outset. When limits are given, however, the implication is that all other clauses except those specified as non-negotiable can be changed. This, of course, is not true. Still, a long list of non-negotiable points presented would be defeating. Instead of doing this, the agent should be prepared to make trade-offs, a compromise by the agent offsetting a demand from the prospect. For example, the leasing agent may agree to a modification of the eminent domain clause, whereby the tenant would be allowed to collect for moving expenses in the instance of condemnation, if the prospect agrees to give up a demand for an additional expansion provision.

Feinting. Making a move in one direction in order to divert attention from an original objection is feinting. For instance, the agent can resist the prospect's request to eliminate the securtiy deposit as a diversion from discussion of an expansion option, which would be impossible to award. After a time, the agent—who has successfully side-tracked the prospect—agrees to eliminate the security deposit and leaves the prospect with a feeling of negotiating success. The distraction gives the agent time to consider alternatives should the expansion clause be reintroduced.

The "How and Where" Strategy

The "how and where" strategy refers to negotiating methods. "How and where" techniques applicable to lease negotiation are labelled participation, association, disassociation, crossroads, blanketing, randomizing, random sample, salami, and bracketing.

Participation. Participation enlists the aid of other parties to work on behalf of the agent. Space planners or contractors, for instance, often are asked to the negotiating table to convince the prospect about tenant improvement provisions. Even the prospect may be an unknown participant, such as when the prospect's opinion is solicited to resolve a problem being discussed.

Association. The association strategy is quite simple: If a tenant, whom the prospect admires, has accepted the lease clause being discussed, it should be stated. Based on association with that tenant, the prospect will accept the provision.

Disassociation. The disassociation strategy is the opposite. To try to win an argument, the prospect may point to something its existing building is offering. In response, the agent should tactfully remind the prospect of its overall dissatisfaction with the building. If the prospect wants to disassociate itself with that inferior product, the agent's argument must be adopted.

Crossroads. Should a prospect be obsessed with one clause, other issues should be introduced, intersecting the prospect's original thought. The agent can make concessions on the less important items while standing firm on major ones.

Blanketing. To hide a weakness, the agent may blanket a discussion. For example, the landlord's tenant improvement allowance may be somewhat inadequate, although it is offset by tenant improvements included in the base building contract and not deducted from the allowance (i.e., ceiling tile, lights, and air conditioning). If dollar value is applied to these items the effective overall allowance is increased. Likewise, a few months' free rent may be applied against tenant improvement costs. The discussion should focus on such fringe benefits and shift away from the insufficient allowance. The agent is a more effective negotiator if the product can be demonstrated to be more desirable than competitive products by blanketing drawbacks with advantages. The prospect is ensured of the assets

Negotiation

to be received, and the gains to be realized by the company are reinforced.

Randomizing. Randomizing is calling a bluff. A tenant may object to signing a lease until certain clauses are altered. Given such obstinacy, the leasing agent must consider the market, the tenant's requirements, and ownership objectives, then play the odds by calling the bluff and refusing any unreasonable requests. For instance, randomizing may be used in a renewal situation: The prospect may state that the company will move elsewhere unless specific changes are granted. The agent is sure the requests are unfeasible. And, the wise leasing agent knows the market is definitely unfavorable for tenants. Secure in the negotiation situation, the agent calls the prospect's bluff. The agent knows that if indeed the prospect moves, it will be extremely difficult. The obvious pitfall in this strategy is the potential loss involved. As with all negotiating tactics, the agent can fail. If the agent calculates the odds incorrectly, this very well could occur. In such an instance, the agent must be flexible enough to adopt another strategy—so that negotiations can be reopened.

Random Sample. This technique requires the use of statistical data to make a point. For example, a prospect may be leery about the degree of accessibility of the office via automobile. By providing information compiled by a transportation consultant as to the time it takes to reach the building from various sites, the random sample may sell the prospect on the product.

Salami. The salami strategy involves taking control of a situation little by little until an entire point has been won. The technique received its name from a Hungarian politician who explained the "salami" operation to his collaborators:

> When you want to get hold of a salami which your opponents are strenuously defending, you must not grab at it. You must start carving for yourself a very thin slice. The owner of the salami will hardly notice it, or at least, he will not mind very much. The next day you will carve another slice, then still another. And so, little by little, the whole salami will pass into your possession. (Gerard I. Nierenberg, *The Art of Negotiating,* [New York: Hawthorn Books, Inc., 1968] p. 119–20.)

If a prospect objects to a lease clause, the conversation should be re-routed to lead to acceptance of specific items within it until the prospect approves of the entire clause.

Bracketing. The agent should use the bracketing strategy every time a lease is being negotiated. Negotiating requires give and take from both sides. The agent cannot refuse to negotiate each clause attacked by the prospect. All items the prospect wants to change should be bracketed. Give and take then can occur on a systematic basis, some changes being fully agreed to (e.g., omit the security deposit for a strong national corporation), some being absolutely forbidden (i.e., elimination of the escalation provision), and some being met midway.

Whether the prospect is represented by the same individual or individuals with whom the agent has dealt throughout the leasing process or by another person experienced at the bargaining table (which is often true of large national firms), negotiating must remain on a professional, stable level.

Summary

Negotiation is very much a part of the leasing effort. Inevitably, the leasing agent and the prospect engage in give-and-take dialogue. It is therefore important that the agent understand the negotiating process and the principles behind it and be able to control the situation. That understanding, coupled with experience and common sense, will bring about results that are beneficial to all parties involved.

The basis for negotiation, which includes the principles of human behavior, perception, and leadership, must be understood. If the agent knows what motivates the prospect to act a certain way or make a certain request, the approach used to deal with the prospect can be more realistically and effectively planned.

Negotiation must be looked upon as a beneficial part of the leasing efforts. If negotiation is carried out in an atmosphere of common concern, rapport between agent and prospect is developed further and mutual respect is strengthened.

The common techniques used in the negotiating process are categorized by Gerard I. Nierenberg as "when" strategy and "how and where" strategy. The leasing agent learns quickly that the type of prospect being dealt with and the personalities involved signal the most effective approach.

15 Concluding the Leasing Effort

The ultimate objective of the leasing program is to obtain signed leases. Once all differences have been settled and negotiations have reached a mutually satisfactory conclusion, this objective can be met. The agent's perseverance and energies do not come to an end at this point, however. The comprehensive leasing effort extends beyond the tenant-signed lease. Final approval must be obtained from ownership. Neither is the relationship between the agent and the prospect severed. Rather, the agent continues to act as liaison during move-in and throughout tenancy. Even after the tenant occupies the building, the leasing agent may deal with that tenant in other situations (e.g., renewal or expansion), and a strong, supportive working relationship can be an asset.

The Close

A closing is the signing of the lease after negotiations have terminated and the document has been reviewed by the prospect and the prospect's attorney. Even though its provisions have been discussed and negotiated, to hand over the lease with a pen and ask for a signature is inappropriate. A lease is a legal document, and it must be fully understood before it is agreed to. The leasing agent should not intercede and offer advice but leave the final decision in the hands of the prospect.

Often, the closing is a mere formality, the prospect being fully committed to leasing office space. At other times, the agent will need to apply pressure, either cautiously or assertively, to secure a signature. The degree of pressure required depends on the prospect's level of decisiveness. In all cases, the pressure must be competently applied if it is to evoke the positive response that is sought rather than a negative one.

If an agent's voice and mannerisms are hurried, self-concern is demonstrated rather than sincere interest in the prospect. The pressure that is exerted must be aggressive.

A signed office lease represents an enormous financial commitment, and it is understandable that some prospects are hesitant at the moment of decision. In dealing with an indecisive prospect, the agent must dispel any last-minute apprehensions through positive reinforcement that the decision to sign is a wise one. Such assurance can be offered by pointing out that the customized suite design fully meets the prospect's needs and that the terms and conditions of the lease are acceptable. This kind of subtle closing pressure strengthens the prospect's ability to be an assertive decisison-maker.

The Direct Close

The direct close relies on being frank and getting right to the point. The most straightforward close is simply to hand the pen to the prospect and ask for a signature. This assumptive attitude on the part of the agent is one of the best ways to motivate the prospect into action. In applying the direct close, any indecisions and queries are bypassed. This is appropriate if the agent and prospect have developed good rapport and previous discussions and actions have been clear and definitive.

Action creates action. If a prospect hesitates about signing the lease, physical action may be effective. The agent should stand up, move around the desk, and assist in turning to the signature page.

If a lease clause has been altered and requires the prospect's initials, the agent should turn first to that page of the lease and say, "All changes to the lease require your initials as well as the landlord's." It is often simpler for the prospect to start with the initials and move to the full signature. Throughout the signing, the agent should continue giving approval while ensuring that signatures and initials are placed wherever necessary.

Another direct close approach is to encourage a final decision on a step-by-step basis. This closing technique is particularly effective if the previous strategy did not cause the prospect to act. By succinctly reiterating everything agreed to and demonstrating the thoroughness of the situation, the agent reinforces the prospect's decision. Throughout the leasing efforts, the agent may have felt the prospect was moving toward tenancy. Thus, the direct close approach supports the prospect's wise decision to secure occupancy in the subject building. However, it is possible that the agent has no inkling one way or another to a prospect's thoughts about occupancy because the prospect has chosen such a position. Thus, the agent, through the direct close, takes a positive approach and leads the decision-making with an air of certainty. The following discourse could apply: "Mr. Prospect, I know that if you sign the lease now, you'll be making the right decision. The office suite was customed designed to meet your exacting requirements. Your input was invaluable. The space is efficient and will work well for your firm. You've provided for growth by insisting upon an expansion option. You've polled your employees, and they want to relocate to these new offices. Both you and your attorney have carefully reviewed the lease, and you agree that the document in front of you is fair. Office space is becoming scarce. Other firms are interested in this space; it won't be on the market long. You couldn't make a better decision. Remember to initial all the changes as well as sign the lease and attachments." With this, the agent flips through the lease to the first section requiring the prospect's attention.

The third direct close method is to direct the discussion to a minor point in the lease which, when agreed to, implies acceptance of the entire lease. For example, the agent could ask the prospect if the occupancy date is acceptable. If the prospect says yes to the date, acceptance of the lease becomes easier. This closing technique is effective in dealing with particularly indecisive prospects. If the prospect continues to hesitate, the process can be repeated numerous times until all parts of the lease have been fully accepted. At this point, the prospect likely will be ready to sign.

The Indirect Close

The indirect close is a more subtle approach to securing the client's signature. Usually in the form of questioning, this close requires an acute awareness on the agent's part of the prospect's needs and demonstrates a willingness to satisfy them.

One type of indirect close is to ask questions designed to uncover hidden objections. Perhaps the prospect agreed to put up a security deposit but is having second thoughts about the matter. This uncertainty may be conveyed through reluctance to sign the lease. Negotiations were not really complete, and the prospect probably will remain hesitant until the problem has been resolved. Sensing the concern, the agent may ask, "Mr. Prospect, if we place the security deposit in an interest-bearing account and allow the interest to accrue to your benefit, will you sign the lease today?"

Rather than having a specific problem, the prospect, especially one inexperienced in leasing office space, may be somewhat plagued by earlier negotiations, during which it seemed the agent had the upper hand. The agent must be sensitive to such a possibility and try to bring objections to the surface. Most importantly, the agent wants to be able to satisfy the prospect's concern. If the objection is one that cannot be rectified, a closing approach should be adopted that focuses on the total package of benefits available to the prospect. In this way, the unreasonable objection is countered.

Although it can be valuable to uncover objections, the agent also must recognize that some prospects never stop negotiating. The questioning type of indirect close cannot be used with these prospects. A non-stop negotiator will translate an indirect close as a weakness and will continue to negotiate until a definite "no" is expressed.

Creating a climate of urgency is another form of indirect close. Simply put, the agent tries to create a now-or-never atmosphere. The approach may be, "Mr. Prospect, we need to complete this transaction now as a rate increase is going into effect soon. If you delay, I won't be able to guarantee this rate. The office you've chosen is choice space and won't be vacant for long." Afraid of a loss, the prospect will sign the lease.

The testimonial is often effective in securing a signature. By listing the tenants who have already signed leases, the agent reinforces the prospect's decision. This is especially useful if the prospect holds those tenants in high esteem. For example, the agent may say, "Mr. Prospect, XYZ Company has signed a lease and will be occupying its space in three months. I know this firm is one of your finest clients. Although you won't be moving in until a month later, that won't create a problem, will it?" The potential tenant, knowing it is joining with other reputable businesses, probably will sign.

Another indirect close is the slow-thinker or Ben Franklin approach. The agent helps the prospect list the reasons the lease should be signed. Then, without the agent's assistance, the prospect lists the reasons for not signing. If the leasing effort has responded to prospect objections, the lists should reveal a few reasons for not signing

Concluding the Leasing Effort

the lease but quite a number of reasons in favor of signing. The merit of this close is that the prospect arrives at the decision through self-evaluation. This tactic is particularly effective when an objection cannot be satisfied but the total package is overwhelmingly favorable.

Another closing is the double-Socratic method—the prospect's question is answered with a question. For example:

Prospect: Can you get me in the office by December 1?
Agent: If I can, will you sign today?

or

Prospect: Will the landlord pay my moving expenses?
Agent: If he will, will you sign today?

Still another indirect close is the subordinate question close. The prospect is asked to make a minor, usually rather easy decision indirect to the lease itself. For instance, "What suite number do you want?" or "Did you decide on wood paneling or grass cloth for your office walls?" These choices usually lead to a major decision, made less of a burden by the agent who has coached the prospect and reinforced affirmative responses.

Whatever closing tractic the leasing agent adopts, perception, sensitivity, self-confidence, and self-trust come into play. Furthermore, the desirability and size of the tenant, market conditions, and ownership goals direct the extensiveness of the closing efforts.

Landlord Acceptance of the Lease Documents

Throughout the leasing process, the agent strives to meet the demands of the prospective tenant. First and foremost, however, the agent must be responsive to the requirements imposed by the owner of the building.

Upon obtaining a tenant's signature on the lease, the agent must secure approval from ownership. The means by which this is done depends upon the agent's relationship with the owner. The authority given to the leasing agency by the owner is contractual and in writing. The degree of involvement from the owner can vary from one situation to the next. Some owners choose to be heavily involved and direct the negotiation through the agent, who reacts directly to the prospect. If the owner has been kept informed throughout the leasing efforts, the lease certainly will be acceptable. Absentee owners, on the other hand, may delegate the entire responsibility for

Figure 15.1

Lease Summation Report

Date of Lease _____   Occupancy Date _____
Date Prepared _____   Prepared by _____

Building _____ I. D. No. _____   Owner _____
Address _____   Mailing Address _____

Lessee _____ I. D. No. _____   Mailing Address _____
Nature of Business _____   Phone _____
Local Contact _____ Position _____

	Sq. Feet	Suite No.	Annual Amt. Rate	Monthly Amt. Rate	Term	Commencing	Ending
Original Lease							
New Totals							

Security Deposit $ _____ Received by _____ Date _____
Changes to Lease Paragraphs _____
_____

Rider _____
_____

Renewal Option _____   Notification Date _____
Expansion Option _____   Area _____
Cancellation _____   Penalty _____
Parking _____
Utilities Exclusion (Describe) _____

---

negotiation, subject to final review and acceptance rights. In this arrangement, the agent is required to sell the signed lease to the owner. Sometimes ownership will delegate the entire process to property management or, if the building is under construction, to a director of development.

Rather than just handing the lease to the landlord, it is ad-

Figure 15.1 (continued)

Janitorial Exclusion (Describe) _____
Percentage Rental (Describe) _____
Escalation Terms _____
Base Year _____ NRA _____ %   Escalation Review Date _____

Leased by (Co.) _____ (Agent) _____   Commission (Co.) $ _____ (Agent) $ _____
Credit Report _____   Reference Source _____
Approved (D.O.L.) (x) _____   Legal Review by (x) _____

Estimated Construction Costs

Total Cost $ _____   Cost per Square Foot $ _____
Allowed Cost $ _____   Cost per Square Foot $ _____
Difference $ _____   Cost per Square Foot $ _____
Lessee to pay extra cost of $ _____   By Cash $ _____
Amortization $ _____ /Yr   Amortized Interest Rate _____%
Approved (D.O.D. or Bldg. Mgr.) (x) _____   Comments _____

Move-In Information

Rent Commencement Date _____   Revised Lease Commencement Date _____
Suite Occupied _____   Termination Date _____
Information Packet Issued _____   Suite Inspected _____
Signs Installed _____   Keys Issued _____ Key Hook No. _____
Parking Permits Issued _____   Directory Listing _____
Move-In Charges to Lessee _____

Keys $ _____   Rent Effective Letter Received _____
Directory $ _____   Approved (Bldg. Mgr.) (x) _____
Construction $ _____   Comments _____
Other $ _____
Total $ _____

visable to first route the lease through the leasing agency. In fact, most firms will have a standard operating procedure requiring that this be done. Furthermore, it may be necessary to complete certain leasing forms. These forms will prove invaluable in future leasing efforts as well as in the management of the building.

A lease summation report, sampled in figure 15.1, is a synopsis of the lease. Its purpose is to provide the reader with the details of the lease, while eliminating the need to constantly refer to the document for information. The typical report calls for: (1) date of lease and occupancy date; (2) building information; (3) tenant information; (4) lease provision details; (5) commission and credit information; (6) construction costs; and (7) move-in information.

The leasing agent can provide all but the move-in information, which must be noted by the property manager when the tenant occupies the space.

Once the lease summation is completed, it is filed with a copy of the lease in an executive approval file, which includes all forms, letters, and other documents pertaining to a single tenant and necessary to the leasing and management of office space. At its most basic, the file contains: (1) a key map (figure 15.2) that shows the entire floor on which the tenant is located and the leased premises; (2) the completed lease summation report; and (3) the lease. If other documents have been prepared, such as construction cost estimates, credit reports, and commission statements, they should be kept in the file.

If a lease gram, such as the one in figure 15.3, is made part of the file, it notes the documents that appear in it and provides a place for approval signatures. Upon being approved by the appropriate individuals, the executive file is sent to ownership for review of the lease.

The owner can either reject, accept, or counter the lease. The response largely depends upon how close the relationship has been between agent and owner throughout the leasing efforts. If the owner demanded a constant reporting of a lease situation, the likelihood of acceptance is great. Conversely, the agent must "sell" the signed lease to the aloof owner with a high risk of rejection involved. The latter situation is not unusual. Many uninvolved owners only want to become involved in the process when the agent approaches with the signed lease seeking approval. Rejection of any or all of the lease suggests the necessity to re-enter the negotiation process with the prospect. Before renegotiating, both prospect and owner must be willing to make concessions to draft a mutually agreeable lease. Although the owner may concede to requests from highly desirable tenants or those that occur in poor markets, any negotiating done at this point should reflect maximum adherence to ownership objectives.

Figure 15.2

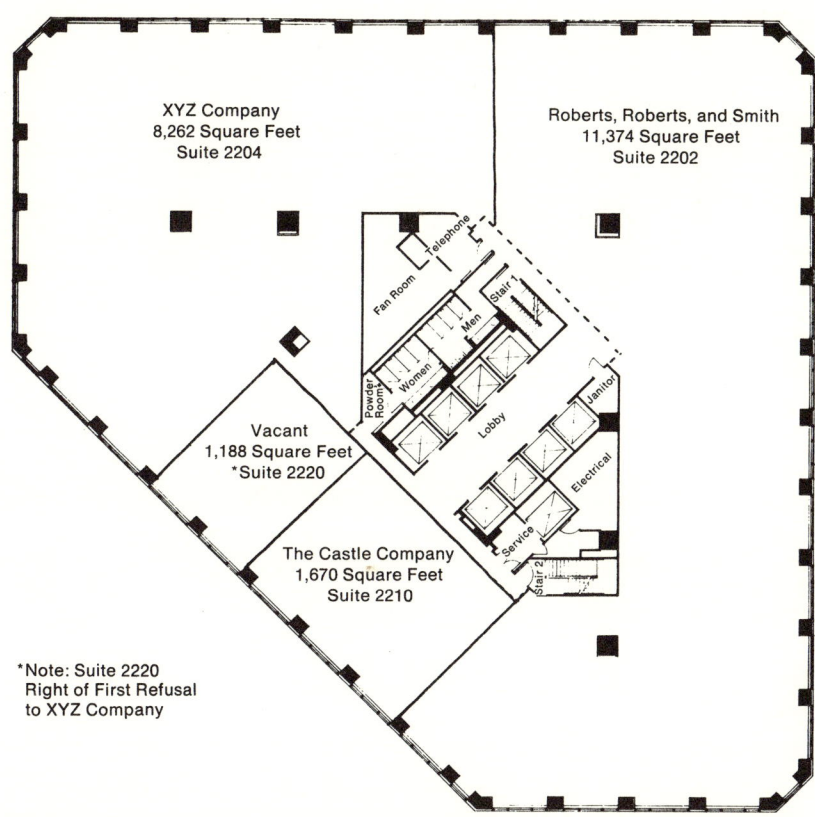

Typical Highrise Floor Plan:
22nd Floor

Figure 15.3

Lease Gram—Executive Approval File

Upon receipt of this Executive Approval File, please review the enclosed documents. By signing and dating the lease gram, you indicate approval. Additionally, please sign or initial the documents, the lease summation report, and related material where applicable. Do not forward this file to anyone except the director of leasing's secretary. If you cannot indicate your approval, return the entire file to the director of leasing's secretary with a cover memo listing reasons.

Lessee _____   Lessor _____
City _____   Building _____
Date Prepared _____   By _____

Executive Approval   Return to
Director of Leasing   Director of Leasing Secy.
_____ Date _____   Date Received _____
Legal Department   Director of Leasing Secy.
_____ Date _____   Date Received _____
Director of Development/Management   Director of Leasing Secy.
_____ Date _____   Date Received _____

Documents Enclosed
Document   Number
Lease   _____
Construction Rider   _____

Immediately upon acceptance by the owner, the lease should be given to the tenant; it is not legally binding until it has been received. The lease may be sent via certified mail, return receipt requested, or delivered by the agent. In the latter case, a lease transmittal letter should be signed to indicate the tenant's acknowledgment of receipt.

Once the lease becomes effective, copies of the entire executive approval file should be given to ownership, the property management agency, and any other party involved in meeting the terms agreed to in the lease.

Again, it is imperative that the leasing agent summarize progress made. A strong prospect report (figure 15.4) must be completed

Figure 15.3 (continued)

Rules and Regulations _____
Other Exhibits:

_____   _____

Addendum/Rider to Lease _____

Sublease and Consent to Assignment _____
Termination _____
Storage Lease _____
Other: _____

_____   _____

Other Enclosures
Item   Number
Lease Summation Report _____
Key Map _____
Credit Report/Credit Memo _____
Agency Commission Statement _____
Agent Commission Statement _____
Memo or Explanation _____
Other _____ _____

and forwarded to ownership on a regular basis. The report indicates the leasing activity within the subject building, and it is a means of evaluating the agent's efforts.

Follow Through

The leasing agent's responsibility does not end when the lease is signed but continues through the construction stage, tenant move-in, and occupancy.

A lease is a formal expression of promises, and the leasing agent must make sure that they are kept. Consequently, the agent often will be involved with the scheduling of everything from telephone

Figure 15.4

Strong Prospect Report

Agent _____
Building Proposed _____
Date _____ Approved _____

Prospect/Floor	Usable Sq. Ft.	Rentable Sq. Ft.	Usable Rate	Rentable Rate	Space Allocation	Space Planning	Space Plan Revision	Credit Report	Lease Transmitted To Lessee	Lease Negotiation	Lease Signed by Lessee	Executive Approval File	Lease Signed by Lessor	Remarks

Concluding the Leasing Effort

installations to furniture delivery, assisting the new tenant in an unfamiliar project. Some agencies have tenant coordinators who oversee a tenant relocation, thereby lessening the agent's workload but not the responsibility. The agent must keep abreast of the status of tenant improvements and move-in through the coordinator.

As a means of maintaining control of tenant construction and move-in, a report such as the one shown in figure 15.5 may be used. By indicating the date each activity is scheduled to be accomplished as well as the actual date of accomplishment, this chart can alert the leasing agent to any problems that may occur. This form may be updated and sent to the owner of the building as a vehicle of regular communication.

When a tenant has moved into the new office space, the leasing agent should make a visit to resolve any problems or correct any deficiencies. Possibly the tenant will be given a small gift, such as a plant for the office.

Other positive reminders of the agent may be extended on an ongoing basis, such as visits at each anniversary of tenancy. These small gestures will prove to be beneficial at renewal, for referrals, or in dealing with problems that may arise during the lease term.

Long-term tenant satisfaction ultimately is the responsibility of a number of professionals. An architect must create working drawings from space plans. An interior designer must select the materials, colors, furniture, and fixtures that combine to reflect the company's image. A tenant improvement contractor must construct the office suite on time, within budgetary guidelines, and according to plans. The property manager must assist with the move-in and provide the services promised in the lease. Nonetheless, the leasing agent instigates the activity and must see that all of these professionals are aiming to satisfy the tenant.

Summary

Although many tenants readily sign leases when negotiations reach a satisfactory conclusion, others require coaxing. To close a deal, the leasing agent may find it necessary to take either a direct or indirect approach. In either case, diplomacy is as crucial in closing as it is in negotiating.

The prospect's signature on the lease does not make it effective. Rather, the document, along with detailed reports of the leasing effort, must be forwarded to the owner of the building for approval.

Figure 15.5

Tenant Status Report

Agent _____
Building Proposed _____
Date _____ Approved _____

Column headers (left to right): Tenant/Floor | Suite No. | Sq. Ft. | Rate | Move-in Date | Final Working Drawings | Approval Working Drawings | Final Cost Estimate | Tenant Work Order | Inspection & Acceptance | Tenant Move-In | Follow-Up & Referral Request | Remarks

Concluding the Leasing Effort

If objections are raised to any lease conditions, they must be resolved accordingly. The lease becomes effective only when it has been signed by ownership and is returned to the tenant.

The agent's responsibility does not end with the signed lease. Concern for the tenant's satisfaction must extend throughout the term of the lease. By displaying genuine interest in the tenant, the agent can look forward to future business in the form of a renewal, expansion, or referrals.

16 Salesmanship and The Leasing Process

By legal definition, an agent is a person employed by a second party to act on that party's behalf in dealing with a third party. Within the office building sector of the real estate management profession, a leasing agent's legal function is to deal with prospective tenants on behalf of a building's owner. Any limitations on the agent's authority are expressed in a written agreement between the two.

Being a successful leasing agent, however, requires much more than an awareness of legal duties and responsibilities. The leasing agent plays a forceful role within the context of the marketing of office space. The agent is the catalyst who successfully coordinates and brings together a company in search of office space with vacant space in need of an occupant. The desired result is a satisfied tenant and a satisfied property owner.

No one specific method of marketing office space will ensure satisfaction of both parties in every situation. The individual personalities confronted in each leasing effort will differ, and market conditions continually change and affect the demands made by both prospective tenants and ownership. What is considered a necessity by a prospect during an overbuilt condition may become unimportant when available office space dwindles; similarly, the market may have an impact on the rental levels that owners will accept and concessions they will agree to. Because of the changing nature of the industry, the leasing agent's task becomes one of tailoring the application of marketing and leasing principles and practices to the individual situation.

Such a task is neither simple nor easy. A foundation based on intense preparation and planning and accumulated knowledge and experience must be built before successful liasion can be established between a prospective tenant and the office building owner. The initial step in laying this foundation is to perform an in-depth analysis of the space to be leased, including its physical and economic environment. Armed with comprehensive knowledge of the product, the general concepts of marketing can be utilized in designing and implementing a marketing plan, establishing a rental schedule, and in creating advertising and public relations campaigns. From this stage, attention may then be turned toward the practical concerns of finding and qualifying prospective tenants, planning office layouts, and negotiating lease terms and conditions.

Woven throughout all of these tasks must be one pervasive activity—salesmanship. In each step, attention must be given to the personal selling of office space, coordination with the leasing and management team, and the agent's own capabilities.

Too often the term "salesman" connotes a fast-talking individual with a canned sales pitch trying to peddle an unwanted product. Such a derogatory image misrepresents salesmanship as a profession that requires specialized training and extensive preparation. For the leasing agent to become a competent salesman, there must be an understanding of the nature of selling, prospect and tenant motivation, and the objectives of promotional activities. Proficiency is required in organizing, planning, and presenting accurate information to prospects, tenants, ownership, and management. Moreover, a constant desire for self-improvement is a key attribute of a competent salesman.

A leasing agent rarely is referred to as a salesman because the relationship between the agent and a prospective tenant is quite different from that between a consumer and salesman. Space is being leased, not sold, for a specified use and a finite period of time. No product is shipped to a buyer; rather, the tenant is moved into the product. But parallels between the leasing and sales functions can be drawn. Records must be kept, communication and marketing skills strengthened, and an allegiance to ownership must be exhibited. Becoming proficient in salesmanship requires concern with appearance and character and familiarity with the tools of the trade. Furthermore, since time is the leasing agent's most important resource, the one on which his livelihood depends, a continuous effort must be made to manage it efficiently and effectively.

Creating the Proper Impression

Because of the one-to-one relationship that the agent has with key representatives of prospective tenants, personal appearance, attitude, and the ability to communicate are important. First impressions can be critical. A prospect, however subconsciously, will make certain assumptions about the agent in the first meeting. If favorable, this first impression may form the basis for a profitable business relationship; if negative, the agent may be denied the opportunity to meet with the prospect again. The agent who is poised, prepared, well informed regarding the product, neatly dressed, and self-assured will inspire confidence.

The most important skill to be developed is that of communication. The agent's voice and speech make an impression and, therefore, should be clear and distinct. A strong vocabulary and precise enunciation decrease misunderstandings and reinforce the agent's self-confidence and self-trust. The art of listening should be perfected as well. Poor listening skills are evidenced by indifference and neglect, which are damaging to the leasing efforts. The more that can be learned, through diligent listening, the easier it becomes to meet the potential tenant's needs.

While some people have more innate ability than others, communication skills can be learned and improved. Speech fundamentals can be exercised in classroom training. Because self-awareness helps refine communication skills, the agent should tape record his own speech and, while playing it, listen for weaknesses in what is being said and how it is being said. This heightens sensitivity to mannerisms, tones, vocabulary, and delivery used in talking with prospects.

The agent should confront himself with these questions: Has thought and preparation gone into what is being discussed? Is my conversation natural? Am I making direct eye contact while speaking to indicate my enthusiasm and sincerity? Are simple nonverbal signs, such as a smile, a nod, or a wide-eyed look of attention, used to convey to a prospect that I am receptive and interested? Are the pitch and volume of my voice flexible and responsive enough to avoid monotony and express my ideas and thoughts?

Assertiveness and enthusiasm are invaluable to the leasing agent. The agent who is persuasively assertive without being obnoxiously aggressive indicates a positive attitude about the product and full knowledge of it. Enthusiasm is contagious; zeal transmits a sense of self-confidence and trust about the leasing agent and the office space being leased.

Other characteristics beneficial to the agent's image are optimism, sincerity, determination, dependability, initiative, imagination, composure, and maturity. All of these will earn the trust and reliance of the potential tenant and lead to success in leasing efforts.

Assembling the Tools of the Trade

The leasing agent can never be over prepared. Potential tenants will always have questions about the office space being considered and want further explanations about the various amenities. Responses to the questions should be immediate. Often, a verbal answer is adequate. At other times, printed materials—brochures, booklets, floor plans—will have greater impact, both on an immediate basis and over the long term, since they can be taken to study, read, and think about over a period of time. If, however, the agent does not have an answer either in verbal or printed form to a particular query, it is imperative that the prospect be told that, "I will get back to you by (a given date) with that information." The promise must be kept. In this way, the agent fulfills the prospect's needs and creates another opportunity for communication.

Printed informational materials represent but one category of "trade tools" that support the leasing agent's efforts, but they are important. The specific situation will dictate the type of materials needed. For example, if the agent is planning to talk with a prospect for the first time, a general brochure about the office building and its features would be necessary. If an agent is re-leasing space, a list of available suites and a short description of each, including the number of private offices, storage areas, and special over-standard improvements, should be at hand. "As built" floor plans, which depict the actual layout of partitions, doors, electrical outlets and the like for existing office suites, also should be made available.

Some prospects may be especially interested in the amenities in the immediate neighborhood. A neighborhood amenity package would respond to this particular interest. The package may include information about: nearby parking facilities, including the distance from the building to the lot and the daily, weekly, and monthly costs; and transportation, including access to public transportation and major thoroughfares and travel time from the building to certain important sites (e.g., airport, train depots, court house, convention center). A map clearly showing the location of parking facilities as well as restaurants, banks, and shopping areas is worth including in the package as well.

Oftentimes, letters written by satisfied tenants and referral sources about the product can be used by the agent as a trade tool. These letters reassure the prospect that a decision to lease space in the office building would be a good one and can be given to a prospect for review and encouragement.

Although it may be difficult to carry all promotional materials at all times, as daily appointments are made with various prospects, the agent can anticipate their interests and take the appropriate items.

Two additional tools the agent might need are a pocket calculator and an architect's scale ruler. The calculator helps in quickly performing various mathematical computations, such as the annual rent for a certain number of square feet; the architect's scale aids in determining measurements in existing or anticipated office space by scaling approximate dimensions off floor plans.

On occasion, materials that do not fit in a briefcase (e.g., scale models of buildings, design boards showing color schemes of building decor, architectural drawings, or oversized photographs and illustrations) will be needed. A model, for instance, often is used in pre-leasing situations to assist prospects who have a difficult time translating floor plans and drawings into actual space and location within a building. The agent who is fully prepared for each prospect meeting takes along the proper visual aids or makes other necessary arrangements. Should, for example, a scale model be too cumbersome or delicate to move, the meeting should be held in the agent's office.

Managing Time

Time is the agent's most valuable resource and must be used efficiently. It should be invested wisely, not spent foolishly. A leasing agent should place high value on time and give top priority to its management.

The process of managing time requires discipline and organization. Before solutions to the time management problem can be offered, however, it is necessary to study work habits and determine how time is being used. A time log facilitates this study.

R. Alec MacKenzie, author of *New Time Management Methods* (Chicago: Dartnell Corporation, 1975), encourages the use of a time

Figure 16.1

Daily Time Log   Date_____

Name_____

Goals: 1. _____( )   3. _____( )

       2. _____( )   4. _____( )*

Time	Activity	Priority**	Comments
8:30			
9:00			
9:30			
10:00			
10:30			
11:00			
11:30			
12:00			
12:30			
1:00			
1:30			
2:00			

*( ) = Check if goal was accomplished

**A = Important, immediate attention required
  B = Important, must be attended to in the near future
  C = Important, must be accomplished within a reasonable amount of time
  D = Routine

log as part of good time management. A daily time log, a portion of which is sampled in figure 16.1, requires: (1) recording activity every half hour; (2) setting daily goals; (3) establishing priorities in daily responsibilities; and (4) evaluating and commenting on the activity recorded.

By keeping a log, the actual time spent on various duties is revealed. A daily time log must be completed regularly, meticulously, and honestly, and certain guidelines should be followed.

First, entries should be made at regular intervals. Waiting to fill in the activities, priorities, and comments until the end of the day is unrealistic and defeats the purpose of the log. Critical details about something done at 8:00 A.M. can be forgotten by 5:00 P.M.

Second, to be effective, daily goals must be realistic yet challenging. They should be: (1) demanding, to insure personal challenge; (2) measurable, to make it clear when and if goals are met; (3) achievable, to avoid frustration; and (4) flexible, to accommodate uncontrollable circumstances. A leasing agent might set these kinds of goals: To complete monthly prospect reports, to make five follow-up telephone calls, and to answer all critical mail.

Third, establishing priorities in goal setting reveals the allotment of time between important matters and routine assignments. The agent can reorganize work habits if it becomes obvious that more time is spent performing routine duties than on important or urgent matters.

Upon completion of a week's or several weeks' logs, it is important to objectively evaluate time usage. The logs help to determine if time spent has been on the essential tasks. In completing the analysis of time recorded, the agent should ask himself such questions as these: Did setting goals improve my effectiveness? Why or why not? Which daily goals helped to draw me closer to long-range goals? If some did not, how can this be corrected? Were long periods of uninterrupted time productive? Why or why not? If numerous interruptions occurred, how can this be stopped? At what time of the day did I seem more productive? Should important priorities be moved to that part of the day so that they may be accomplished more smoothly and efficiently? Analyzing the log is as important as completing it. Only by doing this will the log become an indispensable tool for managing time wisely.

MacKenzie also advocates the dismissal of time wasters. Those that often seem to find their way into daily work activities include procrastination, drop-in visitors, poor communication, incomplete information for making decisions, telephone calls, preoccupation, worries, and the like. The leasing agent learns quickly that in order to end each day on a successful note, poor work habits must be recognized and eliminated.

The leasing agent's livelihood depends on success in leasing office space. Tasks that do not support this key objective should be dealt with as expeditiously as possible and nonproductive activities disposed of altogether. Only by doing this can the agent devote the necessary amount of time to the active marketing of office space.

The Leasing Effort

The marketing and leasing of office space is a systematic and ongoing program of attracting prospective tenants, analyzing and meeting their needs and working within the guidelines set by ownership. The dynamic force behind these efforts is the agent whose physical appearance, mental agility, and thorough knowledge of the market and the product ensure that office space will be filled. The agent plans and manages all leasing activities and guarantees that a proper balance among them is maintained.

Defining the Role of the Leasing Agency

The leasing agency is the business organization that acts for a building's ownership and assumes responsibility for preparing the marketing plan as an expression of leasing objectives and the strategies to be used in meeting them. In some instances, the agency staff performs and is responsible for various marketing functions, such as advertising, public relations, and market research. If marketing tasks are performed by others, they must be harmonious with the total marketing plan, including the role of the individual leasing agent. In other cases, the agent alone is charged with these functions. The leasing agent, however, always personally performs the most vital marketing activity—personal selling.

The leasing agency office is the base from which the agent works. Staff meetings with other agency personnel can be used to evaluate leasing efforts and provide support and guidance from peers and superiors. Regardless of its size, the company can become a valuable resource in the merchandising of the subject property.

Gaining Knowledge of the Product

The agent must be as well versed as possible about the office space being leased, the building in which it is located, and the building's

Salesmanship and the Leasing Process

environment. The decision to rent space in one office building rather than another usually is made after comparing it to other buildings. A complete picture of the product must be drawn if a positive image is to be created of it and comparison to a competitive building is to be favorable.

Establishing Rental Schedules

Rental rates are dependent on the activities and conditions of the local office building market and cannot be set haphazardly. The marketing plan, competitive factors, the building's location, and the market's ability to absorb space must be considered, as should operating expenses, debt service payments, and the return sought by the owner. The agent is, therefore, a rent analyst, not a rent maker.

As a rent analyst, the leasing agent must continuously study the market to evaluate the impact of economic changes, construction or demolition of other office buildings, changes in amenities or services, and the like.

While an analysis of the overall market reveals the average competitive rental rate, specific location of space within an office building must be evaluated in order to increase or decrease the average rate based on desirability. For instance, a suite on the top floor of a building that offers a panoramic view of the city can exact higher rents than less favorably located suites.

Segmenting the Market

All of the companies and individuals who use office space make up the office market. However, because of the diversity in office requirements, no single building can attract every user. The effective marketing effort focuses on those specific types of users whose requirements are compatible with what the subject office building has to offer. In order to achieve this, the overall market must be divided into submarkets or market segments.

The most notable building characteristics that can assist in identifying appropriate submarkets are location, size, and architectural structure. Depending on the nature of these characteristics, a building might appeal to certain users and not to others. From this, it can be concluded that appropriate submarkets can be identified by location, by company size, and by the type of business operation (e.g., government, corporate, institutional, or service).

The purpose of market segmentation is to identify the most logical prospects for a particular office building so that marketing efforts can be designed to reach and appeal to them. By segmenting the market, the agent is increasing the potentiality of success.

The constant changes in the market, and consequently market segments, demand that market research be an ongoing process. Thus, the leasing agent will be aware of these changes (e.g., economic, population, construction, and demolition) as they affect leasing efforts.

Promoting the Office Space

An advertising program is essential to marketing office space. Regardless of the type of advertising used, the image of the property must be given utmost consideration. Advertising supplies product information to prospective tenants who otherwise might never learn of available space.

The high cost of advertising dictates that detailed planning and preparation be undertaken. Promotional dollars must be spent in areas in which a high rate of readership or listenership of prospective tenants is earned. The marketing plan designates the type of overall campaign to be used and the allocations budgeted for it. Advertising experts then implement campaign tactics.

Like advertising, public relations must be handled by experts (whether in-house or an outside agency) in order to successfully win the approval, confidence, knowledge, and preference of the public. Various public relations tools—press releases, promotional aids, community involvement, announcements and ceremonies, and business entertainment—may be used to promote the office building and lend continued credibility to the leasing agency.

Locating and Qualifying Prospects

While promotional activities will attract some inquiries about office space, the most effective means of obtaining prospects is through personal solicitation. Prospective tenants can be located several ways: by contacting sources of referrals and centers of influence, through cold canvassing, and by establishing a program of mutual cooperation with other leasing agents.

Refining the list of prospects requires skill in asking the right questions in the right way at the right times. Answers to these questions should reveal if the prospect is a financially stable organization and provide data to be used in determining if the building can accommodate the prospect's needs.

Salesmanship and the Leasing Process

Planning the Space and Presenting the Design and Lease Proposal

As office interiors grow more important in the business world, so does space planning in the marketing process. An office user has both operational and aesthetic requirements on which financial limitations are imposed, all of which affect the suite design. If the agent successfully plans the prospect's office space within these limitations and helps the prospect visualize the firm within the proposed space, that prospect may well be converted to tenant.

In creating an efficient yet attractive office, the agent must work within a financial framework established by the landlord's tenant improvement allowance and the financial strength and budget of the tenant. Construction cost estimates should be accurately prepared and allocated between the landlord and tenant.

When the suite designs have been completed, they should be formally presented to the prospect. At the same time, the agent should conduct the prospect on a tour of the building and present a lease proposal. The lease proposal outlines the allocation of tenant improvement costs and other general conditions of the lease, such as rental rate, escalation provisions, lease term, and expansion and renewal provisions. This proposal can be a simple listing of information or an elaborate visual presentation.

Negotiating the Lease

The objective of all marketing efforts is to transform a prospect into a satisfied tenant. Consequently, the components of an office lease and the techniques of negotiating its provisions must be known.

The use of a standard form lease eliminates the problem of writing a lease for every new tenant. Although the terms in a standard form lease can be altered, addenda added, riders attached, and wording changed to satisfy the parties involved, it provides a point from which to begin negotiating. The final contract, written with advice from legal counsel, will be tailored to a specific rental arrangement.

Every lease should contain six elements:

1. The correct names and signatures of legally competent parties to the agreement.
2. A description of the leased premises.
3. The term of the lease.

4. The amount of the rent.
5. The purpose for which the tenant is to use the premises.
6. The rights and obligations of both parties to the contract.

Once the lease document is written, it is the point at which negotiation begins. The agent must anticipate those lease clauses that will be challenged by the prospect and be prepared to make a mutually profitable agreement for both owner and prospect.

Closing and Following Through

The final formality in the leasing process is to obtain first the prospect's signature on all legal documents and then the landlord's approval. Although some prospects will be ready to sign the lease, others may require subtle persuasion, calling for the leasing agent to apply recognized closing techniques. Even after the lease is signed by both parties, the agent's involvement should continue through construction of the suite, tenant move-in, and the period of occupancy. Total tenant satisfaction is necessary to the successful leasing cycle.

Summary

This text has repeatedly stressed the many skills that the agent will need and use and discussed the disciplines to be mastered in performance of duty and responsibility. Education, training, experience, salesmanship, business sense, and common sense must all work together if the professional agent is to be successful in the marketing and leasing of office space.

Speculative office buildings—those constructed without substantial preleasing—have become rare. Lenders are not anxious to participate in such risks. The major tenant lease, therefore, precedes the actual development, construction, and management of the building. Leasing leads the way, as new office buildings are virtually created by the efforts of leasing agents in the acquisition of a major tenant. To accomplish this task, the agent is turned to for answers—answers to questions relating to prospective tenants' needs, market conditions, site considerations, building design, development and construction costs, projected revenue and operating expenses, financing arrangements, legal opinions, suite design and layout, tenant improvement costs, management plans, and many other considerations. The leasing agent collates this data and arranges it in a presentable, understandable form that anticipates the major tenant's motivations.

The leasing agent's success or failure is largely dependent upon personal efforts and abilities. The leasing business provides great opportunities for self-motivated, ambitious individuals. Success comes in the form of status and income. No longer merely a salesman, the professional leasing agent with a vast knowledge in many disciplines has become a consultant, dealing with the top businessmen in the community and around the country, and even the world. Owners and developers rely heavily upon the leasing agent's expertise, not only to provide tenants for their space but also to consult in the design and ongoing management of the structures. The leasing agent works with both the owner and tenant to create an office building and leasehold that is mutually beneficial and functional.

Leasing office space is demanding and intense. A constant and growing technology requires that the agent, today, more than at any other time, keep current with innovations in all the disciplines in which he necessarily is involved. The professional agent cannot be satisfied to learn but must relearn and apply new knowledge and methods to meet daily challenges of the industry. By meeting this challenge, the leasing agent will find satisfaction and gratification in the profession.

Appendix

Figure A.1

Standard Method of Floor Measurement for Office Buildings

For Guidance of Owners and Managers, Appraisers,
Architects, Lending Institutions, and Others.

The purpose of a standard is to permit communication and computation on a clear and understandable basis. Another important purpose is to allow comparison of values on the basis of a generally agreed upon unit of measurement. The Building Owners and Managers Association International has sponsored a Standard Method of Floor Measurement for more than fifty years. The BOMA Standard has also been the one accepted and approved by the American National Standards Institute for many years. The result is a unit of measurement that can be used by owners, managers, tenants, appraisers, architects, lending institutions, among others.

It should also be noted that this standard can and should be used in measuring office space in old as well as new buildings. It is applicable to any architectural design or type of construction because it is based on the premise that the area being measured is that which the tenant may occupy and use for his furnishings and his people.

The Standard Method of measuring office space as described in this publication measures only occupiable space, undistorted by variances in design from one building to another. It measures the area of an office building that actually has rental value and, therefore, as a standard can be used by all parties with confidence and with a clear understanding of what is being measured.

The Building Owners and Managers Association International urges all its members and others in the office building industry to use this method in measuring office space.

THE NEW STANDARD

Area measurement in office buildings is based in all cases upon the typical floor plans, and barring structural changes which affect materially the typical floor, such measurements stand for the life of the building, regardless of readjustments incident to tenant layouts.

In the case of buildings designed for divided or multiple tenancy, this typical floor plan must permit of subdivisions to accommodate usual tenant requirements with corridors that reach every reasonable office subdivision. The definition of "Rentable Area—Multiple Tenancy Floor" applies to this typical floor, designed for tenant subdivision.

In the case of buildings designed for whole-floor tenancy, where corridors are omitted, the definition of "Rentable Area—Single Tenancy Floor" applies.

BOMA STANDARD

In 1915 the Association adopted the first Standard Method of Floor Measurement for office buildings. This was readily accepted as a "National Standard," serving the industry more than thirty-five years without occasion for amendment. With the advent of "block type" building design, a revised Standard Method was adopted by the Association in 1952. This was further revised (three years later) to conform to the new "American Standards," of which the Association was co-sponsor. At the Miami Convention in 1971, the Standard was again revised to reflect modern leasing concepts and practices.

Appendix 249

Figure A.1 (continued)

AMERICAN STANDARD

The "American Standard" for measuring office areas in buildings is the result of joint action by participating organizations under the auspices of the American National Standards Institute. Our Association, as a sponsoring organization, is represented by the Chairman of our Rental Committee, Leonard J. Adreon of St. Louis, who serves as ANSI Committee Chairman. The new BOMA Standard has been unanimously approved by the ANSI Committee and was submitted on February 18, 1972, to the parent body for adoption as the new "American Standard."

Originally adopted September 15, 1915—Reissued (without change) December 1, 1925—Revised and reissued December 8, 1952—Revised and readopted December 6, 1955, and reissued January 10, 1956—Reprinted April, 1963; April, 1966; April, 1970—Revised and readopted June, 1971, and reprinted April, 1972; February, 1973; August, 1976.

AMERICAN NATIONAL STANDARD

Z65.1–1972 Areas in Office Buildings, Method of Determining (revision of ANSI Z65.1–1956 (R 1964) Approved August 14, 1972)

Copyright 1977 by
Building Owners and Managers Association International

Figure A.1 (continued)

RENTABLE AREA—MULTIPLE TENANCY FLOOR

The Net Rentable Area of a multiple tenancy floor, whether above or below grade, shall be the sum of all rentable areas on that floor.

The rentable area of an office on a multiple tenancy floor shall be computed by measuring to the inside finish of permanent outer building walls, or to the glass line if at least 50% of the outer building wall is glass, to the office side of corridors and/or other permanent partitions, and to the center of partitions that separate the premises from adjoining rentable areas.

No deductions shall be made for columns and projections necessary to the building.

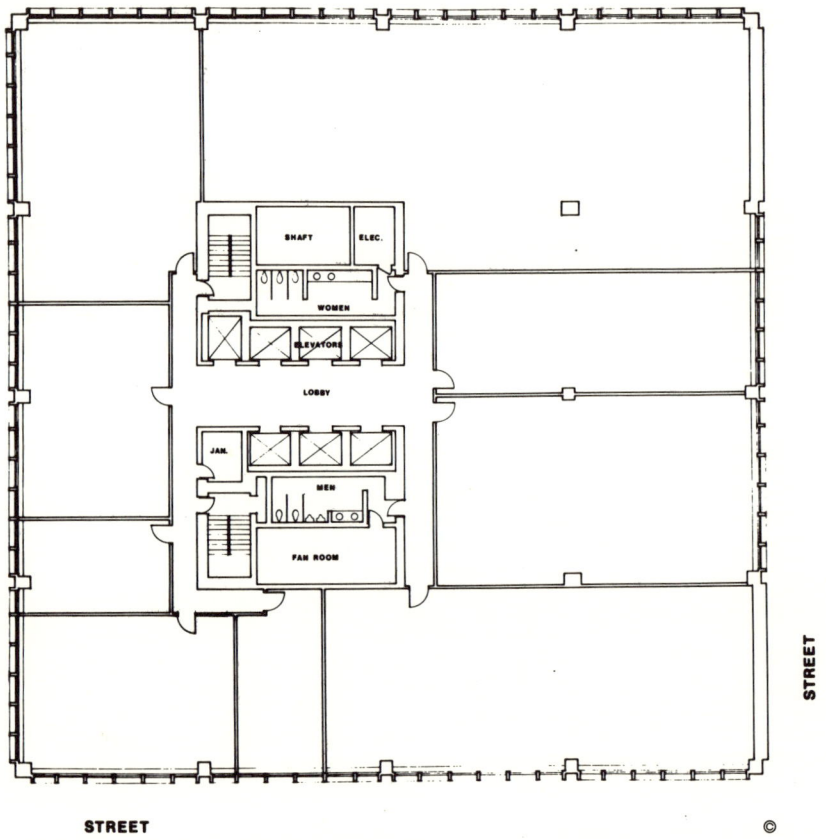

Appendix 251

Figure A.1 (continued)

RENTABLE AREA—SINGLE TENANCY FLOOR

Rentable area of a single tenancy floor, whether above or below grade, shall be computed by measuring to the inside finish of permanent outer building walls, or from the glass line where at least 50% of the outer building wall is glass. Rentable area shall include all area within outside walls, less stairs, elevator shafts, flues, pipe shafts, vertical ducts, air-conditioning rooms, fan rooms, janitor closets, electrical closets—and such other rooms not actually available to the tenant or his furnishings and personnel—and their enclosing walls. Toilet rooms within and exclusively serving only that floor shall be included in rentable area.

No deductions shall be made for columns and projections necessary to the building.

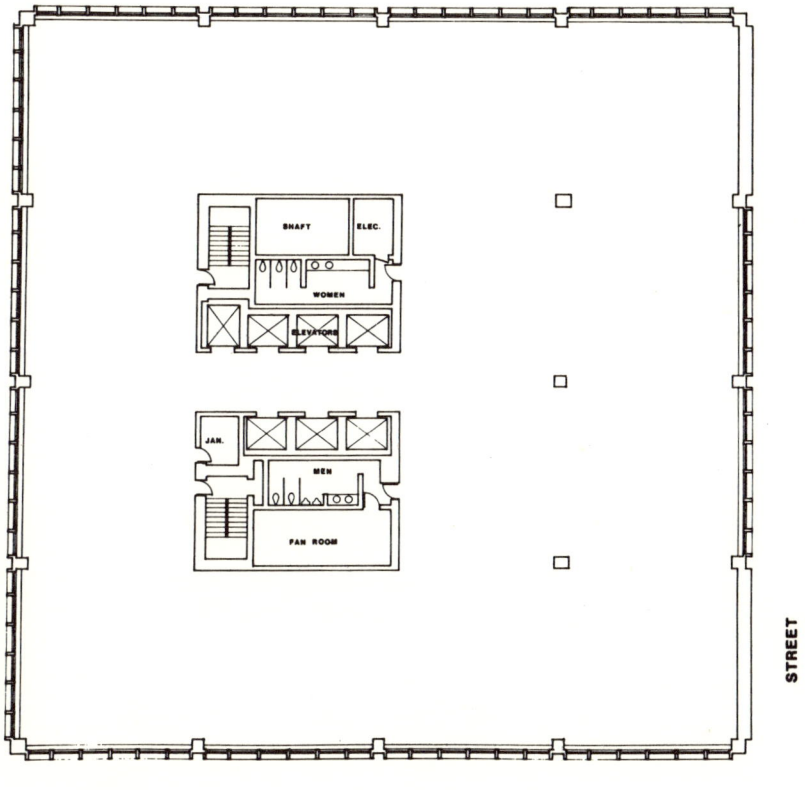

Figure A.1 (continued)

STORE AREAS IN OFFICE BUILDINGS

To determine the number of square feet in a ground floor rentable store area, measure from the building line in the case of street frontages and from the inner surface of other outer building walls and from the inner surface of corridor and other permanent partitions and to the center of partitions that separate the premises from adjoining rentable areas.

No deduction should be made for vestibules inside the building line or for columns or projections necessary to the building.

No addition should be made for bay windows extending outside the building line.

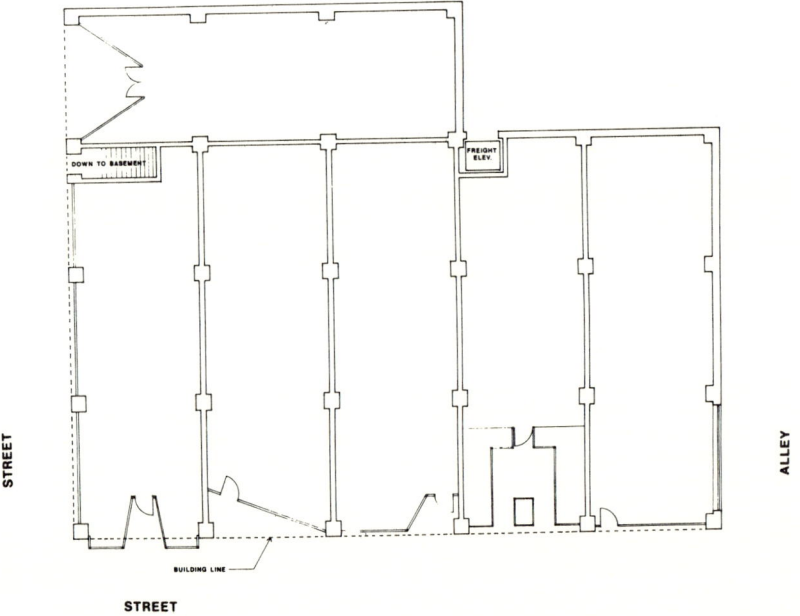

Appendix

Figure A.2

Standard Method of Floor Measurement for Office Buildings
Sponsored by
The Real Estate Board of New York, Inc.

General

Architectural plans when available are to be used. Tenant special installations including, but not limited to, private elevators, stairs, special flues, dumbwaiter shafts and special air conditioning facilities are included within the rentable area of such tenant. In determining whether a floor is, and in computing the aggregate rentable area of, a single tenancy floor, any special installation on said floor of another tenant shall be disregarded. In computing the aggregate rentable area of any multiple occupancy floor, any special installation of a tenant who is not a tenant of any other part of such floor shall be disregarded.

Single Tenancy Floors

Three steps to be followed to determine the rentable area:
  a) Compute gross area.
  b) Deduct certain areas.
  c) Add applicable share of areas to be apportioned.
     (see below paragraph c).
a) Gross Area:
The gross area of a floor shall be the entire area within the exterior walls. If the exterior wall consists in whole or part of windows, fixed clear glass or other transparent material, the measurement shall be taken to the inside of the glass or other transparent material. If it consists solely of a nontransparent material, the measurement shall be taken to the inside surface of the outer masonry building wall.
b) Deductions From Gross Area:
The following non-rentable building areas with their finished enclosing walls are to be deducted:
  1. Public elevator shafts and elevator machine rooms.
  2. Public stairs.
  3. Fire tower and fire tower court.
  4. Main telephone and electric switchboard room except:
     (a) where the same is leased by tenant, or
     (b) is a special installation.
  5. Areas within the gross area which are to be apportioned.
     (see below paragraph c).
(NOTE: *If a base building area to be deducted and a base building area that is rentable have a common wall, the thickness of the wall is to be equally divided; e.g. if an elevator shaft is adjacent to a telephone closet, the elevator shaft and half of the finished dividing wall are to be deducted.*)
c) Areas To Be Apportioned:
1. Air conditioning facilities: All air conditioning floors and other areas throughout and within the building (exclusive of tenant's special air conditioning facilities) including their finished enclosing walls containing equipment or enclosing pipes, ducts, or shafts serving the facilities are to be apportioned to the areas they serve.
2. Whenever the height of an air conditioning facility room or floor above the grade floor shall exceed the average story height in the building by more than 25%, then the area of such room or floor shall be determined by multiplying the floor area by the percentage that the height of the room or floor exceeds the average story height, and adding the area so determined to the area of the room or floor.

Multiple Occupancy Floors

The total of the rentable areas for two or more tenants on a floor shall be the rentable area for that floor as computed in the manner for single tenancy floors, except that public corridors of the floor shall be included.

Figure A.2 (continued)

Three steps are to be followed:
  a) Compute the net area for such floor.
  b) Compute the net area for each tenant.
  c) To determine the rentable area for any tenant, multiply the rentable area of such floor by a fraction whose numerator is the net area for such tenant and whose denominator is the net area for such floor.

a) Net Area For Any Floor:
The net area shall be the gross area as described for single tenancy floors less the entire core areas (including the finished enclosing wall thereof but excluding any part of the core rented to a tenant) and corridors (excluding the enclosing walls thereof).

b) Net Area For Each Tenant:
Exterior walls are to be measured as described in procedure for gross area. Demising walls between tenants are to be equally divided. Corridor walls to the finished corridor side are to be included in the net area of each tenant.

Stores
1. The rentable area of a store shall be computed by measuring from the building line in the case of street frontages, and from the inside surface of other outer building walls to the finished surface of the corridor side of corridor partition and from the center of the partitions that separate the premises from adjoining rentable area.
2. No deductions shall be made for columns and projections necessary to the building.
3. Rentable area of a store shall include all area within the outside walls, less building stairs, fire towers, elevator shafts, flues, vents, stacks, pipe shafts, vertical ducts with their enclosing walls if serving more than one tenant.
4. Private stairs, private elevators, toilets, air conditioning facilities, janitors' closets, slop sinks, electrical closets and telephone closets, with their enclosing walls exclusively serving only that store, shall be included in rentable area. When air conditioning facilities serve more than one tenant area, they shall be apportioned in the same manner as that used for single tenancy floors.
5. Where a store fronts on a plaza or arcade which is intended for use by the general public and is not for the exclusive use of the store tenants, its customers, etc., the area of the plaza or arcade shall not be included in determining the rentable area of the store.

Basements
1. If the rentable area extends beyond the building line under the sidewalk, the rentable area shall be computed by measuring from the finished surface of the retaining wall to the finished surface of the corridor or other permanent partition, and from the center of the partitions that separate the premises from adjoining rentable area, provided such partitions are not bearing walls.
2. If the rentable area is entirely inside the building line the rentable area shall be computed by measuring from the inside surface of the outer building wall to the finished surface of corridor side of corridor partition or to other permanent partition and from the center of the partitions that separate the premises from adjoining rentable area, provided such partitions are not bearing walls.
3. No deductions shall be made for columns, projections or footings necessary to the building.
4. Rentable area of a basement shall include all area within the outside walls, less building stairs, fire towers, elevator shafts, flues, vents, stacks, pipe shafts, and vertical ducts, with their enclosing walls serving more than one tenant.
5. Private stairs, private elevators, toilets, air conditioning facilities, janitors' closets, slop sinks, electrical closets, and telephone closets, with their enclosing walls, exclusively, serving only the tenant, shall be included in rentable area.
6. Where air conditioning facilities serve more than one tenant area, they shall be apportioned in same manner as that used for single tenancy floors.

Figure A.2 (continued)

Single Tenancy Buildings

The rentable area of a Single Tenancy Building shall be the gross aggregate area thereof without any deductions.

Effective April 16, 1968

Figure A.3

Form 50A

THE INSTITUTE OF REAL ESTATE MANAGEMENT
of the
NATIONAL ASSOCIATION OF REALTORS®

_____ 19____

OFFICE BUILDING INSPECTION REPORT

Name of Property .... Address ....

Type of Property .... Office Area Rental Rate ....

No. of Stores .... Store Area Rental Rate ....

Report Submitted By .... Basement Area Rental Rate ....

Owner ....

EXTERIOR

Items	Character & Condition	Needs	Est. Expenses
Roofs			
1. Type			
2. Flashing			
3. Valleys			
4. Drains			
Walls - North			
5. Type			
6. Base			
7. Top			
8. Tuck pointing			
9. Stone sills			
10. Coping			
11. Parapet walls			
12. Terra cotta			
13. Metal trim			
Walls - East			
14. Type			
15. Base			
16. Top			
17. Tuck pointing			
18. Stone sills			
19. Coping			
20. Parapet walls			
21. Terra cotta			
22. Metal trim			
Walls - West			
23. Type			
24. Base			
25. Top			
26. Tuck pointing			
27. Stone sills			
28. Coping			
29. Parapet walls			
30. Terra cotta			
31. Metal trim			
Walls - South			
32. Type			
33. Base			
34. Top			
35. Tuck pointing			
36. Stone sills			
37. Coping			

Appendix 257

Figure A.3 (continued)

GENERAL EXTERIOR

Items	Character & Condition	Needs	Est. Expenses
Walls - South (cont'd)			
38. Parapet walls			
39. Terra cotta			
40. Metal trim			
Walls - Court			
41. Type			
42. Base			
43. Top			
44. Tuck pointing			
45. Stone sills			
46. Coping			
47. Parapet walls			
48. Terra cotta			
49. Metal trim			
Chimney			
50. Type			
51. Comment			
Sidewalk Elevators			
52. Permits - expiration date			
53. Make			
54. Type			
55. Capacity			
56. Parts, oil, grease contr.			
57. Sidewalk doors			
58. Shaft			
59. Platform size			
60. Shaft gates			
61. Motors			
62. Pumps			
63. Tanks			
64. Generator			
65. Signal			
66. Safety locks			
67. Controls			
68. Pits			
69. Signs			
70. Comments			
Bldg. Entrance			
71. Doors			
72. Hinges			
73. Locks			
74. Checks			
75. Side lights			
76. Transoms			
77. Canopy			
78. Signal button			
79. Lighting			
80. Building name			
81. Street numbers			
82. Entry steps			
Exterior Fire Escapes			
83. Signs			
84. Access windows			
85. Access ladders			
86. Maintenance			
87. Ladder treads			
88. Hand rails			
Sidewalks			
89. Comments			

Figure A.3 (continued)

GENERAL EXTERIOR

Items	Character & Condition	Needs	Est. Expenses
Light Walls			
90. Skylights			
91. Roof			
92. Comments			
Fire Hazards			
93. Defective wiring			
94. Trash and rubbish			
95. Oil, gasoline or paint storage			
96. Gas leaks			
97. Self-closing doors			
98. Breeching and flues			
99. Dumbwaiter enclosures			
100. Hot ash disposal			
101. Defective fire hose			
102. Fire extinguishers			
Windows - Office			
103. Type			
104. Frames			
105. Stops			
106. Sash			
107. Sills			
108. Lintels			
109. Anchor bolts			
110. Glass			
111. Glazing			
112. Caulking			
113. Weather strip			
114. Screens			
115. Locks			
Windows - Store			
116. Frames			
117. Transoms			
118. Sash			
119. Glass			
120. Caulking			
121. Glazing			
122. Screens			
123. Hinges			
124. Sash			
125. Locks			
Penthouse - Elevator			
126. Roof			
127. Walls			
128. Steps			
129. Doors			
130. Windows			
131. Flooring			
132. Fire protection devices			
Other Roof Structures			
Miscellaneous Extras			

Appendix 259

Figure A.4

THE INSTITUTE OF REAL ESTATE MANAGEMENT
of the
NATIONAL ASSOCIATION OF REALTORS®

Form 50B

_____ 19___

OFFICE BUILDING INSPECTION REPORT

Name of Property _____ Address _____

Type of Property _____ Office Area Rental Rate _____

No. of Stores _____ Store Area Rental Rate _____

Report Submitted By _____ Basement Area Rental Rate _____

Owner _____

INTERIOR

Items	Character & Condition	Needs	Est. Expenses
Lobby			
1. Ceiling			
2. Walls			
3. Floors			
4. Lighting fixtures			
5. Glass			
6. Directory			
7. Signs			
8. Mail box			
Interior Doors			
9. Type			
10. Glass			
11. Rails			
12. Stiles			
13. Hand rails			
14. Hinges			
15. Locks			
16. Pulls			
17. Push plates			
18. Kick plates			
19. Mail slot			
Stairway			
20. Treads			
21. Risers			
22. Gates			
23. Bannisters			
24. Handrails			
25. Walls			
26. Ceilings			
27. Windows			
28. Skylights			
29. Electric lights			
Corridors			
30. Ceilings			
31. Walls			
32. Wood trim			
33. Floors			
34. Hardware			
35. Doors			
36. Glass			
37. Lighting fixtures			
38. Lighting switches			

Figure A.4 (continued)

GENERAL INTERIOR

Items	Character & Condition	Needs	Est. Expenses
Corridors (Cont'd)			
39. Convenience outlets			
40. Waste paper receptacle			
41. Sand jars			
42. Fire hose			
43. Fire extinguishers			
44. Required signs			
45. Safety code violations			
46. Hopper rooms			
47. Maintenance			
Office Interiors			
48. Ceilings			
49. Walls			
50. Floors			
51. Lighting			
52. Fixtures			
53. Switches			
54. Elec. outlets			
55. Radiators			
56. Air conditioning			
57. Doors			
58. Transome			
59. Hardware			
60. Baseboards			
Windows			
61. Type			
62. Frames			
63. Sash			
64. Sills			
65. Stops			
66. Weights			
67. Glass			
68. Glazing			
69. Caulking			
70. Weaterstripping			
71. Locks			
72. Screens			
Elevator-Passenger			
73. Permit expiration date			
74. Serviced by			
75. Contract			
76. Full maintenance			
77. Parts, oil, grease contr.			
78. Make			
79. Type			
80. Capacity (weight)			
81. Capacity (passengers)			
82. Lobby door fronts			
83. Corridor door fronts			
84. Operatorless			
85. Pit			
86. Full automatic			
87. Self leveling			
88. Door operator			
89. Electric			
90. Air			
91. Manual			
92. Cab-size			
93. Cab trim			

Appendix 261

Figure A.4 (continued)

Items	Character & Condition	Needs	Est. Expenses
Elevators-Passenger (Cont'd)			
94. Cab walls			
95. Cab doors			
96. Cab lighting			
97. Cab ceiling			
98. Cab floor			
99. Cab ventilation			
100. Position indicators			
101. Floor indicator			
102. Signal lanterns			
103. Signal buttons			
104. Emergency switches			
105. Telephone			
106. Elevator shafts			
107. Pits			
108. Walls			
109. Guide rails			
110. Hoisting cables			
111. Compensating cables			
112. Governor cables			
113. Sheaves			
114. Motors			
115. Generators			
116. Governors			
117. Signs in shaft			
118. Floor numbers on shaft walls			
119. Floor numbers on door			
120. Miscellaneous			
121. Control panels			
122. Threshold lights			
Elevators-Freight			
123. Permit expiration date Contract			
124. Serviced by			
125. Full maintenance			
126. Parts, oil, grease contr.			
127. Make			
128. Type			
129. Capacity, pounds			
130. Platform size			
131. Platform lighting			
132. Shaft doors			
133. Cab gates			
134. Hoisting cables			
135. Compensating cables			
136. Governor cables			
137. Pit			
138. Motors			
139. Generators			
140. Signal buttons			
141. Signal buzzers			
142. Shaft numbers			
143. Shaft safety signs			
144. Guide rails			
145. Comments			
Public Rest Rooms-Men			
146. Floors			
147. Floor drain			

Figure A.4 (continued)

Items	Character & Condition	Needs	Est. Expenses
Public Rest Rooms-Men (Cont'd)			
148. Walls			
149. Wainscote			
150. Ceiling			
151. Watercloset enclosure			
152. Watercloset type			
153. Tank			
154. Flushing valve			
155. Vacuum breaker			
156. Seat			
157. Bowl			
158. Lavatory			
159. Trim			
160. Soap dispensers			
161. Urinal			
162. Type-wall-floor			
163. Flushing valve			
164. Stall panel			
165. Hardware on door			
166. Locks			
167. Deodorants			
168. Ventilation			
169. Light fixtures			
170. Switches			
171. Window			
172. Waste receptacle			
173. Towel cabinets			
174. Mirrors			
175. Signs			
Public Rest Rooms-Women			
176. Floors			
177. Floor drain			
178. Walls			
179. Wainscote			
180. Ceiling			
181. Watercloset enclosure			
182. Stall doors			
183. Stall doors hardware			
184. Watercloset type			
185. Tank			
186. Flushing valve			
187. Vacuum breaker			
188. Seat			
189. Bowl			
190. Toilet tissue holder			
191. Lavatory			
192. Trim			
193. Soap dispenser			
194. Mirrors			
195. Vanity shelf			
196. Deodorants			
197. Ventilation			
198. Light fixtures			
199. Switches			
200. Windows			
201. Waste receptacle			
202. Sanitary napkin vendors			
203. Signs			

Appendix

Figure A.4 (continued)

Items	Character & Condition	Needs	Est. Expenses
Basement Stairway			
204. Entrance door			
205. Treads			
206. Risers			
207. Hand rails			
208. Walls			
209. Landings			
210. Ceilings			
211. Light			
Basement Area			
212. Floors			
213. Sump pumps			
214. Walls			
215. Ceilings			
216. Fire doors			
217. No. of exits			
218. Sprinkler system			
219. Lighting			
220. Convenience outlets			
221. Ventilation			
222. Elevator service			
223. Storage space			
224. Heating			
225. Utility space			
226. Carpenter shop			
227. Plumber			
228. Paint shop			
229. Superintendent office			
Men Employees Rest Rooms			
230. Showers			
231. Watercloset			
232. Type			
233. Lavatory			
234. Urinal			
235. Lavatory trim			
236. Floor			
237. Walls			
238. Ceilings			
239. Lighting			
240. Heating			
241. Ventilating			
Men's Locker Rooms			
242. Floors			
243. Walls			
244. Ceiling			
245. Lighting			
246. Switches			
247. Heating			
248. Ventilation			
249. Doors			
250. Fire hazards			
Women Employees Rest Rooms			
251. Showers			
252. Watercloset			
253. Type			
254. Lavatory			
255. Trim			
256. Floor			
257. Walls			

Figure A.4 (continued)

Items	Character & Condition	Needs	Est. Expenses
258. Ceiling			
259. Doors			
260. Heating			
261. Ventilation			
262. Lighting			
263. Switches			
Women's Locker Rooms			
264. Floors			
265. Walls			
266. Ceiling			
267. Lighting			
268. Heating			
269. Ventilation			
270. Doors			
271. Fire hazards			
Boiler Room			
272. Floor			
273. Walls			
274. Ceiling			
275. Fire doors			
276. Fire hazards			
277. Ventilation			
278. Lighting			
279. Switches			
Boilers			
280. Type			
281. Pressure, high			
282. Pressure, low			
283. Flues			
284. Tubes			
285. Draft control			
286. Valves			
287. Blow-off pit			
288. Vents			
289. Grates			
290. Fire box			
291. Pointing fire brick			
292. Steam line insulation			
293. Fuel, kind			
294. Storage tanks			
295. Coal chutes			
296. Coal bins			
297. Stokers			
298. Oil burners			
299. Gas burners			
300. Injectors			
301. Low water cutout			
302. Pop-off valves			
303. Gauges, pressure			
304. Gauges, water level			
305. Automatic controls			
306. Diaphragms			
307. Flanges			
308. Gaskets			
309. Packing glands			
310. Draft regulators			
311. Smoke detectors			
312. Steam condensate return			

Appendix 265

Figure A.4 (continued)

Items	Character & Condition	Needs	Est. Expenses
Vacuum Pump Make			
313. Storage tank			
314. Control (elec.) make			
315. Control (elec.) voltage			
316. Water level float switch voltage			
317. Combination negative & pressure gauge			
318. Strainer			
319. Motor			
320. Type			
321. Horse power load			
Hot Water Heaters			
322. Inside lining			
323. Steam coils			
324. Insulation			
325. Gaskets			
326. Thermostat			
327. Steam trap			
328. Safety valve			
329. Fire box			
330. Fuel			
331. Burner			
Pumps			
332. Sump			
333. Pressure			
334. Feed water			
335. Circulating			
336. Vacuum			
Water Softeners			
337. Type			
338. Sand filters			
339. Valves			
340. Differential gauges			
341. Tank, filter			
342. Softener			
Salt Tank			
343. Coating			
344. Float valve			
345. Overflow			
346. Tank			
Compressors			
347. Filters			
348. Automatic switch			
349. Safety valve			
350. Drive			
351. Motor H.P.			
352. Tank capacity			
353. Purpose of comp. air			
Vacuum Pump-Cleaning System			
354. Automatic switch controls			
Air Conditioning			
Window Units			
355. Miscellaneous			
a.			
b.			
c.			

Figure A.4 (continued)

Items	Character & Condition	Needs	Est. Expenses
Window Units (cont'd)			
d.			
e.			
Central system			
356. Type			
a.			
b.			
c.			
Original Installation			
357. Age			
358. Refrigeration			
359. Unit			
360. Refrigerant			
361. Compressor			
362. Capacity			
363. H.P. connec. load			
364. Performance			
365. Cooling tower			
366. Air distribution			
367. Ducts			
368. Insulation			
369. Grills			
370. Thermostats			
371. Zones			
372. Fans			
373. Performance			
Electric Panel Room			
Electric Energy Service			
374. Transformer capacity			
375. Voltage			
376. Cycle			
377. Power			
378. Lighting			
379. Phase single			
380. Phase three			
Panel Board			
381. Maker			
382. Amperage capacity			
383. Power circuits			
384. Lighting circuits			
385. Emergency circuits			
386. Stand by circuits			
387. Spare circuits			
388. Fuses			
389. Circuit breakers			
390. Meters			
391. Lighting meter			
392. Power meter			
393. Tenants meter			

Figure A.5

Design and Construction Criteria for Office Premises

I. General

The information contained herein is intended to assist the Tenant in the planning, design and construction of his leased space and to bring to his attention at the earliest opportunity those building conditions that his design must accommodate.

1. Tenant Improvements Coordination.

   All requests for information and approvals as described herein shall be addressed to: (name, address, and telephone number of agency)

   When reference is made herein to specific approvals by the Landlord these approvals are obtained by application to the Tenant Coordinator.

2. Specifications and Drawings.

   Specifications and Drawings for Base Building work are available for review by the Tenant or his Agent at the above address and show the typical architectural, mechanical and electrical details applicable to the Base Building construction of the leased space. The Landlord reserves the right to change the drawings and specifications at any time. The Drawings and Outline Specifications showing Building Standard details and requirements are attached to this document.

3. Changes to the Base Building Construction.

   The Landlord reserves the right to approve any revision or change to the Base Building desired by the Tenant and to require all approved revisions or changes to be carried out by the Landlord's contractor at the Tenant's expense. When necessary, drawings indicating the revisions and/or additions to the basic systems required by the Tenant will be prepared by the Landlord's consultants and submitted to the Tenant for approval. Design and drafting fees covering the production of such drawings will be at the Tenant's expense.

4. Approval of Leasehold Improvements.

   The Tenant shall submit all drawings, specifications and schedules to be used in the construction of the Leasehold Improvements to the Landlord for approval prior to construction commencing. The submission shall consist of four sets of Blue-Lines of all drawings and specifications.

   The Landlord reserves the right to require such additional information and drawings from the Tenant as may be necessary to identify and describe the nature of the Leasehold Improvements.

   The Tenant or Tenant's Agent will be responsible for obtaining all necessary permits, including the City of _____ Building Department permits and any other approvals and permits of Authorities having jurisdiction over this work. Tenants must furnish evidence of such approvals and permits prior to the commencement of construction of their Leasehold Improvement work. The Tenant shall not make any change to the drawings, specifications and schedules approved by the Landlord without informing and obtaining the written approval of the Landlord to the change.

5. Consultants.

   The consultants for the Tenant Improvements Building Standard Design work are as follows:

   Architect—

   Structural Engineer—

   Mechanical Engineer—

   Electrical Engineer—

   Although *not mandatory,* Tenants are encouraged to use the services of the above consultants for Tenant Extra work, particularly with respect to structural, mechanical and electrical design. In the event that the Tenant selects consultants other than those named above, the design work carried out by the Tenant's consultants will, as it effects the Base Building work, require checking and approval by the Building Consultants at the Tenant's expense.

Figure A.5 (continued)

6. Contractor Requirements.
   The contractor for the Base Building Tenant Building Standard construction work is:

   The Tenant may employ a contractor of his own choice for Tenant Extra work except that if the contractor is not the Tenant Standard Building contractor, the Landlord will require the contractor to meet the following requirements:
   a. Have a Union affiliation compatible with the Union affiliation of the Base Building Contractor(s);
   b. Be acceptable to the Landlord;
   c. Comply with (name of building) *Tenant Construction Requirements* available from the Tenant Coordinator.

   In the event that the Tenant selects a contractor other than the Base Building Contractor, the Tenant shall pay to the Landlord the sum of $_____$ per square foot of rentable area for such services as coordination, temporary power source, lighting and heat, security and water, provided by the Landlord's contractor.
   The mechanical and electrical contractor(s) that may be employed by the Tenant to perform all mechanical and electrical work of the Leasehold Improvements must be specifically approved in writing by the Owner. This requirement is to ensure that warranties and guarantees applicable to the Base Building electrical and mechanical systems are not invalidated.

II. Building Standards and Building Standard Allowances.
   1. Partitions.
      The Building Standard Partition, to be selected by Landlord, will be either: (1) conventional painted drywall or (2) demountable, prefinished vinyl faced gypsum board. The partitions will have extruded aluminum pre-finished door frames, header channels and trim pieces as required. A _____" vinyl base will be provided. Special acoustic details will be provided to insure privacy between tenancies and public corridors.
      a. *Demising Partitions* consist of the basic system with special wall cavity sound batt and security baffle above the ceiling plenum between tenants to reduce flanking noise. A special curtain wall closure piece is provided at the curtain wall intersectoin to insure tight fit and allow for removal of glazing sections should this be necessary. The Building Standard quantity allowance is one (1) lineal foot of partition per sixty (60) square feet of leased area.
      b. *Corridor Partitions* will be supplied in the basic system with wall cavity sound batt insulation. Vinyl will be provided on the corridor side. The Building Standard allowance is quantity required to demise the leased premises.
      c. *Interior Partitions* will be provided in the basic partition system. The Building Standard allowance quantity is one (1) lineal foot of partition per fifteen (15) square feet of leased area.
   2. Doors.
      All doors will be ___'___" full height x ___'___" wide, solid core wood, red oak finish compatible with the Base Building millwork. Doors will be hung in an extruded Duralac aluminum frame supplied as a standard component of the basic partition system.
      a. *Entry Doors* will be provided one (1) door per tenant based on open space within the leased premises as a Building Standard allowance. Additional entrances occasioned by the tenant's partitioning will be at the Tenant's expense. Entry Doors are supplied with Building Standard lockset, closer and hinges.
      b. *Interior Doors* will be provided as a Building Standard of one (1) door per five hundred (500) square feet of leased area and will be provided with Building Standard hardware consisting of latchset, hinges and stop.
   3. Hardware.
      a. *Entry Doors*—(specify locks, finish, hinges, etc.)
      b. *Interior Doors*—(specify latchset, dome stop, hinges, etc.)
   4. Flooring.
      Building Standard finish is carpet (specify type) applied at the Building Standard allowance rate of one (1) square foot of carpet per one (1) square foot of leased area. Carpet will be applied directly to concrete floor slab.
   5. Ceiling.
      A suspended ceiling at a height of ___'___" consisting of (specify size) concealed spline acoustical tile supplied on the floor by the Landlord and installed into mechani-

Appendix

Figure A.5 (continued)

cal suspension system by Landlord's Base Building Contractor. Building Standard allowance provides for installation of tile in ratio of one (1) square foot of tile per one (1) square foot of leased area.

6. Electrical Systems.
   a. *Lighting.* The lighting arrangement consists of one (1) light fixture for every eighty (80) square feet on an open area basis. The individual fixtures are 2' x 4' with four (4) 40-watt lamps, return air and heat extraction type. The Base Building Contractor will provide these fixtures stacked on the floor with installation being made by the Tenant Improvements Contractor. The Building Standard allowance provides for installation of these fixtures in the ratio of one (1) fixture per eighty (80) square feet of leased area.

   Emphasis is placed on the modular lighting pattern and the need to maintain this in the exterior perimeter zone of the building. Particular emphasis should be placed on this in the design of the lighting in the perimeter zone of approximately twelve (12) feet. One (1) Building Standard wall switch with accessories will be provided as a Building Standard allowance for one thousand (1000) feet of leased area.

   b. *Power Outlets.* One (1) wall duplex outlet will be provided as the Building Standard Allowance for each two hundred (200) square feet of leased area.

   c. *Telephone Outlets.* One (1) wall telephone outlet will be provided as the Building Standard allowance in the ratio of one (1) outlet per three hundred (300) square feet of leased area. Wall outlet shall be 4" x 4" box with drag line from hung ceiling cavity to outlet box.

   (Floor mounted code acceptable poke-through type telephone and/or power outlets may be provided by the Tenant at their expense only when specifically approved by the Landlord.)

   d. *Electrical and Telephone Rooms.* These rooms are provided on each floor to provide basic communication and electrical services to each floor and are not accessible to tenants. Any space of this nature which a Tenant requires for his own equipment or use must be provided within the leased premises.

7. HVAC.
   The Base Building provides a Variable Air Volume type air conditioning system, complete with air distribution dust network. Diffuser units and thermostats only are provided by the Base Building Contractor to be installed under Tenant Improvements. The Base Building Standard provides one (1) diffuser per two hundred (200) square feet of leased area, and one (1) thermostat per twelve hundred (1200) square feet of leased area. Return air shall be through the return air opening provided in the lighting fixtures.

8. Fire Protection.
   The leased area is provided with complete automatic sprinkler protection with one (1) head per two hundred twenty-five (225) square feet on a Building Standard open space layout. Relocation or additional heads required for approval by insurance and jurisdictional bodies based on Tenant's interior layout will be at Tenant's expense.

9. Venetian Blinds and Windows.
   Windows are sealed, double-glazed, insulated units with a heat reflective mirrored glass for temperature and sun control. Mullions and sills are extruded aluminum, painted white. Slim line venetian blinds with nylon cords are hung at each window. Venetian blinds for the full exterior exposure are provided under the Building Standard allowance. Drapes and drape tracks may be supplied by the Tenant if desired, but subject to approval by Landlord. Drapes must be open-weave type to prevent heat build-up at the glass line and to allow air circulation within the leased space.

10. Elevator Lobbies and Public Corridors.
    Elevator Lobbies and public corridors are provided under the Building Standard allowance to provide carpet flooring, vinyl-covered walls, painted metal elevator entrance doors and frames, 1' x 1' concealed ceiling and recessed cove lighting to complement the Building Standard Tenant interiors.

11. Graphics.
    Tenant must submit drawings and description of its proposed signs for the Landlord's approval. A standard letter type for the project is Helvetica Medium in polished aluminum finish. Tenant Graphics to be at Tenant's expense.

Glossary

Absorption rate The estimate of the rate at which office space will be leased or occupied each year.

ACCREDITED MANAGEMENT ORGANIZATION® (AMO®) A designation conferred by the Institute of Real Estate Management to real estate management firms that are under the direction of a CERTIFIED PROPERTY MANAGER® and comply with stipulated requirements as to accounting procedures, performance, and protection of funds entrusted to them.

Action program One of six components in a marketing plan; a statement that defines the means of implementing the marketing strategy.

Addendum A legal document that adds to or amends the terms of a standard form lease. (*See* **Rider to lease**.)

Advertising The purchase of time (radio and television) or space (periodicals, outdoor, transit) to provide information, shape attitudes, and benefit a product's image.

Aesthetics, general The landscaping, greenery, views, maintenance of surrounding territories, and the like of the subject property.

Agency A legal relationship created when an individual (the principal) delegates to another (the agent) the right to act on behalf of the principal in business transactions, specifically, the leasing of office space.

Agent An individual authorized to represent and act on behalf of another person or entity (referred to as the principal).

Alteration provision A provision which prohibits a tenant from making any alteration of or improvement to the leased premises without the expressed consent of the landlord.

Amenities Tangible and intangible features that enhance and add to the desirability and value of a subject property, e.g., cafeteria, indoor parking, special janitorial services.

Assignment of lease The transfer of all title, right, and interest that a lessee possesses in certain real property. Also, the document used to convey a leasehold is called an assignment of lease rather than a deed. (*See also* **Sublease**.)

Audit An inspection of accounting records and procedures conducted by a trained person to check their accuracy, completeness, and reliability.

Bay depth The distance from the corridor wall to the real window or wall.

Billboard A large panel designed to carry outdoor advertising.

Broadcast media All media for advertising prepared for transmittal by television or radio.

Bubble schematic Used in early stages of space planning, a simplified diagram which indicates activity centers, personnel interactions, and people circulation without a formalized layout.

Building Owners and Managers Association (BOMA) A national organization of professionals in the office building industry.

Building standards The specific items of construction which the developer or the owner decides to use throughout a building; for example, in an office building, building standards would offer a certain type of carpet, wall and floor coverings, etc.

Calendar and budget summary One of six components in a marketing plan; a statement which puts a time frame on and a ceiling on spending for the marketing plan.

Canvassing Often referred to as cold prospecting or cold calling; involves visiting users of office space and encouraging them to consider space in a particular building.

Central business district (CBD) Downtown area of a major city.

CERTIFIED PROPERTY MANAGER® (CPM®) The professional designation conferred by the Institute of Real Estate Management on individuals who distinguish themselves in the areas of education, experience, and ethics.

Glossary 273

Classified advertisement Newspaper and magazine advertising subdivided according to the types of items offered or sought. Often referred to as want ad.

Close The signing of a lease after negotiations have terminated.

Company An association of individuals for the purpose of carrying on some joint business or enterprise, whether incorporated or not.

Competition A state of rivalry among sellers, each of whom is trying to gain a larger share of the market and greater profits.

Competitive office space The office space in a building in which there is possible turnover within the next 10 years.

Computer program The process of producing a sequence of instructions which, when carried on a computer, results in specific data processing results; often referred to as software.

Construction rider That part of the lease pertaining to all work that is to be done for the tenant by the landlord; also called a workletter.

Consumer good A product used directly to satisfy human needs or desires.

Core space The area in a building which includes the square footage used for public corridors, elevators, washrooms, stairwells, and electrical and janitorial closets.

Corporation A form of business organization created by statute law and consisting of owners who are regarded legally as a single entity.

Corridor A hallway or a passageway which provides a common way of travel to an exit, another office, and the like.

Cost book A list of unit costs of labor, materials, and service submitted by a general contractor to a prospective tenant for work to be done.

Cost-plus method The method a general contractor uses to estimate cost based on costs of labor (time) and materials plus a percentage fee; also referred to as time-and-material method.

Covenant A promise by one party to another ensuring certain performance or nonperformance of certain acts or a promise that certain conditions do or do not exist.

Credit rating Evaluation of the financial trustworthiness of a company or individual, particularly with regard to meeting obligations.

Curb appeal The aesthetic image and appearance projected by a building creating a first impression.

Debt service The total annual payment (principal and interest) on a mortgage.

Default Nonperformance of a duty or failure to meet an obligation when it is due.

Deferred maintenance Ordinarily, maintenance of a property that has not been performed and which noticeably affects the use, occupancy, welfare, and value of the property.

Demand In the theory of economics, the willingness of buyers to purchase a given amount of goods or services for a given price at a given time. (*See* **Supply**.)

Demographics The social statistics—age, race, density, distribution, wealth, education, occupation, nationality, and religion—of a population.

Destruction provision A provision within a lease stating the applicable procedure and rights in the event that the leased premises are damaged or destroyed by fire or other mishap. As a rule, the lessee will be held financially liable if deemed responsible.

Direct mail Any advertising piece sent through the mail, such as broadsides, form letters, circulars, catalogs, booklets, postcards, and portfolios.

Display ad A type of print media ad, usually of more than one column in width, that may have a border, headline copy, and possibly an illustration or logo.

Economics The study of the production, distribution, exchange, and consumption of goods and services.

Electric spectacular A large illuminated sign with special lighting and action effects.

Electronic data processing (EDP) The gathering, interpreting, and transmitting of data for reference and as the basis for decision-making. EDP is used primarily in connection with mechanical and electronic equipment, such as computers.

Eminent domain The right of a government body to acquire private property for public use through court action.

Equity The excess of a firm's assets over its liabilities; the interest or value an owner has in real estate over and above any mortgage on it.

Escalation clause A clause in a lease, contract, etc., permitting an adjustment of certain payments either up or down in order to cover certain contingencies.

Ethics The rules of conduct or code of principles recognized in respect to a particular class of human actions.

Glossary

Exhibit Attachment to a lease that elaborates on points agreed to within that lease.

Finish schedule A list of items, such as floor coverings, wall coverings, and paint colors, that finish off a suite design.

Fixed-bid basis The method of cost estimating which requires the contractor to state that a project will cost a certain amount based upon the plans and specifications provided.

Floor plan The architectural drawings showing the floor layout of a building including precise room sizes and their interrelationships.

Form Printed piece of paper that provides space for inserting specific information that is to be conveyed to other persons.

Garden office building An office building, usually one to three stories, often referred to as a suburban office building because of its typical location.

General contractor A construction specialist who enters into a formal construction agreement or contract with a real property owner to construct a building or complete a remodeling project.

Geographics Those variables which pertain to the region, climate, and size of a city and county and whether the location of the potential customer (or tenant) is in an urban, suburban, or rural area.

Gross lease A type of lease under which the tenant pays a fixed rental and the owner pays all other operating expenses related to the property.

Guaranty A pledge or security used to insure the landlord that the rent will be paid and all other terms, covenants, and conditions required in the lease will be performed.

High rise A building 11 or more stories in height.

Hold harmless lease clause A standard provision that states that the owner will not be liable for damages or injury sustained in, on, or about the leased premises; also referred to as indemnification clause.

HVAC system The heating, ventilating, and air conditioning system of a building.

Improvement Something done or added to real property in order to increase its value.

Income The returns that come in periodically from all sources.
Institute of Real Estate Management (IREM) A professional association affiliated with the NATIONAL ASSOCIATION OF REALTORS® for persons who meet professional standards of experience, education, and ethics with the objective of continually improving their respective managerial skills by mutual education and exchange of ideas and experiences.
Insurance provision A lease clause that requires the tenant to obtain a certain amount of public liability insurance and have the landlord named as co-insured in that policy.
Interest The charge, usually quoted as an annual percentage, for borrowing money.
Interest rate The price of borrowing money.

Job estimate form An organized, at-a-glance means of computing an estimate of the cost of tenant improvements.

Labor The human effort expended to produce income.
Labor cost The total salaries and wages paid to workers.
Labor pool The individuals available to perform human effort to produce income.
Landlord The owner of the leased premises; under a lease, the landlord is referred to as the lessor.
Lease A contract that transfers the right to use and enjoy a given piece of real estate from the owner of a property to a tenant for a definite period of time and under specific conditions.
Lease conditions The provisions setting forth the agreed privileges, obligations, and restrictions under which a lease is made; also referred to as lease terms.
Lease proposal A presentation made to a prospect regarding the general terms and conditions of a proposed lease.
Lease summation report A record or report which summarizes the content of a lease.
Lessee The individual or entity to whom property is rented or leased; often referred to as tenant.
Lessor The individual or entity who rents or leases property to another; often referred to as landlord.
Life-support system The security and protection services of a building, e.g., security systems, communication systems.
Live load The variable weight per square foot to which a building is subjected.

Glossary 277

Loan A sum of money borrowed at interest for a specific period of time with the promise of repayment.
Loan payment The payment of an installment on the principal balance plus accrued interest on the entire prepaid balance.
Loan payment cost The cost paid by the borrower for securing a loan.
Logo A trademark or company name or other identifying device.
Low rise A building up to five stories in height.

Maintenance Care and work necessary to keep a property in good physical and operating condition and appearance.
Management The job of planning, organizing, and controlling a business enterprise; the persons in an organization who are engaged in management.
Market analysis A determination of the characteristics, purchasing power, and habits of a given segment of the population.
Marketing All business activity involved in moving goods and services to consumers.
Marketing mix A segment of the marketing strategy which outlines the use of controllable marketing variables (namely, product strategy, price strategy, distribution strategy, and promotion strategy) to achieve specified marketing goals.
Marketing objectives and payout calculations One of six components in a marketing plan. A quantitative statement that evaluates the viability of the overall plan.
Marketing plan A short-term business tool used to generate profits by increasing business. The typical marketing plan contains six components: situation analysis, statement of marketing problems and opportunities, statement of objectives and payout calculations, statement of marketing strategy, action program, and calendar and budget summary.
Marketing problems and opportunities One of six components in a marketing plan; a statement which reveals what the product will face in the marketplace.
Marketing strategy One of six components in a marketing plan; the plan of action for meeting marketing objectives.
Market segmentation The division of the market into identifiable submarkets.
Market survey Up-to-date information collected and analyzed on other products distributed in a given area. In the office building market, a survey is made of comparables within the area sur-

rounding the subject property and includes such information as net rental area, amenities, number of stories, and the like.

Merchandising An aspect of marketing that involves advertising, promoting, and organizing the sale of a particular product or service.

Mid rise A building six to 10 stories in height.

Mortgage A legal agreement that pledges real property as security for the payment of a debt.

Mortgagee The lender in a mortgage loan transaction.

Mortgage lien The claim on real estate given to the mortgagee when the mortgagor executes a mortgage or trust deed to secure his note.

Mortgagor The borrower; the owner of the real estate who conveys his property as a security for the loan.

Multiple-tenancy floor A floor of an office building that houses several businesses.

Negotiation The art of making mutually profitable agreements; a transaction of business aimed at reaching a meeting of the minds among the parties involved.

Neighborhood A district or locality, often defined in reference to its character or inhabitants; a limited area as to size and use for residential, commercial, or other purposes or a combination of such use integrated into an accepted pattern.

Net lease A type of lease under which the tenant assumes the obligation to pay for utilities, real estate taxes, and other special assessments associated with the leased premises.

Net-net lease A type of lease under which the tenant assumes the obligation to pay for utilities, real estate taxes, and other special assessments associated with the leased premises plus ordinary repairs and maintenance.

Net-net-net lease (triple net lease) A type of lease under which the tenant assumes the obligation to pay for utilities, real estate taxes, and other special assessments associated with the leased premises plus ordinary repairs and maintenance and some capital improvements.

Noncompetitive office space The office space in a building occupied by owners or long-term tenants (those with leases with 10 or more years remaining) and which consequently is not available to satisfy immediate demand.

Glossary

Obsolescence A loss in value brought about by change in design, technology, taste, or demand.
Occupancy report Statement on the number of units in a building occupied and, consequently, the vacancy factor.
Office building A single- or multistory building designed for the conduct of business, generally divided into individual offices and offering space for rent or lease.
Operating expenses Periodic and necessary expenses essential to the operation and maintenance of an enterprise or a property.
Option A provision that gives a tenant some right or privilege not otherwise granted within the standard rental agreement, e.g., option to expand, option to renew, option to cancel.
Outdoor advertising A type of advertising used outside, such as billboards, electric spectaculars, painted displays, and transit ads.
Ownership Legal right of possession.

Partnership A form of business organization formed by agreement in which two or more enter into business as co-owners to share in profits and losses.
Policy A statement of general intent that tells what is permitted or expected.
Population Total of all individuals in a fixed or stipulated geographical area.
Portable presentations Items such as drawings, models, slide programs, movie film, and easel presentations used to promote a product.
Press release Also referred to as a news release; a straightforward, newsworthy story prepared for release to the media.
Price The exchange value of a good or service at a particular time as expressed in terms of money.
Primary demand A category of advertising campaigns designed to increase the demand for a generic type or class of product.
Principal In law, the individual being represented in a business transaction by an agent authorized to do so; in finance, the original amount of capital invested.
Print media All media for advertising prepared by printing, e.g., periodicals, posters, etc.
Pro forma An unofficial financial statement that treats hypothetical events as though they actually had occurred.

Promotional aid   Often referred to as a hand-out or give-away and used as part of a promotional campaign of a product or service.

Property management   A professional activity in which someone other than the owner oversees the operation of a parcel of real estate and assists the owner in achieving the investment objectives.

Prospect   A potential customer or tenant.

Prospect card   A card on which information about a potential tenant is kept for purposes of future contact.

Prospecting   The systematic search for potential tenants based on personal interaction, including referrals, canvassing, and cooperation with other colleagues in the business.

Psychographics   The life-style measurement of the consumers in the area in which the product will be distributed.

Psychology   The study of human behavior.

Public relations   A business function used to secure publicity, contacts, and market exposure by means other than advertising. Public relations is aimed at developing a good rapport between the public, a business, and the business's clients.

Qualify   To determine whether or not a potential tenant will be acceptable to the office building and whether or not the building will be compatible with the tenant.

Quiet enjoyment   A clause in most leases which states that the owner is obligated to protect the tenant against the claim of another firm that it is really the tenant of the specified space.

Real estate   Land and objects permanently attached to it.

Referrals   Potential users of office space as suggested by satisfied tenants, business associates, persons in influential positions, and friends.

Rendering   A perspective drawing finished with ink or color to bring out the effect of the design (as in an architect's rendering of a proposed office building).

Rent roll   A record of rents and other income payable and paid by tenants.

Rentable area   The total interior area in a building, usually expressed in square feet, that may be leased to tenants.

Rental clause   In an office lease, a provision that states the amount of rental to be paid, the method of payment, and to whom the payment is to be made.

Glossary

Rental schedule The listing of rental rates for units, suites, or space in given building.

Rider to lease A legal document that adds to or amends the terms of a standard form lease. (*See* **Addendum**.)

Rights and obligations A section of a typical office lease which clearly outlines the rights and obligations of the parties named in the lease.

Security deposit A means of guaranteeing the owner that the tenant will comply with the conditions of the lease.

Selective demand A category of advertising campaigns designed to increase the demand for a certain brand or product.

Single-tenancy floor A floor of an office building that houses a single business.

Situation analysis One of six components in a marketing plan; a detailed analysis of the marketplace in which a given product seeks to secure a place.

Space planning The planning and preparing of how space will be efficiently and effectively used based on operational and aesthetic requirements and financial limitations of the potential tenant.

Strategy Specification of programs for attaining desired objectives.

Strict performance A lease article which permits the landlord to collect rent and still insist on strict performance of other lease provisions.

Sublease A lease given by a lessee for a part of the leasehold interest but holding on to some reversionary interest in the lessee.

Submarket A segment or part of the market made up of entities which share certain characteristics.

Subordination clause A lease clause usually required by the mortgagee which makes the lease subject to any first mortgage.

Substitution of premises clause A clause within a lease which reserves the owner's rights to relocate various tenants to comparable offices within the building.

Supply In the theory of economics, the willingness of producers or manufacturers to sell a certain amount of goods or services for a given price at a particular time. (*See* **Demand**.)

Target market The specific segment of the market to which marketing efforts are directed for a particular good or service.

Tenancy Occupying or holding land or other real estate on a rental basis, with or without a written lease.

Tenant The individual or entity who exclusively possesses or holds property for a specified time period.

Tenant mix The combination of occupant types within a building.

Tenant profile A study and listing of the similar and dissimilar characteristics of the present tenants of a property.

Time-and-material method. *See* **Cost-plus method.**

Time log A record that facilitates recording time usage.

Transit advertising All types of advertising signs on or in trains, subways, taxis, buses, and other similar public transportation vehicles or the stations from which they operate.

Usable area On a multitenant floor, usable area is the gross area minus core space. (Core space includes the square footage used for public corridors, elevators, washrooms, stairwells, and electrical and janitorial closets.) On a single-tenant floor, the usable area is the gross square footage excluding the building lobby, ducts, stairwells, and elevators.

Use clause A clause within a lease that indicates the purpose for which the leased office space is to be used.

Utilities and services clause A clause within a lease that details any and all services that the owner is to provide for the tenant.

Vertical leasing plan A judgment by the leasing agent of which types of tenants would be suited to certain spaces within a highrise building.

Workletter That part of the lease pertaining to all work that is to be done for the tenant by the landlord in detail; also referred to as a construction rider.

Yield Rate of return on any investment.

Zoning Establishment of districts in which specific enterprises may be located, designed to regulate and control the character and use of the property.

Index

Absorption rate, defined, 65
ACCREDITED MANAGEMENT ORGANIZATION® (AMO®), 25
Action program, as part of marketing, 11
Adler, Dankmer, 4
Advertising, 67–78, 242
  analyzing effectiveness of, 77, 78
  defined, 67–8
Advertising campaign, 68, 69, 76–7
Aesthetic requirements
  impact of, on space planning, 132, 133, 134, 149
  of prospective tenants, 126–27, 243
Agent (*See also* Leasing agent)
  defined, 233
Amendment to lease, 197, 198–99, 206
Apparent withdrawal, as negotiating technique, 212–13
Architect's scale, as trade tool, 237
Armour, Philip D., 2
Assignment of lease, 175, 177, 197, 201, 206
Association, as negotiating technique, 214
Averaged rental rate, 145–46

Base rental rate, 43–4, 48–50
Baumann, Frederick, 3
Bay depth, defined, 16
Billboard, as advertising medium, 71–2
Bland withdrawal, as negotiating technique, 212

Blanketing, as negotiating technique, 214–15
BOMA (Building Owners and Managers Association) method, of space measurement, 17
Bracketing, as negotiating technique, 216
Breakdown clause, of standard form lease, 170
Broadside, as direct mail piece, 74–5
Brochure, as promotional medium, 74–5, 236
Bubble schematic
  as space planning tool, 134, 136
  for determining operational requirements, 124–26
Building Owners and Managers Association (BOMA), 17, 85
Building standard improvements, 18, 186
Burnham, Daniel, 4
Business entertainment, as public relations tool, 86, 87
Business stability, as tenant selection criterion, 114–16

Calculator, as trade tool, 237
Calendar and budget summary, as part of marketing plan, 12
Canvassing, 92–4, 242
Cash flow, formula for calculating, 45
Center, Allen H., 79, 80

Centers of influence, as referral source, 90, 242
Ceremonies, as public relations vehicle, 82, 85–6, 87
CERTIFIED PROPERTY MANAGER® (CPM®), 25
Chicago Fire, 1–2
Chicago School of Architecture, 4
Circular, as direct mail piece, 74
Circulation factor, impact on space planning of, 136
City directory, as source of prospective tenants, 96
Classified advertisement, 70
Closing
　description of process, 217–18
　techniques for, 218–21, 229, 244
Communication, as required skill, 235
Community involvement, as public relations vehicle, 82, 84–5, 87
Comparable analysis, of competition, 39–43
Comparable analysis worksheet, 41–3
Competency, of parties to lease, 164–65
Competition, impact on marketing, 39
Competitive office space, 36, 39
Concessions, 55–6
Conference room, operational requirements of, 123
Consent of assignment, 201
Consent to sublease, 199
Construction rider. See Workletter.
Contingency expense, tenant improvement costs and, 143
Cooperative arrangement, as source of prospective tenants, 94–6
Copy center, operational requirements of, 122
Corporations
　as office submarket, 62–3, 66
　as tenants, 164–65
Corridors, as product component, 21
Cost book, 141
Cost-effectiveness, of advertising, 77, 78
Cost-plus method, of estimating tenant improvement costs, 140
Credit verification, of prospective tenants, 114–16
Crossroads, as negotiating technique, 214
Curb appeal, as product component, 28
Cutlip, Scott M., 79, 80

Default, of lease, 175
Demised premises, 165, 182
Demographics, impact on rental rates of, 30, 31
Departmental areas, operational requirements of, 118, 120–21
Design and construction criteria, 186
Destruction clause, of standard form lease, 173
Dining facilities, operational requirements of, 122–23
Direct advertising, 73
Direct close, 218–19
Direct mail, 73–5
Directory board, lease provision for, 170, 195–96, 206
Disassociation, as negotiating technique, 214
Display advertisement, 70–1
Distribution, as element of marketing mix, 11

Economics, impact on rental rates of, 30–1
Effective rental rate, 55–6
Electrical system, as product component, 24
Electric spectacular, as advertising medium, 71, 72
Electronic data processing, operating requirements of, 121
Elevator
　history of, 3
　impact on rental rates of, 47
　as product component, 19–21
　service of, as provided by lease, 170
Eminent domain clause, of standard form lease, 173–74
Empire State Building, 6
Energy conservation, as lease covenant, 170–71
Energy conservation techniques, as product component, 23
Escalation clause, 166, 167–69
Executive approval file, 224, 226
Executive offices, operational requirements of, 118, 119
Exhibits, to lease, 181–87
Expansion
　space planning and, 126, 144–46, 149
　tenant improvements and, 192–93

Index

Fait accompli, as negotiating technique, 212
Feinting, as negotiatng technique, 213–14
Field, Marshall, 2
Field, research form, 41
Financial limitations
   impact on space planning of, 132, 133, 149
   of prospective tenants, 127–29, 243
Finish schedule, 151, 156, 160
Fire control, as product component, 22–3
Fixed-bid method, of estimating tenant improvement costs, 140
Floor plans
   for identification of leased premises, 181, 182
   as marketing tool, 236
Forbearance, as negotiating technique, 211
Form letter, as direct mail piece, 74–5
Freight elevator, as product component, 20

Garden office building
   defined, 47–8
   pricing space in, 48–50
General office areas, operational requirements of, 119, 120
General Services Administration (GSA), 62, 133
Geographics, impact on rental rates of, 30, 32
Government
   as office submarket, 62, 66
   impact on rental rates of, 31
Gross lease, 162
Ground floor space, establishing rental rate of, 46
Guaranty, 197–98

High-rise office building
   defined, 45–6
   pricing space in, 45–7
Holabird, William, 4
Hold harmless clause, in standard form lease, 172
Holding over, of lease, 176
Home Insurance Building, 1, 3
Homogenized rental rate, 154–46

Horizontal factors, in establishing rental schedule, 46, 47, 48–50, 53
"How and where" negotiating strategy, 210, 214–16
Human behavior, as factor in negotiation process, 208–09
HVAC (heating, ventilating, air conditioning) system
   impact on operational requirements of, 121
   as product component, 23–4

Image, of prospective tenant, 116, 127, 134
Indemnification clause, in standard form lease, 172
Indirect close, 219–21
Information retrieval system, 65–6
Institute of Real Estate Management (IREM)
   founding of, 5
   as promotional vehicle, 25, 85
Institutions, as office submarket, 62–3, 66
Insurance clause, in standard form lease, 172–73, 177
Interested prospect report, 99
Invoice, for monthly rental, 167

Janitorial cleaning specifications, 170
Janitorial service
   as product component, 21–2
   as provided by lease, 170
Jenney, William LeBaron, 1, 3
Job estimate form, 141, 143

Karkow, Waldemar, 44
Key map, 224

Laboratory, operational requirements of, 124
Labor pool, as product component, 26
Landlord's allowance. *See* Tenant improvement allowance.
Lease
   assignment of, 197, 201, 206
   characteristcis of, 163–64, 179, 243–44
   covenants within, 164–79
   defined, 161

Lease—Cont.
  gross, 162
  maintaining records of, 224
  making alterations to, 187–90, 204–06
  net, 162
  net-net, 162
  ownership acceptance of, 221–26, 229, 244
  parties to, 164–65
  percentage, 162
  special provisions to, 195–97, 206
  term of, 166
  termination of, 173, 176, 197, 201, 206
  transmittal of, to tenant, 226
  triple net, 162
Lease addendum, 189–90
Lease amendment, 197, 198–99
Leased premises, 165–66
Lease escalation clause, 167–69
Lease exhibit, 181–87
Lease gram, 224
Lease proposal, 151, 157–60, 243
Lease summation report, 223–24
Leasehold improvements. *See* Tenant improvements.
Leasing agency, role of, 240
Leasing agent
  in leadership role, 209, 233, 240, 244–45
  relationship to property management, 7–9
  as rental analyst, 241
  role in development process, 244
  as salesman, 234, 240
  skills required of, 8
Leasing plan, 50–3
Lessee, tenant as, 162
Lessor, landlord as, 162
Library, operational requirements of, 123
Life-support system, as product component, 22–3
Limiting, as negotiating technique, 213
Live load, impact on space planning, 121
Lobby, as product component, 19
Loss factor, 16–7
Low-rise office building, defined, 45

MacKenzie, R. Alec, 237, 239
McCormick, Cyrus H., 2
Mailing list, as source of prospective tenants, 96
Maintenance and repair clause, of standard form lease, 171–72
Management agreement, 25
Market, defined, 29–30
Market analysis, 29–43
Market conditions, impact on leasing program of, 33–4, 53, 56, 116, 186, 233, 241
Marketing, defined, 9
Marketing mix, 11, 67
Marketing objectives, 10
Marketing plan, 9–13, 16
Marketing strategy, 10–2
Market research, 64–5
Market segmentation, 11–2, 59–66, 241–42
Market survey, 34–9
Market survey form, 36
Measurement, of office space, 16–8
Mid-rise office building, defined, 45–6
Move-in, coordination of, 229

Neighborhood amenities, marketing value of, 27–8, 154–55, 236–37
Neighborhood analysis, 32–3
Negotiating techniques, 208–09, 210–16
Negotiation, 207–16
  conceptual basis for, 208–09, 216
  defined, 207
  of lease terms, 191–94, 207, 244
  standard form lease and, 161–62, 164, 179
Net lease, 162
Newspaper advertising, 69–70
News release. *See* Press release.
New York method, of office space measurement, 17
Nirenberg, Gerard I., 210, 216
Noncompetitive office space, 36

Objections, responding to, 109–10, 112, 219–20, 231
Office building (*See also* High-rise office building; low-rise office building; garden office building; mid-rise office building; suburban office building)
  categories of, 36
  defined, 15
  history of, 5–7
  as product, 15–28

Index

Office leasing, history of, 4–7, 12
Office market, defined, 59
Office space, measurement of, 16–8
Ogden, William, 2
Operational requirements
 of prospective tenants, 116–26, 243
 space planning and, 132, 133, 134, 136, 148
Option
 defined, 191
 to cancel, 194–95, 206
 to expand, 126, 191–93, 209
 to renew, 193–94, 206
Ownership, objectives of, 44–5, 197

Painted display, as advertising medium, 71, 72
Palmer, Potter, 2
Parking
 lease provision for, 195, 206
 as product component, 26–7
Participation, as negotiating technique, 214
Partnership, as tenant, 164, 165
Percentage lease, 162
Periodical advertising, 69, 70–1
Portable presentation, as marketing tool, 76, 237
Portfolio, as direct mail piece, 74
Postcard, as direct mail piece, 74–5
Pre-call preparation, 103–05
Preleasing
 effect on space planning of, 148, 149
 trends toward, 8, 244–45
Presentation, of space plans, 151–54, 160, 243
Press release, as public relations vehicle, 82–4, 87
Prestige, impact on marketing of, 25–6
Price, as element of marketing mix, 11
Primary demand advertising, 68
Private offices, operational requirements for, 119–20
Product
 as element of marketing mix, 11
 obtaining knowledge of, 15–28, 234, 240–41
 office building as, 15–28
Promotion, as element of marketing mix, 11, 67, 242
Promotional aids, as public relations vehicle, 84, 87
Property management
 history of, 5–6
 as product component, 24–5
 relationship to leasing function, 7–9
 types of, 25
Prospect card, 99–100
Prospecting, 89–100
Psychographics, impact on rent rates of, 30, 31–2
Public relations, 79–87, 242
 as distinct from advertising, 79
 scientific program of, 80–1, 86–7

Qualifying, of prospective tenants, 113–29, 242
Quantity allowance sheet, 18
Questioning
 as closing technique, 219, 221
 mastering art of, 108–09, 11
 as qualifying technique, 242
Questions, types of, 108–09
Quiet enjoyment clause, of standard form lease, 171, 175

Radio advertising, 75
Randomizing, as negotiating technique, 215
Random sample, as negotiating technique, 215
Reception area, operational requirements of, 118–19
Record keeping, of leasing activity, 99–100, 101, 224–26
Referral system, establishment of, 89–92, 237, 242
Referral source card, 92
Refurbishment clause, of standard form lease, 196
Region, defined, 30
Regional analysis, 30–2
Relocation, space planning and, 147
Renewal, space planning and, 144, 149
Rentable area
 measurement of, 16–8
 relationship to rent escalation, 166–68
Rental
 invoicing for, 178
 recovery of, 167
Rental rate (*See also* Rental schedule)
 adjustments to, 167–69
 averaging of, 145–46
 lease provision for, 166–67, 196, 206
 method of quoting, 53–5

Rental schedule, establishment of, 29–57, 241
Repairs, as provided by lease, 171–72
Reversal, as negotiating technique, 213
Rider to lease, 189–90
Roche, Martin, 4
Root, John Wellburn, 4
Rules and regulations, 177, 181, 187

Sales and Marketing Executives Association (SMEA), 85
Salesmanship, 103–12, 234–36
Sales presentation, 105–08
Security. *See* Life-support system.
Security deposit, 167
Selective demand advertising, 68
Service industry, as office submarket, 62–3, 66
Services, lease provision for, 169–70, 196
Sheridan-Karkow formula, 44
Sherdian, Leo J., 44
Signs, as advertising medium, 72–3
Singer Building, 5
Situation analysis, as part of marketing plan, 10
Skyscraper, history of, 2–5
Space planning, 131–49, 243
  alternate methods of, 132—33
  authorization for, 134
  for contracting tenant, 143, 146–47, 149
  cost of, 133–34, 144
  for expanding tenant, 143, 144–46, 149
  history of, 131–32
  preleasing and, 148, 149
  preliminary steps in, 137–38, 148, 151
  for relocating tenant, 143, 147, 149
  for renewing tenant, 143, 144, 149
  for tenant in previously occupied space, 143, 147–48, 149
Speaking engagements, as public relations vehicle, 84–5
Special-purpose areas, operational requirements of, 120–24
Speculative office space, 244
Stairways, as product component, 21
Standard form lease, role of, 161–63, 179, 187, 243
Storage areas, operational requirements of, 122
Strict performance clause, in standard form lease, 176
Strong prospect report, 226–27
Sublease, 177, 197, 199–201, 206
Submarkets, identification of, 59–64, 66
Subordination clause, in standard form lease, 174–75
Substitution clause, in standard form lease, 174
Suburban office building
  defined, 47–8
  history of, 6–7
  pricing space in, 48–50
Suite, defined, 133
Sullivan, Lewis, 4
Supply and demand, impact on rental rates of, 33–4
Surprise, as negotiating technique, 211–12
Swift, Gustavas F., 2

Take-off, cost estimating procedure of, 141
Target market (*See also* Market segmentation; Submarket), 12, 93
Telephone, as canvassing tool, 93–4
Telephone/communications room, operational requirements of, 120–21
Television advertising, 75–6
Tenant improvement allowance, 145, 147, 149, 156, 243
Tenant improvements (*See also* Financial limitations; Space planning; Tenant improvement allowance)
  allocation of costs of, 116–17, 128–29, 134, 137, 139, 149, 151, 156–57, 160, 186–87
  estimating cost of, 139–43, 149, 243
  expansion and, 192–93
  lease and, 172
  ownership of, 176
  as product component, 18–9
  workletter and, 184–87
Tenant mix, 26, 155
Tenant relations, 229, 231
Tenant selection criteria. *See* Qualifying
Termination of lease, 197, 201, 206
Testimonial, as closing technique, 220
Tickler, 92, 99–100
Time log, 237–39
Time management, 237–40
Tour of building, as marketing tool, 151, 154–56, 160, 243

Index

Transit advertising, 71, 72
Transportation, as product component, 26–7
Trial close, 110–11

Usable area, 16–8
Utilities, lease provision for, 169–70, 196, 206

Vertical factors, impact on rental schedule of, 46–7, 48–50, 53
View, impact on rental rates of, 43–4, 47

Walk-ins, as source of prospective tenants, 96

Weather, impact on rental rates of, 47
"When" negotiating strategy, 210, 211–14, 216
Woolworth Building, 5
Work flow, space planning and, 124, 136
Workletter, 181, 184–87. (*See also* Tenant improvements)
Wright, Frank Lloyd, 4
Wright, John Stephen, 2

Yellow pages, as source of prospective tenants, 96

Zoning, impact on rental rates of, 31